AF531813

CONGRESS-MUSLIM LEAGUE TUSSLE
1937–40
A Critical Analysis

CONGRESS-MUSLIM LEAGUE TUSSLE 1937–40

A Critical Analysis

ABIDA SHAKOOR

Compiled & Edited by
Q.Z. Hasan
Hajira Kumar

AAKAR BOOKS

CONGRESS-MUSLIM LEAGUE TUSSLE
1937-40
A Critical Analysis

First Published, 2003

ISBN 81-87879-08-4

Published by
AAKAR BOOKS
28-E, Pocket-IV, Mayur Vihar Phase-I, Delhi-110 091
Phone : 22795505 Telefax : 22795641
E-mail : aakarb@del2.vsnl.net.in

Typeset at
Nidhi Laser Point, Delhi-32
Ph. : 22825424

Printed in India on behalf of M/s Aakar Books by
Arpit Printographers, B-7, Saraswati Complex,
Subhash Chowk, Laxmi Nagar, Delhi-110 092

Dedicated to Prof. Irfan Habib who has given a new meaning to the concept of intellectual honesty. Late Ms. Abida Shakoor greatly admired his academic excellence and scholarship. He was a source of inspiration for her during the course of this research work.

Dedication to Prof. Irfan Habib who has given a new meaning to the concept of intellectual honesty. Late Ms. Abida Shakoor greatly admired his academic excellence and scholarship. He was a source of inspiration for her during the course of this research work.

Acknowledgements

On behalf of Abida Shakoor, the author of this masterpiece, I am deeply indebted to one and all who have assisted in her endeavour.

I express my gratitude to Dr. Neeti Mahanti for taking initiative and providing moral courage to me to take up the gigantic and complicated task of editing and compiling these scattered papers in the form of a book.

I am also obliged to those who have provided technical assistance and helped in proof reading.

I am thankful to my family members who have helped me in collating documents and papers from various sources.

This study is based on intensive and extensive work. Any shortcomings are due to my humble efforts in compiling the study.

Hajira Kumar

Preface

This is a moment of happiness as well as grief. With mixed feelings I am presenting this book as an addition to the treasure of historical literature. I am happy that ultimately these papers could be published but at the same time, grief stricken, that Abida Shakoor who took this research as a mission of her life, unfortunately could not see it in published form.

I believe that life goes on whatever may happen. Abida Shakoor is not amongst us but she will forever survive in the form of her invaluable contribution. **Congress-Muslim League Tussle—1937-40,** is a research work based on at least fifteen years of intensive study. The topic has now gained a new meaning in the present socio-political context. Hope friends and colleagues from the field of history are able to appreciate the authenticity and hard work which will, hopefully, make this publication a noteworthy piece of research.

Hajira Kumar

Contents

Preface ix

Introductory Profile 1

1. Eve of 1937 Elections—A Political Prognosis 7
2. Aftermath of the Elections 16
3. Mohammad Ali Jinnah and the Emergence of Muslim Nationalism 30
4. The Congress Regime and the Muslim League 63
5. And Then Came the War 115
6. Lahore Conference and After 171
7. The U.P. Ministry Episode 184

Conclusive Corollary 198

Appendix 203

Bibliography 205

Index 211

Introductory Profile

The metamorphic political development in India in the three years between 1937 and 1940 was the sprouting and political exploitation of Muslim nationalism. I.H. Qureshi in *A History of the freedom Movement* rightly observes : "The events after the elections of 1936-37, ...triggered the forces of Muslim separatism into speedy activity."[1] The only all-India Muslim party of any consequence at that time was the All-India Muslim League, which however had performed poorly in the general elections of 1937, attracting less than five per cent of the Muslim vote, and manifesting little symptoms of separatist tendencies. M. A. Jinnah, who had finally returned to India after some years of retirement in England to resume leadership of the Muslim League and to marshal the party for the election, was still calling for Hindu-Muslim coordination, as he had been doing in the past. Though in the Legislature he had assailed the federal part of the 1935 Act as "totally unacceptable" , yet he had asserted that he was not against all-India federation as such, but merely to the scheme embodied in the Act.[2] And even after the rout of his party in the elections, after the Indian National Congress had formed ministries, and his failure to reach any kind of Congress-League accord in the United Provinces and Bombay, Jinnah, condemned Congress policies as they would result in communal animosity. He still emphasized the need for a "complete united front with an honesty of purpose" to obtain "full national democratic government for India."[3] "There was no suggestion" as yet, affirms C. H. Philips, "of Muslim secession."[4]

How did it come about that the Muslims, politically

impotent and disjointed in the 1930s, were able to put forward a telling demand for a separate state in the 1940s? Was Muslim nationalism a spontaneous growth, a widespread movement of the grass roots which for long was not discerned in the centres of power, or was it the wilful creation of the Muslim League? Did the League merely represent the feelings of the bulk of the Muslims or did its leaders fabricate a nationalist movement by manipulating the many existing economic, social and political tensions focussing on the one goal of seeking a separate homeland for Muslims?

The political ideal of nationalism was not widespread among Muslims until the last few years before the transfer of power. It took a concrete shape as late as 1940, crystallizing rapidly thereafter. Moreover, this Muslim nationalist movement did not show its head in those parts of north-west and north-east India where Muslims were in the majority, but appeared first among middle and upper class conservative Muslims in the United Provinces, where they were in a minority. A detailed study of the politics of both minority and majority areas before the Pakistan bandwagon drove most Muslims into the League camp might help to show how a party of a conservative minority became a great mass movement. On the evidence at present available, it seems most likely that it was the adoption of a simple and inspiring slogan, the creation of an effective all-India organization, and the extremely capable and single-minded leadership of Jinnah were among the chief reasons. They worked upon the separatist tendencies of the Muslims, and utilized every opportunity offered by the Congress and the British to further the League cause, which explains the success achieved by the League in such a short period.

Many Pakistani scholars—like Mumtaz Hasan and M.A.H. Ispahani[5]—do not accept this view, believing that the demand for separation came up from the grassroots and would sooner or later have had to be taken account of, that it was not the creation of the Muslim League, but that the League leadership merely provided flesh to the aspirations and convictions of the masses.

What was the precise role of Jinnah? No one doubts that he played an important and positive part in these crucial years. He dominated the League organization, in fact he was the League organization. But how did he come to be so established? He was not a new star rising on the horizon, but a prominent politician of very long standing. He was the League's guiding personality and president during the 1920s when the party was at a low ebb. It seems therefore, that it was not Jinnah's personality alone which brought about the renovation of the League after 1937. It was rather the combination of his drive and authority, his steadfastness and capacity to inspire devotion in his associates, together with the exhilarated call for Pakistan.

The period of Congress rule in its eight provinces created among Muslims a basis of resentment on which 'atrocity' charges could be built, thus providing Jinnah with his first strong assault weapon against the Hindus. The Congress governments evinced a woeful lack of realism, of foresight and of high statesmanship, and this put Jinnah at a vantage point. For however unfounded or exaggerated the charges of Hindu atrocities might have seemed, there is no doubt that Muslim opinions and sentiments were disregarded by the Congress ministries, and that Muslims felt themselves threatened. The grim realities of the Congress raj were being unfolded; dread of Hindu raj reinforced and nothing substantial was done to reassure them or to assuage their fears which became an irritant. By rotation, Jawarharlal Nehru, Abul Kalam Azad, Sardar Patel and others took important initiatives in governance but these were not vigorously pursued and no definite line of Congress policy was evolved or maintained.

Two major decisions on policy, both of which revealed a fundamental lack of appreciation of the realities of power were mostly responsible to enervate the foundations of Congress power. The first was the resignation of all Congress ministries as a protest to the commitment, by the British Viceroy Linlithgow, of India to war. The second was the ill-devised attempt in 1942 at rebellion to press the hard-pressed British to quit India.

To follow the Congress line of thinking as to the first decision: It has been said that Congress had only taken office recently (in 1937) after great hesitation and misgivings, and by a narrow majority, and in face of strong opposition from the left-wing; it could not honourably allow itself to be dragged into war on behalf of an India which was not free.[6] Such considerations fitted well with inner and peace-time politics. The situation now was that at the most critical period of Britain's existence, Congress adopted a negative attitude, voluntarily relinquished the gains of twenty years, tamely surrendered the political initiative and position of authority for little apparent gain, and at the same time opened to its opponents a route hitherto blocked to the centre of Indian government. This was an irreparable loss to the Congress, and a prestigious gain to its rivals. No wonder Jinnah was so exultant, and he was a man equal to the new situation.

The subsequent move of Congress into rebellion[7] manifested its sense of frustration and uncertainty of purpose and it proved to be a great miscalculation of the forces at work. The leaders of Congress were condemned to a long periods of imprisonment and the Congress organization was disjointed for nearly three years at a very crucial time. A God-sent opportunity which Jinnah and his associates could not and did not fail to turn to account.

In their evaluation of Muslim League, Nehru and Congress committed the same type of mistake as the Britishers did in respect of Congress by belittling its importance by describing it as the organization of the English-educated classes constituting a microscopic minority.

Congress opinion which conditioned all of the decisions taken by the party in respect to the Pakistan movement was largely created by Gandhi and Nehru. It denounced and denied the validity of Jinnah's 'two-nation theory' India, it affirmed, was one nation and the Congress stood for its unity, but at the same time Gandhi made it clear that under no circumstances would the Congress forcibly resist Pakistan; perhaps assuming, along with most Congressmen, that British policy and presumably force of arms would, in the last analysis, be thrown on the side of maintaining the unity of India. Gandhi declared: "We are at present a joint family. Any member may claim a division." This view he frequently expressed. Nehru's response to the Pakistan demand was to say that those who insisted on Pakistan and people like him could not live together in India.

The practical effect of taking this attitude towards the Pakistan movement was drastically to reduce Congress's power of manoeuvre *vis-a-vis* the Muslim League, and to place sole emphasis on persuasion and negotiation, without reference to Congress's power.

Looking back into the pages of the history of the Indian freedom movement, one comes across several instances wherein one has reason to feel that the Congress as the leading party and the oldest, due to wrong moves and careless action, had to face ominous consequences. Faced with a human problem involving large numbers of people with a different way of life and outlook, nay, different set of values, the major communities should in their own interest and in the larger interest of the country as a whole, have adopted a conciliatory and sympathetic attitude which would make for a friendly response. The lessons of history seem to have been lost on the Congress leadership, and, as months and years rolled on, whether one liked it or not, partition became inevitable and a *fait accompli.*

NOTES AND REFERENCES

1. Qureshi, I.H. *A History of the Freedom Movement*, 1936-1947, (Karachi : Pakistan Historical Society, 1970), Vol IV, Part I, p. 2.
2. "Speech on the Report of the Joint Parliamentary Committee on Indian Constitutional Reforms in the Legislative Assembly on 7th February, 1935", In: *some Recent Speeches and Writings of Mr. Jinnah*, (4th edn.). Ahmad, Jamiluddin, (collat. ed.), (Lahore: S.M. Ashraf, 1946), pp. 9-11.
3. "Presidential Address Delivered at the Lucknow Session of the all India Muslim League, October 1937," Ibid, p.29.
4. *The Partition of India—Policies and Perspectives, 1935—1947*, Philips C.H. and Wainwrights M.D. (eds.), (Massachusetts :

Cambridge, The M.I.T. Press, 1970), p. 11.

5. Hasan, Mumtaz *"The background of Pakistan"*, pp. 319-30; and Ispahani M.A.H. , "Factors Leading to the *Partition of British India"*, Ibid. pp. 331-59.
6. It was too much to expect that India should fight for the freedom of other nations while she was being denied her own freedom.
7. Long before all other possible paths had been explored.

Chapter 1

Eve of 1937 Elections—A Political Prognosis

The 'ifs' of history have always tantalized statesmen no less than scholars. Conservative British statesmen who were instrumental in making the Government of India Act of 1935 have aired an 'if' of pivotal importance to students of recent Indian history: if the Act's federal provisions[1] had become implemented before the war then the partition of the country could have been averted.[2] Speculation on what might have been, although apparently futile, does at least have the merit of not assuming that the course of events in the past was inevitable.

When the Government of India Bill 1935 was being steered through the House of Commons during the winter of 1934-35, Jawaharlal Nehru was in jail and writing his autobiography. "It is an illusion to imagine", he wrote in this book, "that a dominant imperialist power will give up its superior position and privileges unless effective pressure amounting to coercion is exercised."[3] Nehru did not therefore, foresee much expectations by the Act of 1935.[4] He described it as "a Charter of Slavery to strengthen the bonds of imperialist domination and to intensify the exploitation of our masses."[5] In his presidential address to the Lucknow session of the Indian National Congress in March 1936, Nehru, fresh from Europe and in full flush of a socialist phase of thought, declared that the new Constitution offered India only responsibility without power, and therefore deserved to be rejected "in its entirety".[6] Sensing the mood of the party, he acquiesced Congress participation in the elections, but made it clear that he did not expect India's salvation through the new Constitution.[7]

If the same Act had been enacted soon after the first world war it would have been hailed as a welcome step on the road to self-government. But in the circumstances and mood of the 1930s, the Act received a frigid reception in India.[8] It was condemned by almost all political groups and parties, though not always for the same reasons. The Congress, with its avowed nationalist and democratic-socialist viewpoint, was the strongest in its denunciation of the Act declaring that it in no way represented the will of the nation.[9] The cardinal objection to it was that "it was the product neither of self-determination nor even of joint determination but of 'other determination'."[10] The Congress deprecated the 'safeguards', checks and balances as rendering responsible government, a sham. It demanded absolute authority in the provinces and at the centre. The Congress coupled its censure of the Act of 1935 with the far reaching demand that the future Constitution of India should be framed by Indians themselves by means of a "Constituent Assembly", elected on the basis of universal adult suffrage and invested with the power to determine finally the Constitution of the country.[11]

But while reprobating the Act, both the Right and Left in the Congress were agreed on the desirability of contesting the elections for the provincial legislatures though they were divided on the question of 'acceptance of office'.[12] So the Congress resolved not to commit itself in any way at the stage and left it to be decided at the proper time by the All India Congress Committee (AICC) after consulting the Provincial Congress Committees. But the Lucknow session left no doubt that the orthodox or the Gandhian wing reigned supreme, while the socialist section formed a feeble opposition.[13]

The party resolved to contest Muslim seats as well as the seats of the Scheduled Castes, to permeate the farthest crevices of the country through the election manifesto, the draft of which was duly approved on 22nd and 23rd of August, 1936. The essence of the manifesto is given below :

> The Manifesto dwelt upon the economic crisis in India and the poverty and unemployment of the peasantry and the industrial workers....The Congress has rejected the Government of India

> Act of 1935 and has resolved to develop internal strength by working in the legislatures. The policy of Congressmen will be to resist British imperialism. ... It stands by the Karachi Resolution relating to fundamental Rights and Duties.... In the domain of industrial labour, decent standard of living, regulated hours of work and conditions of labour, settlement of disputes and relief against old age, sickness and unemployment and the right to form Unions and to declare strikes, will be the reforms aimed at. Removal of sickness-disability, maternity-benefits and protection of women workers, equality with men.... the removal of untouchability and uplift of the *Harijans* and backward classes, ... readjustment of communal claims will largely constitute the programme of the Congress in the legislatures.[14]

Accordingly at its Faizpur session in December 1936, the Congress finalised the decision to contest the elections to the provincial legislatures due in early 1937 but kept in abeyance the disposal of the controversial issue of 'acceptance of office' till after the elections.[15] Though Nehru, the president of the Faizpur session, had considerably mellowed down in his enthusiasm for Communism—there was a marked change in his views between Lucknow and Faizpur[16]— he still expressed himself very definitely against the acceptance of office, and the question was again to be decided by the AICC immediately after the provincial elections were over.

As regards the position of the Muslim League during these months prior to the elections of 1937; Muslim politics was in a state of hopeless confusion, with interests clashing at all levels, provincial, local and personal. No Muslim organization appeared capable of smoothing out the discord that corroded the Muslim body politics. Organizations such as *Jamiat-ul-Ulema-i-Hind, All-India Muslim Conference* and even the All-India Muslim League were deliberative bodies. Since the non-cooperation days the Jamiat had been in oblivion and was not sufficiently organized. It continued to plough its lonely furrow until the time when it unconditionally joined the Congress in 1937.[17] The All-India Muslim Conference had been inactive. In 1936, it decided to withdraw from the election campaign. Like other Muslim organizations, the Muslim League too during the last few years had been in a moribund condition.[18] After the second session of the Round Table Conference, Jinnah had stayed in England, and during his absence the Muslim League had 'lived on paper'. But the League was older than other Muslim organizations and it had played a part in the past in organizing the Muslim community on an all-India basis. It was still the only party in the field to fight elections but, however, had to set its own house in order before it could start organizing the machinery for a national effort.[19]

Jinnah had come back and started the revival process of the League. At its 24th annual session at Bombay in April 1936, while condemning the federal scheme, the League decided to utilize the provincial part of the Act for "what it was worth" and empowered Jinnah to form a central parliamentary board, consisting of not less than thirty-five members, and authorized to affiliate provincial boards in the various provinces to contest the elections on the ticket of the Muslim League.[20]

On May 21, 1936, Jinnah announced the personnel of the parliamentary board consisting of fifty-six members,[21] who were nominated with much difficulty. Provincial leaders representing different political Muslim parties had already formulated programmes and embarked upon their election campaigns. Jinnah was late in the field and had, perforce, to depend on those leaders who were still unattached to any parties or those whom he could persuade to merge their organizations with the League.[22] Leaders like Fazlul Haq (Krishak Praja Samity, Bengal), Syed Abdul Aziz (United Party, Bihar), Sheikh Abdul Majid Sindhi (Azad Party, Sind), and other local leaders, though originally nominated on the board had already organized their respective parties to fight the elections under the auspices of their own organizations.[23] Personal and provincial rivalries and fear of rival groups, rather than the differences with the Muslim League, lay behind the unwillingness of some of the leaders of provincial parties to serve on the Muslim League Parliamentary Board. Such were the divisive forces that convulsed Muslim politics in 1936.

It was against such divisive politics in the Muslim ranks that Jinnah raised his voice and sought to boost Muslim politics from the provincial and local to an all-India level, not realizing that these splinter organizations had no public sanction behind them. Only a cohesive Muslim party would have the authority and sanction to speak powerfully. Nevertheless, in organizing the Muslims under the banner of the Muslim League, Jinnah did not believe that he was diminishing the chances of Hindu-Muslim cooperation. In the words of Z. H. Zaidi :

> When Jinnah embarked on rallying the Muslims on the League platform and asked them to stand by its policy, he was far from running the Muslim League as a counter to the Congress. For him the memories of the Lucknow pact were still fresh.[24]

The main aim of the Muslim League programme was to maintain the solidarity of the Muslims. The election was to be fought—and this is an important point—not essentially between the Congress and the League (as some of the members of the Muslim League continued to be the members of the Congress) but between the Muslim League and the local Muslim parties. The issue was whether local interests should be subordinated to national interests of the community or vice versa.[25]

The manifesto adopted by the League on June 9, 1936, while affirming that the position of Muslims should be protected and safe-guarded in any future constitutional fabric, asserted that such a demand did not "savour of communalism."[26] For it was not only "natural, but essential for securing a stable national government by ensuring whole-hearted and willing cooperation of the minorities who must be made to feel that they can rely upon the majority with a complete sense of confidence and security." The manifesto also stressed the need for a new social order with specific attention to poor and backward Muslims.

The League adopted the following programme :

1. To protect the religious rights of the Mussalmans. In all matters of purely religious character, due weight shall be given to the opinions of *Jamiat-ul-Ulema-i-Hind** and the *Mujtahids.***
2. To make every effort to secure the repeal of all repressive laws.
3. To resist all measures which are detrimental to the interest of India, which encroach upon the fundamental liberties of the

people and lead to economic exploitation of the country.

4. To reduce heavy cost of administrative machinery, central and provincial, and allocate substantial funds for nation-building departments.
5. To nationalize the Indian army and reduce the military expenditure.
6. To encourage development of industries, including cottage industries.
7. To regulate currency, exchange and prices in the interest of economic development of the country.
8. To stand for the social, educational and economic uplift of the rural population.
9. To sponsor measures for the relief of agricultural indebtedness.
10. To make elementary education free and compulsory.
11. To protect and promote Urdu language and script.
12. To devise measures for the amelioration of the general conditions of Muslims.
13. To take steps to reduce the heavy burden of taxation.
14. To create a healthy public opinion and general political consciousness throughout the country.[27]

The League manifesto further hailed the Lucknow pact as "one of the greatest beacon lights in the constitutional history of India" and as "a signal proof of the identity of purpose, earnestness and cooperation between the two great sections of the people of India."[28] Indeed there was every indication, as I. H. Qureshi states, "that the Congress could rely on the support of the League in its twin tasks of winning freedom and ameliorating the lot of the masses."[29]

In the words of Ram Gopal :

> The Muslim League itself now talked least of communalism, and raised itself almost to the level of the Congress in the economic content of its election programme. The Congress had never been hostile to the League, but as the election drew nearer, its attitude towards the League grew softer. An impression was allowed to prevail that the two organisations would not come into conflict with each other. In U.P., the Congress and the League pronouncedly arrived at an understanding of mutual help in the election campaign.[30]

NOTES AND REFERENCES

1. "The federal part of the Act was to become operative only when and if a sufficient number of states were (i) to occupy 52 of the 104 seats allotted to the states in the upper house of the federal legislature and (ii) to make up half the total population of all states, had acceded to the federation." Mehrotra, S.R. "The Congress and the Partition of India" In : *The Partition of India, Policies and Perspectives, 1935-1947*, Philips C.H. and Wainwright., M.D. (Massachusetts : The M.I.T. Press, 1970), p. 188. "The part of the Government of India Act which proved to be a still-born child as the rulers of states turned their faces against it," Majumdar, R.C. (gen. ed.), *Struggle for Freedom.* (Bombay : Bharatiya Vidya Bhavan, 1969), p. 574.
2. Lord Templewood and Lord Halifax expressed such views : for instance Lord Halifax states, "Federation, if only it could have been quickly implemented, might have saved the situation." Earl of Halifax, *Fullness of Days* (London : Collins, 1957), pp. 126-27.
3. Nehru, Jawaharlal. *An Autobiography*, (Bombay : Allied Publishers, 1962), p. 554.
4. For text of the Act, *Select Documents—The Evolution of India and Pakistan—1858 to 1947*, Philips C.H. (gen. ed.)., (London: Oxford University Press, 1962), pp. 320-35.
5. Nehru, Jawaharlal, *India and the World*, (London : George Allen and Unwin, Ltd., 1936), Vol. I, p. 86.
6. Mitra, Nripendra Nath, (ed.,), *The Indian Annual Register* Calcutta, The Annual Register Office, 1936, Vol. I, p. 249.
7. Nehru, Jawaharlal, *India and the World*, op. cit. p. 86.
8. Templewood wrote to Halifax in 1953: "When Willingdon succeeded you and I became Secretary of State, I came to the conclusion that it was we in London who were pressing the reforms, and that the brake came not from Whitehall but from Delhi," Templewood Collection, cited by Moore, R.J. "The Making of India's Paper Federation, 1927-35", Philips, *Partition of India* op. cit. pp. 54-55.
9. Mitra, op. cit., p. 248.
10. Sitaramayya, Pattabhi, *The History of the Indian National Congress*, 1935-1947, (Bombay: Padma Publications, 1947), Vol. II, p. 12.
11. Ibid., p. 35.
12. Ibid, p. 12, Majumdar, op.cit. p. 558.

13. "Nehru's views coincided with those of the latter, but his personal allegiance was to the leader of the former... Nothing is more remarkable in the history of the next decade than the gradual conversion of Nehru, step by step and stage by stage, to the views and practices of Gandhi. One might well ponder how and why a dynamic personality like Jawaharlal Nehru made an abject surrender to Gandhi—about whom he himself said that 'ideologically he was sometimes amazingly backward', and again 'much that he says seems to fit in with a medieval Christian saint and not at all with modern psychological experience and method'. Fortunately, Nehru has himself answered this question on behalf of himself and many others who were insensibly drawn within the magnetic circle of Gandhi: '... He attracted people... They did not agree with his philosophy of life or even with many of his ideals. Often they did not understand him. But the action that he proposed was something tangible ...and we went with him although we did not accept his philosophy. Majumdar op. cit., p. 559.
14. Sitaramayya, op. cit, p. 24.
15. Ibid, pp. 12 and 35.
16. The official history of the Congress attributes this change to the "schooling that the President of Lucknow had had for well nigh a year in the University of life." Ibid, p. 31. "It would, perhaps, be more correct to say that the schooling really took place in the University of Sabarmati under its presiding genius, Gandhi. In any case, the change was significant. The Congress said the President, "today stands for full democracy in India and fights for a democratic state, not for socialism." Majumdar, op. cit., p. 560.
17. Zaidi, Z. H. "Aspects of the Development of Muslim League Policy, 1937-47" In : *'Partition of India,'* Philips, C.H. (ed.), op cit., pp. 245-46.
18. Ibid, p. 246.
19. In 1933, with a total income of Rs. 1318. 11.6, its annual expenditure showed a deficit of some 564 rupees." *'Annual Report of the All India Muslim League for the Years 1932 and 1933;* Ibid, p. 10.
20. *'Star of India'*, April 13, 1936, Ibid. p. 10.
21. "Bengal 8, Punjab 11, Sindh 4, North West Frontier Province 4, Madras 4, United Provinces 9, Bihar 5, Central Provinces 2, Delhi 1, Assam 2, Bombay 6," *State of India*, May 23, 1936. Ibid, p. 247.

22. *Civil and Military Gazette,* May 23, 1936, Ibid. p. 250.
23. Ibid. p. 251.
24. Ibid p. 251.
25. *Civil and Military Gazette',* June 11, 1936, Ibid. p. 251.
26. Ibid., p. 252.
27. *Civil and Military Gazette,* June 12, 1936, also "*Star of India,* June 12, 1936. Ibid p. 252, and Gopal, Ram. *Indian Muslims—A political History 1858-1947* (Bombay : Asia Publishing House, 1959), p. 244.
28. Coupland, Reginald, *Report on the Constitutional Problem in India* (London : Oxford University Press, 1944), Part II, pp. 14-15.
29. Qureshi, I.H. '*History of Freedom Movement,* op. cit., p. 2.
30. Gopal, Ram, op. cit. p. 243.

* Group of Indian men of learning

** Muslim divines

Chapter 2

Aftermath of the Elections

The experience of contesting the elections of 1937 and forming ministries under a responsible government revealed the inner dynamics of Indian politics. It brought to fore both majority and minority attitudes in a new and striking way. The most significant of these was the Congress tendency towards a one-party polity in India that assumed the submersion of other Indian parties. Another was the emergent unity of Muslim India.

The results of the elections considerably altered the outlook of the different political groups and the British authorities. The Congress emerged as the largest party in seven provinces out of eleven, with a clear majority in five—Madras, U.P., C. P., Bihar and Orissa.[1] Of the 1,585 seats in the provincial legislatures, Congress contested 1,161 and won 716. Congress victory is all the more impressive when it is borne in mind that of the 1,585 seats less than half, 657, were 'general' or open, that is not allotted to a separate, closed elect group such as Muslims, Sikhs, Christians, Europeans, Anglo-Indians and landholders.[2]

The performance of the Muslim League as such was modest. It won only 109 of the 482 seats allotted to the Muslims, securing only 4.8 per cent of the total Muslim vote. It did not win a majority of seats in any of the four Muslim majority provinces—Punjab, Sind, North West Frontier Province and Bengal.[3] In fact, its performance in these provinces was far worse than in the Muslim minority provinces. In the Sind legislative assembly the League had won three seats, in Punjab only one, and in the North West Frontier Province, none at all. In Bengal, it had won a third of the Muslim (and one-sixth of the total) seats in the legislative assembly, but did not enjoy a commanding position even there. Party alignments in Muslim majority provinces had cut across religion; Sir Sikandar Hayat Khan in Punjab, Fazlul Haq in Bengal, and Sir Ghulam Husain Hidayatullah in Sind had not responded to Jinnah's appeal for Muslim solidarity. They seemed to be swayed little by religious affiliations. Among minority provinces, it did not win a single seat in the lower houses in Bihar, the Central Provinces and Orissa. Only in two it did rather well, winning 27 out of 64 seats in U.P. and 20 out of 29 in Bombay.[4]

In Punjab, the Unionist Party—and not the Muslim League—under the leadership of the redoubtable Sir Sikandar Hayat Khan, secured a majority, and he formed a cabinet of six ministers consisting of three Muslims, two Hindus and a Sikh. In Bengal Fazlul Haq., the leader of the Krishak Praja Samity Party, came to the fore with a strong programme. His plea for the abolition of the Permanent Settlement Act and the release of political prisoners and detenus brought him and his party considerable Congress support before and during the elections.[5]

The success of Congress Party in U.P. was due, in large measure, to the solid backing of the peasantry. Nehru claimed that the election had proved that the Congress had the complete confidence of the people in U.P. He said :

> The election has brought a patent fact to the forefront, which is this: the masses are hungry and they want bread. Education is starved and the children of the poor classes should be given proper education. The peasantry is crushed by the burden of debt. How to give bread and education and how to relieve the masses from their debt should be the concern of all.[6]

Repressed for generations and hard hit by the economic depression of the early thirties, the peasants rallied to the election appeal of the Congress. Their hopes of a better life had been stirred up by Nehru's personality and his socialist programme. They felt elated that in installing a Congress government in power in U.P., they would have a share.

But this success was by no means unqualified. Nehru acknowledged that the party had not done so well in Muslim constituencies. The performance of the Congress in Bengal, and the NWF Province was not bad, but cut a rather sorry figure in Sindh and Punjab. The election of 1937 showed that Hindu communalism was stronger in the Muslim majority provinces than in the Hindu majority provinces, and that Muslim communalism was more firmly entrenched in the same way in the Hindu majority provinces. But on the whole, the electorate all over India had preferred non-communal parties and individuals.

The Congress was naturally jubilant and optimistic for the future. Weary of trying to promote an agreement between the various communities of India through private parleys and public conferences, the Congress had appealed directly to the masses[7] over the heads of communal leaders on the basis of its own political and economic programme and scored a notable triumph. The results had seemingly vindicated the propriety of its new approach to the solution of the communal problem in India.[8] Congress leaders thought it was possible to wean the masses away from their communal organizations and rally them under the banner of the sole national organization in India. The year 1937 in a sense, therefore, may be called the acme of Congress prestige and popularity. It accelerated its campaign of contacting the masses, especially the Muslims. The communal leaders on the other hand saw in the Congress move, a menace to their very existence. They felt that unless they organized themselves like the Congress they cannot win popularity with the masses.

The outstanding success of the Congress in the polls—especially when contrasted with the miserable perfomance of the Muslim League—was not only galling to the pride of the leaders of the Muslim League, it also disrupted many of their complacent postulations. The results of the elections showed that while the vast majority of the Hindus especially those in the Hindu majority provinces, were at the back of the Congress, only a very small percentage of the Muslims supported the Muslim League, and that, despite their numerous divisions the Hindus were capable of greater coherence in political action than the socially more homogeneous Muslims. While the Congress leaders occupied the centre of the political stage in India in 1937, and decided the fate of ministries, M.A. Jinnah and his colleagues, in the Muslim League, were in political ostracism, sadly learning the lessons of their debacle and straining every nerve to check their small following from defecting to the Congress. According to calculations, while the Hindus would dominate all the Hindu majority provinces, the Muslims could not be sure of dominating two of the Muslim majority provinces which they considered to be their main props, namely the Punjab and Bengal.[9] The lessons of the elections were clear and unmistakable and the Muslim League did not fail to learn them. The prospect that was starkly obvious to the League leaders was this: either they must soon retire from active public life or they must accept a position of permanent inferiority and exclusion from office in the Hindu majority provinces and the proposed all India federation. Only in the Muslim majority provinces was there some scope for the leaders of the League, provided they could make their organization as effective as that of the Congress. With characteristic daring, the Muslim leaders clutched at this off-chance, but very soon they realized that their ambition could not be fulfilled without detaching the Muslim majority provinces from the main body.[10]

It is significant that even at that stage, Jinnah's thoughts were not in the direction of a separate state of Pakistan. Shortly after the elections he declared : "Nobody will welcome an honourable settlement between the Hindus and the Muslims more than I, and nobody will be so ready to help it"; and he followed it with a public appeal to Gandhi to tackle this question. The latter's response was prompt but somewhat depressing: "I wish I could do something , but I am utterly helpless. My faith in unity is bright as ever; only I see no day-light but impenetrable darkness; and in such distress I cry out to God for light."[11]

Despite its previous disclaimer and Nehru's personal misgivings, the Congress finally agreed to take office. "The

AICC authorised and permitted the acceptance of office in provinces where the Congress commanded a majority in the Legislature, provided the Congress Party in the legislature was satisfied and was able to state publicly that the Governor would not use his special powers of interference or set aside the advice of ministers in regard to constitutional activities,"[12] (17-18 March, 1937). Not until June 22, 1937, did the Governor General Lord Linlithgow make a public statement which was regarded by the Congress as satisfactory on this point.[13] Congress ministries were formed in due course as follows : Bombay, Madras, the United Provinces, Bihar, the Central Provinces, and Orissa. Later in the same year the Congress was able to form a ministry in North West Frontier Province. Sind came in Congress fold early in 1938 and Assam was incorporated the same year in September.[14]

The Congress in office initiated two unfortunate moves which brought to surface the latent forces of Muslim separatism: one was the so called ministry episode, the other, the programme of Muslim mass contact. The first has acquired much prominence since the publication of Maulana Abul Kalam Azad's memoirs in which he details the negotiation with the Muslim League in the formation of the ministry in U.P. which was a key province so far as Hindu-Muslim relations were concerned. Muslims, who constituted only about 15 per cent of the population, had played a leading role in the cultural and political development of this region for centuries. Until the general elections, the relations between the Congress and some of the prominent Muslim leaders were generally cordial and even friendly. The Congress Party, though confident of challenging the landlords' influential position in the provincial government, was not hopeful of securing a clear majority.[15]

Choudhry Khaliquzzaman and Nawab Ismail Khan were then the leaders of the Muslim League in U.P. They assured Maulana Azad that not only would they cooperate with the Congress, but would fully support its programmes. They naturally expected that the Muslim League would have some share in the new government. The local position was such, Azad would have us believe, that neither of them could enter the government alone. Either both would have to be taken or neither. Azad gave hopes that both would be taken into the government. If the Ministry consisted of seven members only, two would be from the League and the rest from the Congress. In a cabinet of nine, the Congress majority would still be more marked. "After discussion with me," says Azad, "a note was prepared to the effect that the Muslim League Party would work in cooperation with the Congress and accept the Congress programme. Both Nawab Ismail Khan and Choudhry Kaliquzzaman signed this document."[16]

"After some days", Maulana Azad continues, "I ... found to my great regret that Jawaharlal had written to Choudhry Khaliquzzaman and Nawab Ismail Khan that only one of them could be taken into the Ministry. He had said that the League could decide who should be included, but in the light of what I have said above, neither was in a position to come in alone. They therefore, expressed their regrets and said that they were unable to accept Jawaharlal's offer."[17]

Azad regretfully points out :

> This was a most unfortunate development. If the UP League's offer of cooperation had been accepted, the Muslim League Party would for all practical purposes have merged in the Congress. Jawaharlal's action gave the Muslim League in U.P. a new lease of life. All students of Indian politics know that it was from U.P. that the League was reorganized. Mr. Jinnah took full advantage of the situation and started an offensive which ultimately led to Pakistan.[18]

Apparently becoming wise after the event, Azad shifts the blame on Jawaharlal Nehru. But as Mohamed Raza Khan says : "He was himself in a way greatly responsible for the breakdown in those days."[19] In the opinion of Ram Gopal, "the terms Azad himself offered to the League do not vindicate but implicate him."[20]

The terms were :

> The Muslim League group in the U.P. Legislature shall cease to function as a separate group.
>
> The existing members of the Muslim League Party in the United Provinces Assembly, shall become part of the Congress party....

> The Muslim League Parliamentary Board in the United Provinces will be dissolved, and no candidates will thereafter be set up by the said Board at any by-election.[21]

Understandably, the League leaders characterized this as the death warrant of the League, which, curiously enough, they of all people, were asked to sign. Was it, it was asked, for this that the League had built itself up as an all-India party, issued an election manifesto, presented itself before the Muslim voters and contested the elections?[22] And, having miserably failed in Muslim constituencies, was it ethically proper for the Congress to suggest that the Leaguers should virtually enter the Congress through the back door? Why the Congress would not accommodate the League? No straight answer to these questions was ever given, though the anxiety of the Congress to make its actual form reflect its creed was an answer; but it was an answer which was naturally more repulsive to the League.

Congress in U.P. was undoubtedly tactless in not taking two Leaguers into the ministry, but in the opinion of C.S. Venkatachar, the distinguished Indian Civil Servant, the action of the Congress is not altogether unjustifiable. Let us follow Nehru's line of thinking in 1937. He had no understanding with Jinnah on an all-India basis for a coalition with the League. In principle there was no case for such a coalition after the poor demonstration of the League in the recent provincial elections. The formation of ministries was of secondary importance to Nehru. To him the ministries, being the creation of Congress, could be set aside any time. His attention was focused on the impending struggle with the British to wrest power at the centre. In this contest the League Muslims were questionable allies, as they did not share Congress ideology.

This was the reasoning part of Nehru, but, in the opinion of Venkatachar, "in action he (Nehru) was led by his friend Rafi Ahmed Kidwai, a curious influence in U.P. politics." Kidwai could not get elected in the general election from any Muslim constituency but managed to slip through the Graduates constituency and Nehru would not exclude his nationalist Muslim friend from the U.P. ministry. "Nehru's attachment to his friend led by winding and devious steps", so says Venkatachar, "to the creation of Pakistan."[23]

As a matter of fact, before the elections, the Congress Party, working on the assumption that a decisive majority in the U.P. legislature could be ruled out, had virtually agreed to a coalition with the Muslim League.[24] This had engendered a working arrangement between the two organizations during the elections. According to Shiva Rao if the Congress had stuck to its pre-election intention of forming a coalition ministry, "the Hindu-Muslim problem might not have assumed formidable dimensions."[25] But it preferred to exercise the right of forming a party government, since that was held to be the verdict of the electorate. A coalition, it was argued, could not combat and wreck the constitution' the avowed object of a section of the Congress. But the Muslim leaders in U.P. regarded it as a breach of faith.[26]

Nehru or the Congress could have ameliorated the situation. The Muslims of U.P. had much personal affection for Nehru, whom they considered their friend, an idealist in politics who had been caught in the trap of communalist Hindus. "Even today Nehru is entitled to the benefit of doubt on the ministry question."[27] Where he went wrong was in his failure to realize the extent to which the faith and confidence of the Muslims in the majority party had been shattered. They argued that if this was the attitude of the Congress in the restricted range of provincial autonomy, how would Muslims fare in the all-vital field of the central government?[28]

V. P. Menon states :

> When the Congress decided to accept office there was a proposal that it should form coalition ministries with the Muslim League... The Congress decided to have homogeneous ministries of its own and chose Muslim ministers from amongst those who were members of the Congress Party. This was the beginning of a serious rift between the Congress and the League and was a factor which induced neutral Muslim opinion to turn to the support of Jinnah.[29]

In the opinion of Prof. M. Mujeeb, Congress victory was overwhelming, and a ministry could be formed without the assistance of any other party or independents, so, "The attitude of the Congress leadership to the informal arrangement made with the Muslim League leaders gradually changed." Mujeeb is critical of the agreement between the Congress and the League. "I was at home in Lucknow when the draft of the agreement proposed by Maulana Azad on behalf of the Congress was sent to Choudhry Khaliquzzaman. My immediate reaction on reading it was that the Muslim League was being asked to abolish itself. This was an attack not on the persons who wanted to become ministers but on the whole class that had painfully organized itself and was still feeling very shaky." Jawaharlal Nehru made matters still worse, Mujeeb adds, by writing to the Muslim League president that there were only two forces in India at that time—British imperialism and Indian nationalism. It was very poor statesmanship that transformed a difference of opinion over a ministerial post or two into a national struggle in which a class felt that it was fighting for its very existence. "It would not have shattered Nehru's prestige", Mujeeb goes on, "if, because of him, the Muslims had got one ministerial post more than they were entitled to; if Khaliquzzaman had been made a minister, the League in Uttar Pradesh would most probably have dissolved of itself." Indeed "Nehru and Azad together cleared the way for his becoming the valiant knight of an insulted and injured community."[30]

In the words of C.H. Philips :

> The sad fact was that temperamently and perhaps through his upbringing and early education in the cosmopolitan setting of Oudh and England, Nehru seemed incapable of evaluating the difference between Hindus and Muslims or of appreciating the full force of the Muslim case.[31]

Had the Congress "behaved more wisely and met the Muslim League half way and formed a coalition government in the United Provinces, the way could have been opened for Hindu-Muslim collaboration throughout India. 'Power corrupts and absolute power corrupts absolutely'."[32]

The Congress High Command wanted no truck with Jinnah. Kanji Dwarkadas discloses a similar attitude of the

Congress High Command in Bombay :[33]

> To sacrifice collaboration with the Muslim League in the name of ideals which did not at all correspond with existing facts was an extremely unwise—almost fatal—step for which India had to pay very dear .... The Muslims now fully realized that as a separate community they had no political prospects in future. The Congress ultimatum was the signal for the parting of ways which, by inevitable stages, led to the foundation of Pakistan.[34]

The breakdown of the talks between Khaliquzzaman and the Congress leaders in July 1937, though regretted by some, caused little surprise. The most suggestive commentary on the whole episode was provided by Khaliquzzaman himself. "I am afraid", he said in a statement issued on July 30, "I was trying to accomplish the impossible."[35]

The Ministry episode was bad enough, and the programme of Muslim mass contact was singularly foolish. Nehru declared immediately after the elections :

> We have too long thought in terms of pacts and compromises between communal leaders and neglected the people behind them .... It is for us now to go ahead and welcome the Muslim masses and intelligentsia in our great organisation and rid this country of communalism in every shape.[36]

Nehru launched this scheme in U.P. to establish direct contact with the people without the mediation of nationalist Muslim organizations. There was opposition to this within the Congress itself. Muslims inferred that Congress was out to obliterate them. Seized with a panic they gave mass support to the Muslim League, which in Nehru's opinion was no more than a reactionary body for safeguarding the vested interests of the Muslim upper classes and loyalists.

Ram Gopal observes :

> For the Congress secularism was an article of faith, and the provision as it stood in Clause VIII of the Instrument of Instructions seemed to hold out the hope of the evolution of a secular party system of government in India. The Congress believed it could provide flesh to this hope by its Muslim mass contact programme. In the communal atmosphere that had been

> advancing, and not receding, ... it was a forlorn hope. It really proved to be so. In the first place, the mass contact programme was never taken up seriously; and in the second, it was crushed, wherever it was launched, by the wheels of the League, which were rapidly gaining speed, strength and mobility.[37]

According to Menon, this scheme "did not meet with any success; on the other hand it widened the gulf between the Congress and the League. Jinnah took serious umbrage at what he described as an adroit effort on the part of the Congress to take advantage of the weakness of the League and the presence of splinter parties among the Muslims, and so to divide the community."[38]

Instead of conciliating the League, the Congress considered it to be a safer and more feasible course to destroy even the little influence it still possessed.[39] It recruited more and more Muslims to its fold. There may be nothing wrong in a political party trying to enroll members from various communities, but the campaign was run by Congress workers while the Congress was in office, which conveyed to the Muslim mind that this enrolement was being carried out, not by the Congress Party, but by the provincial government. This was the factor responsible for the failure of the campaign and added to Hindu-Muslim bitterness. Perhaps the Congress did not realize that a party in power is more exposed to criticism of every kind by the opposition, without always being able to justify its policies. In this respect the League worked from a point of vantage, and Jinnah, supreme tactician that he was, fully used this advantage. The Raja of Mahmudabad, whose family had been intimately connected with top Congress and League leaders, says :

> "To my great disappointment I found that .... Jawaharlal Nehru showed nothing but contempt for the Muslim League and its leaders.... The more Nehru spoke contemptuously and violently about the League and Jinnah, the more I disliked the Congress."[40]

The official Pakistan *History of the Freedom Movement* states:

> Oblivious of the trend of events and all warnings, the Congress persisted in its Muslim mass contact campaign, hoping to gain

> by governmental authority what it could not do through political activity. But it misjudged the temper of the Muslims who proved their mettle in times of peril and adversity.... Inspite of all its advantages including exercise of official pressure, the Congress was defeated in each of .... by-elections. Thus, by the close of the year 1937 the Congress campaign of Muslim mass contact had met with utter failure.[41]

In the words of Raza Khan :

> In fact, it used religion in its mass contact campaign. *Moulanas* and *Moulvis** were freely brought in to use the name of Islam to secure support for the Congress. It was paradoxical that while it opposed the mixing of religion and politics, it used this means very freely, but lo! it produced the opposite result.[42]

A series of Muslim by-elections in U.P. after the general elections afforded an opportunity to the two parties to test their relative strength. A Congress candidate (who had stood in the general elections as a Muslim Leaguer and was returned on that ticket) retained his seat and was taken into the cabinet.[43] Nehru started a mass contact scheme to attract Muslims of all persuasions to the Congress creed. Muslims even outside U.P. felt that the League's existence was being jeopardized; and in the later by-elections, the results evinced that Nehru's tactical error did not take long to show tangible repercussions.

Congress-League relations in the United Provinces touched a new low in June-July 1937 when the two parties set up rival candidates to contest the Jhansi-Jalaun-Hamirpur Muslim seat in the by-election.[44] The contest became a veritable trial of strength between the Congress and the League who strained all their available resources to win it.

The defeat of the Congress candidates in these by-elections had a visible psychological effect. The status of Muslim League rose all over India. Other parties which had been defeated in the elections, saw in the Muslim League a rallying point for a combined opposition to the Congress. Landlords, in particular apprehensive of the Congress agrarian programme, naturally clung to the League for indirect assistance and in return gave it support.[45]

NOTES AND REFERENCES

1. Sitaramayya, Election Results, op. cit. pp. 38-40.
2. Mehrotra, S.R. *The Congress and the Partition of India* In : Partition of India, Philips (ed.), op. cit., p. 189.
3. Ibid. p. 190.
4. Nanda, B.R. "*Nehru, the Indian National Congress and the partition of India*", Philips, op. cit, p. 157.
5. Rao, Shiva, "*India, 1935-47,*" in Philips, Ibid. p. 417. Sitaramayya, op.cit, p. 64.
6. Rao, Ibid. p. 417.
7. "It (election) forced the Congress to come in close contact with the masses, and this aroused political consciousness among them." Majumdar, op. cit. p. 560. "The enfranchisement of 3.5 crores of voters, including the wives of men voters and those who could sign their names, gave an impetus to the awakening of women with their civic consciousness on the one hand, and to the progress of literacy in one bound on the other. Thousands of women came forward to register their names as voters, and thousands more of illiterate men who had just learnt to sign their names." Sitaramayya, op.cit. p. 36.
8. Mehrotra, op.cit. p. 190.
9. Ibid, p. 191.
10. Ibid. 192.
11. Ahmed, Jamiluddin, *Historic Documents of the Muslim Freedom Movement* (Lahore: United Publishers, 1970), p. 220. Jamiluddin Ahmed (ed.), *Some Recent Speeches and Writings of Mr. Jinnah* (Lahore: S.M. Ashraf, 1952), Vol. I, pp. 25-26.
12. Gwyer Maurice L. and Appadorai, A. (eds,) *Speeches and Documents on the Indian Constitution* (New York: Oxford University Press, 1957), Vol. I, pp. 392-93. Sitaramayya, op. cit., p. 43, Majumdar, op. cit. p. 561.
13. The Marquess of Linlithgow, *Speeches and Statements 1936-43,* (New Delhi : Bureau of Public Information, Govt. of India, 1945), pp. 73-82.
14. Sitaramayya, op. cit., pp. 53 and 93.
15. Rao, op cit, p. 419.
16. Azad, Maulana Abul Kalam, *India Wins Freedom* (New York: Longman Green and Co., 1960), p. 188.
17. Ibid. p. 188.
18. Ibid, pp. 188-89.
19. Khan, Mohamed Raza, *What Price Freedom* (Madras : The Nuri

Press Ltd., 1969), p. 34.

20. Gopal, op cit, p. 248.
21. Khan, op. cit. pp. 34-35, Gopal, Ibid. p. 248.
22. Gopal, Ibid, p. 249.
23. Venkatachar, C.S. *1937-47 in Retrospect : A Civil Servant's View* in Philips, op.cit. p. 470.
24. Rao, Ibid. p. 419.
25. Ibid, p. 419.
26. Ibid, p. 419.
27. Venkatachar, op.cit. p. 470.
28. Ibid, p. 470.
29. Menon, V.P., *The Transfer of Power in India* (Princeton New Jersey: Princeton University Press, 1957), p. 56.
30. Mujeeb, M. *The Partition of India in Retrospect* in Philips, op. cit, pp. 411-12.
31. Philips *The partition of India 1947*, (Leeds : Leeds Univ. Press., 1967), p. 14.
32. Sinha, Sasadhar *Indian Independence in Perspective* (Bombay: Asia Publishing House, 1964), p. 96.
33. Dwarkadas, Kanji, *India's Fight for Freedom 1913-1937*, (Bombay: Popular Prakashan, 1966), pp. 466-67.
34. Majumdar, R.C. *History of the Freedom Movement* (Calcutta: Firma K.L. Mukhopadhyay, 1963), Vol. III, pp. 563-65.
35. *'Leader'* August 4, 1937: cited by Mehrotra, op. cit. p. 199. For details Khaliquzzaman, *Pathway to Pakistan* (Lahore: Longman Pakistan Branch, 1961), pp. 160-63.
36. Rao, B. Shiva, "They too Served India with Distinction", in *Swarajya* Annual Number (1968), p. 88.
37. Gopal, op. cit, p. 254.
38. Menon, op. cit., p. 56.
39. The Raja of Mahmudabad, *'Some Memories,'* Philips (ed.), op.cit. p. 387.
40. Ibid, p. 386.
41. Ahmed, Jamiluddin, *"The Congress in Office 1937-39"* In: *"A History of the Freedom Movement,"* 1936-1947, Vol. IV, Part II, op. cit., p. 50.
42. Khan, op cit, p. 29.
43. Rao in Philips, op cit, p. 419.
44. Mehrotra in Philips, op. cit. p. 198.
45. Rao, Ibid, p. 419.

* Muslim theologians and clergymen.

Chapter 3

Mohammad Ali Jinnah and the Emergence of Muslim Nationalism

In the perspective of Indian Muslim life and thought, M. A. Jinnah emerges as a most remarkable and enigmatic personality. His career is an intriguing paradox. He showed little solicitude and love for Islam and Islamic thought, reportedly disliked the *mullah* 'nonsense', and yet developed a lasting interest in the problems of the Muslim community. Considered as a 'European of Europeans', he rendered the indigenous Indian Muslims the singular service of carving out a separate homeland for them.[1]

Undergoing a metamorphosis in the late thirties, Jinnah—who had been the leader of the left wing section of the League in the cause of Hindu-Muslim unity—so drastically changed his ideals and objectives to call for the creation of a separate Muslim state on the basis of a newly propounded theory that Hindus and Muslims formed two distinct national entities which could not co-exist, that the so-called Indian entity was an artificial construct maintained solely by the British sword.[2] He argued that the differences between Hindus and Muslims were so fundamental that they could not be hushed up, and must be handled by all as realists. Since Muslims were a separate nation, a beleaguered one, things must be so arranged that they could have a sense of security and honour. The assertion that the Muslims and Hindus were "two completely and irrevocably opposed civilizations," was repeated as self-evident truths that required no proof, only repetition with vehemence.[3] Indeed the very demand for freedom for a united India, Jinnah said, was just an euphemism for establishing the domination of Hindus over Muslims. With a resoluteness rare among our politicians, he ensured the League was recognized as the sole representative of the Muslims, and he, in turn, was recognised as the League. As the spokesperson for the *millat* (Islamic community), he said, "Those who did not agree with him were betraying their religion."[4]

The question comes to the fore, how a convinced advocate of Hindu-Muslim unity for most of his political career could turn into the foremost advocate of Hindu-Muslim separation. For this, it would be worthwhile to study Jinnah's make-up vis-a-vis certain significant developments. It may be said "there were two Jinnahs," as Khalid B. Sayeed observes, "the Jinnah of the twenties and the Jinnah of the late thirties and of the forties." During the twenties Jinnah aimed at reaching a Hindu-Muslim settlement on the basis of a workable compromise. Later when this approach failed, he adopted a rigid attitude and negotiated from a position of strength based on the political power that he had mobilized.[5]

Jinnah belonged to the class of Macaulay's dreams which was, Indian in blood and colour, and English in thought and mannerism. He was steeped in the creed and philosophy of stalwarts like Spencer and Comte, Bentham and Mills. Besides imbibing the British influence, he was also associated, as Moin Shakir says, with the top most liberal leadership of the country, having come in contact with Naoroji, Gokhale, Surendranath and C.R. Das.[6] He was free from sectarian prejudices and was not prepared to think in terms of Hindu or Muslim nationalism.[7] In 1925, speaking at the All-Parties Conference, Jinnah had declared: "I have not come to say what Musalmans want..... Let us put our heads together not as Hindus or Mohamedans but as Indians.[8] He had warned Gandhi against encouraging the religious fanaticism of the Muslim priest which would lead to disaster, a warning which of course went unheeded. He felt that passionate religious excitement would do more harm than good, to Muslims in particular. As predicted, the mixing up of religion and politics initiated the element of irrationalism and mysticism in the political life of the country.[9]

Jinnah wished to get rid of the political ideology of the Aligarh school which was out for exploring ways and means for Muslim security vis-a-vis a non-muslim majority in a future independent India. Any ideology short of liberalism would do, as he believed, a permanent damage to the community and to the country. Nor did he consider Pan-Islamism—or an Islamic League of Nations—a sound ideology for the Muslims in this country. He feared that the consequences would be unfortunate if religion were brought into politics. "It would lead to the emergence of religious and fanatic leadership," to quote Moin Shakir, "while the country needed a secular and rational leadership." His conviction that politics and religion should be kept separate was an expression of his apathy to the theology or religious dogma. A liberal and secular nationalist, Jinnah did not approve either "the extremist Hindu view of nationalism or the separatist or communal nationalism of the Muslims. He held that the well-being of the country demanded cooperation between the two communities and sticking with its leaders that if the British left the country Hindu raj would be established. His liberalism implied nationalism, democracy, secularism and the unity of the country. He was of the opinion that British civilization had exerted a profound influence on all aspects of life in India, and believed that the new national consciousness of the Indian people owed much to the attitude and policy of the British government. He wished to drive home the point that if politics were rational the terms religious minority and religious majority would lose their importance. Jinnah adhered to his doctrine of liberalism honestly "until the logic of events convinced him of its futility."[10]

According to Jawaharlal Nehru, Jinnah had been largely responsible in the past for bringing the Muslim League nearer to the Congress. Till as late as 1936, Jinnah emphasized that without a united stand of two major communities, India's drive towards freedom would come to nought. Recalling his role at the Round Table Conference, he said early in March 1936: "I displeased the Muslims" at the said Conference. He further said, "I displeased my Hindu friends because of the 'famous' 14 Points. I displeased the princes because I was deadly against their underhand activities, and I displeased the British parliament because.... I rebelled against it and said that it was all a fraud. .... But whatever I have done, Let me assure you, there has been no change in me, not the slightest, since the day when I joined the Indian National Congress. It might be that I have been wrong on some occasions. But it has never been done in a partisan spirit. My sole and only object has been the welfare of my country," As for communal cooperation and harmony he emphatically asserted, "I will not, and I cannot give it up. It may give me up. But I will not."[11]

It speaks much for Jinnah that even from outside, he continued to cooperate with the Congress in the pursuit of unity, until he was hard hit, in 1937, by Nehru's declination to take two Muslim Leaguers in the U.P. ministry.[12]

At the time of his return to India in 1935, Jinnah could hardly be regarded a top-ranking politician. He was moreover not easily approachable, understandable or likable, being aristocratically arrogant and fastidiously scrupulous in his ways; and keeping a disdainful distance from the multitude.[13] Nor was he animated by any spirit of service to his fellowmen. A cold-blooded logician as he described himself to be, Jinnah was never a man of religion or of the masses. His knowledge of Islam was rudimentary, and this had not improved even when, later, he used religion unbridledly as an instrument to gain his political objectives.[14] And yet—or was it because of that—within the span of a lustrum he had risen not simply as Quad-i-Azam (the Great Leader), the creator of a popular, even zealotical movement, but as one capable of forcing his will on other parties, and showing that he too like the Congress had a nation at his beck and call. "This personal transformation, one of the most dramatic and decisive in modern history," states C.H. Philips "offers some explanation of the partition."[15]

Even though Jinnah had worked closely with leading men of different political organizations, he not only remained personally aloof, but advanced a point of view which was often at variance with most of his collaborators. With the advent of M.K. Gandhi his political lonesomeness became more marked.

He was dismayed to see during the late twenties that his constitutional adjustments and patterns were being submerged by the Congress nationalist upsurge that Gandhi was leading.[16] He had tried to steer the League as close to the Congress political wind as possible, but to his chagrin, he found his advances repulsed by the Congress leaders.[17] The so called Nehru report had decisive effect upon the aggravation of the communal problem.[18] Jinnah was cold-shouldered.[19] It seemed unsmart to pursue a communal point. The secularists dismissed it as an archaic force.[20] Nor did he receive much approbation or encouragement from his own community which feared his liberalism. As for the British, they made no bones about their apathy for Jinnah. "Till the first six years of the thirties, including the Round Table Conference period, the policy of the British government had always been." Writes M.H. Kidwai, "to project the arch British loyalist Agha Khan as the leader of the Indian Muslims and leave Mr. Jinnah high and dry."[21] Jinnah seemed to be doomed to political ostracism.

Rejected by his peers and deeply hurt by the sad—almost synchronous—finale of his marital venture—to be discussed presently—Jinnah's initial reacton was to withdraw from Indian politics. It may be said that during 1929-35, there took place in his thinking a searching self-introspection, a probing of the entire situation and of the role that he could play in it.[22] He was indeed to traverse a long way from his earlier posture of compromise making. He felt that his will and character were so strong that neither disappointments in public life nor personal griefs could shatter him.

In February 1929, Jinnah suffered a great personal loss in the death of his wife. Kanji Dwarkadas, a close personal friend of both Jinnah and his wife Ruttie, tells us that her death left him a total wreck. His loneliness added, writes Dwarkadas, "to the bitterness of his life; and I must add that this bitterness, born out of his personal loss and disappointment, travelled into his political life." This, Kanji Dwarkadas feels, "is the correct analysis of Jinnah's political bitterness which lasted throughout the nineteen years that he lived after his wife's death, and influenced his political life and opinions." He withdrew into his "Ivory Tower" and "became a perfect isolationist." His ego-centricism and sensitivity to criticism increased.[23]

"It is futile to contemplate and speculate," observes the same author, "how Jinnah's political life would have shaped if Ruttie had been by his side through the fateful thirties and forties." She was a great nationalist with no communal bias, and Jinnah, influenced by her, would have remained non-communal.[24]

One cannot deny, in the light of the above, the importance of psychology and psychiatry to historical understanding. The individual, as Veronica Wedgwood has sagely remarked, is at once infinitesimal dust and the cause of all things, an amazingly overwhelming and beauteous paradox. History may be sighted as the product of human nature in action, a projection of individual human nature, ideas and impulses on to the collective plane; hence, the new importance of biography as an indispensable adjunct to general history.[25]

To Carlyle, history was no more than a collection of a number of biographies, and he was of course exaggerating. Indeed the basic elements of history are, as V. B. Kulkarni says, social, economic and cultural forces which obviously overstep the lives of individuals. And yet, individuals have always played a momentous role in shaping the course of history.[26] There is not the slightest doubt that Jinnah, Gandhi and Nehru played a decisive part in the contemporary history of India.

Psychoanalytical probings of why and how the outsize men of history, generally speaking, yearn and struggle for power have lately acquired much currency and intellectual respectability. Harold D. Lasswell, a pioneer in these studies, has remarked, "Our key hypothesis about the power seeker is that he pursues power as a means of compensation against deprivation. Power is expected to overcome low estimates of the self, by changing either the traits of the self or the environment in which it functions."[27] A whole human being, Jinnah perhaps existed "only in being acknowledged". This, Hegel would say, entailed a "process of recognition"[28] and implied a search for solidity and security.

While recovering from his gnawing mental pang, with his ego bruised but taut, Jinnah must have had recourse to massive totalisms from which he derived the foundation stones for a new wholeness. Here what Erik Erikson, the eminent psychoanalyst, has said pertaining to ego will bear perusal for its great intrinsic merit, and may be quoted :

> To the ego the past .... is part of a present mastery which employs a convenient mixture of forgetting, falsifying, and idealizing to fit the past to the present, but usually to an extent which is neither unknowingly delusional nor knowingly dishonest. The ego can resign itself to past losses and forfeitings and learn not to demand the impossible of the future. .... To the healthy ego, the flux of time sponsors the process of identity. .... it is afraid of losing mastery over the negative conscience, over the drives, and over reality. To lose any of these battles is, for the ego, living death; to win them again and again means to ego something akin to an assumption that it is causing its own life.[29]

The strong ego element in Jinnah's make-up was both visible and audible. He was going through an agonizing identity crisis. He was reported to have said that one could break him but never bend him. Lasswell has mentioned cases in which a severe deprivation relatively late in life has led to frantic concentration upon power.[30] "It could be said," states Khalid B. Sayeed, "that Jinnah's mind was groping for a new solution to India's constitutional and political problems." He was drifting away from the traditional methods and pattern of thinking.[31] Badly mauled, he needed an instrument to recoup his self-confidence. Since he could not toe in line with others he had to have an organization under his sole charge, a forum to put forward his view-point. He must have seen that Indian politics had undergone a tremendous change by the induction of the masses into the national movement under Gandhi's leadership. Under such circumstances power would be magnetized towards leaders with a popular backing. The British government, he felt, was always thinking of the Congress, of the repercussion of the British stand in the Congress camp, because Congress was organized and enjoyed immense mass following. Therefore, the League had also to establish its solidarity and mass appeal. For Jinnah it may be said that it was practical politics which finally determined his ideology and thought. He had now to be "pragmatic, practical, beguilingly reasonable and logical," Moin Shakir says. It seems he was maturating, overhauling his ideology, making it down to earth and adequate for purposes of effective leadership in the country.[32] He planned to weld the different Muslim classes and sections into a monolithic organization. The lesson had come home that one could not play a dominant role in politics by merely acting as a negotiator or an intercessor.[33] Taking an audacious plunge he immersed himself complete into Muslim politics. Daringly he argued that there was no such thing as the Indian "nation" and the notion was pure intellectual luxury nurtured by the leaders of the majority community.[34]

So, Jinnah made Muslim politics both methodical and motivated. Election was a rough jolt. The supreme objective of Jinnah thenceforth was the acquisition and concentration of enormous power in his hands, an objective which he could rationalize in terms of the success and well-being of the *millat*. Bare manoeuvring could not produce results. It had to be backed by power. Jinnah found that his voter regarded askance the language of temperance and harmony. The League's election manifesto could not incense communal hatred and dogmatism and this default laid the League low, and consequently the extremist organizations swept the polls.[35]

Some of the commentators, impressed by the seeming Congress-League concurrence of the election period, failed to discern the dissension that was brewing between Jinnah and Nehru.[36] At the time the League election manifesto was penned, Jinnah was virtually a nationalist Muslim. "But the manifesto," remarks Atulananda Chakrabarty, "was the beginning of the road to two nations."[37]

Separate nationhood had always been in the subconscious mind of the Muslims. It was the Hindu extremist element which brought this latent desire to the fore, Moin Shakir says, Jinnah only crystallized and exacerbated it, and gave it an ideological and religious twist. His compromise with Muslim reactionary leadership on the political level had to be a concomitant to a compromise in ideology. Jinnah's two nation theory was the natural corollary of this mode of thinking, the ideological and political fulfilment of League's anti-Congress and anti-Hindu attitude.[38]

Learning his lesson, he switched on to demagogic tricks with alacrity; saw that he could beat mass contact all hollow by tuning his speeches to induce crude and raw passions. He plunged into the fray and gained the large and zealous following that gave him the mandate to frame the Lahore Resolution. On January 19, 1940, Jinnah wrote: "To conclude, a constitution must be evolved that recognizes that there are in India two nations, who must share the governance of their common motherland." But with his increasing hold on the Muslim mind, he soon turned impatient of any faint oneness. Even the conditional love of the common motherland rapidly died away when the fateful resolution was promulgated.[39] Nehru and others had never thought Jinnah would go that far, having taken him for granted.

As the Congress mass contact was beaten, Gandhi for the first time recognized Jinnah as the key man to bring about any Hindu-Muslim unity[40]—a late recognition. Jinnah was already past the "Rubicon."

Much can be understood if Jinnah's ambition, pride and Nehru allergy are taken into consideration. It was a gross political mistake to have ignored and alienated Jinnah to regain whose support there was a frantic, if belated, effort. "Any objective analysis will bring to light the carefully overlooked fact that the progress of national disintegration was," observes A. Chakrabarty, "more or less concomitant with the progressive alienation of Jinnah.[41] Besides, ambition, an essential element of his personality could hardly find sufficient scope for personal glory in the Congress which claimed the cream of intelligentsia in its fold.[42]

It appears, Jinnah was particularly allergic to Nehru's utterances and stances. When he sojourned in England in the early thirties, after the failure of the Round Table Conference, Nehru is reported to have said that Jinnah was "finished". The latter became furious at the remark. He packed up and sailed back to India to "show Nehru" Louis Fisher says.[43] This anecdote "is so typical of the personalities involved," argues Chakrabarty, "as to have the ring of truth." Evidently "it is in the power of the great ones to do great harm."[44] To Cleopatra and the elegant contour of her nose "as a factor in history one should perhaps add Jinnah's pride," Fischer remarks.[45]

In 1937, from a position of power and prestige Nehru wrote to Jinnah that there were two forces in India at that time, British imperialism and Congress representing Indian nationalism, implying that Muslim League was not a factor to reckon with.[46] Nehru was astride on the fancy, and Gandhi gave countenance to it, that power was the monopoly of the Congress, that the League was practically fading away.

The disappointed man turned an angry man. Clearly "this letter was no gesture of spiritual kinship with a people struggling to build together a single nation" but the presumptuousness of a politician aglow with a sense of superiority having a party in majority at his command. Proud and sensitive, Jinnah must have got sharply stung to see the insolent letter. "Here was the seed of the two nations dogma," Chakrabarty points out.[47]

He started to fight this Nehruvian totalitarianism. His politics assumed the character of aggressiveness, and he rapidly mastered the communal technique which he had so long persistently shunned. Muslim isolationism at last attracted him. Before long, he converted the communal to a national cause.[48]

The ascent of Jinnah to greatness is a remarkable proof for the potency of the psychological appeal of shrewd leadership, for the rationale of his cause was dubious and flimsy. Jinnah took to support the two nation theory despite its theoretical and practical unsoundness because of the great emotional excitement it evoked. The two nation concept, and the consequent demand for Pakistan, signifies the non-rational trait of the Muslim mind. It offered an escape from grim realities and inclement posture of things.[49]

In the astounding role that Jinnah played in Muslim politics since the autumn of 1937, he found a good vent for the political acumen that he was gifted with. In the attention that Muslims showed him, he could gain the better of his personal frustration.[50] It has been suggested that Jinnah sought power as a means of compensation for the deprivations that he had suffered. But "the mere possession of a strong will and the desire for power," K.B. Sayeed vigorously states, "could not have made him the Quad-i-Azam." There came about the lucky congruence between his needs and characteristics and the needs of his community. It is only when spurred by despair and doubt that the people resign themselves to the leadership of desperate, domineering and charismatic men. Such men can conceive a great idea, they can mould big crowds. They have been characterized as crowd pullers.[51]

However, it remains baffling how the Muslims of India, a warm hearted people, turned to a leader who was so austere and so distant from them. One explanation—not a complete one—is that this power conscious man promised to them the much coveted political power which their forefathers had wielded in India.[52] Muslims also clung to him as to a great saviour. After the death of Maulana Mohammad Ali there was no political leader of sufficient stature to lead them. On his part Jinnah would now lean on Muslims alone, and would leave no stone unturned to bring their desires to fruition. This now brings us to the other phase of our topic, the emergence of Muslim nationalism.

Nationalism is a comfortable mean between universalism and individualism. It is the old herd instinct, on an elevated plane "with an aroma of sublimity," observes A. Chakrabarty. It is afterall the desire to expand and magnify the "self".[53] At the same time love of humanity finds itself conveniently narrowed down to one's fatherland or motherland or still more narrowed down to race or religion. There is no set rule, however, where religious or regional cohesibility will prevail.[54]

How a particular people came to share this nationalist urge by merging a great many individuals into a "bigger oneness" has evidently not been uniform in all cases. But behind a nation there is this urge. The most appropriate definition of a nation seems to be, according to F. W. Coker : "A nation is a group which chooses to call itself a nation". Circumstances have differed in the evolution of different nations.[55]

The chronicle of mankind is largely a tale of sorrow and misery engendered by the selfishness, rancour and cupidity of man, and India is no exception to the rule. The reaction of the British impact on the psyche of Muslims and Hindus was bound to be very different. The former looked upon the English as their bitterest enemy who had monopolized the political power and the resulting privileges which they had so long enjoyed. The latter, on the other hand, not only welcomed the European rule, but even regarded it as a deliverance from the oppressions and sufferings of the Muslim rule. This Hindu attitude inevitably resulted in creating a dichotomy between the two major communities of the country.[56]

There can be no denying the fact that the Aligarh upsurge was to the Muslims what the Renaissance and nationalist movement of the nineteenth century was to the Hindus. It boosted the Muslim morale and lifted the community from the state of hopeless dejection in which it had fallen after the Mutiny.[57] Sir Syed Ahmad Khan, a man of extraordinary vision, saw that the "old order" had had its final exit, and that the future would be determined by modern education, science and technology. To cling to the crumbling "old regime" evinced a diseased mind. Aligarh soon became a symbol. It developed a pattern of its own.[58]

There may be some truth in K.M. Panikkar's statement that "till the establishment of British authority, the Muslims had felt no rivalry towards the Hindus," but after the Mutiny the situation showed a change. Once Congress was in order, the British authorities, apprehensive of the growth of nationalism, took to encouraging Muslim separatism.[59] To them imperialism had become a sanctified philosophy. Lord Morley, a liberal and a nationalist later had qualms of conscience and felt uncomfortable over the communal manoeuvring of 1909. But the growing complexities of events and attitudes made it advantageous for the authorities to play upon the susceptibilities of both the communities at the same time.[60]

However, if the British played their role of spoiling the national movement, this at least may be acknowledged that it was they who initiated this country into the national concept, and brought. Indians in touch with the lusty, revolutionary western world with its thrilling cry of national liberty, to say nothing of the unifying influences of British rule in India.[61]

It may also be pointed out that "no imperial power in history has been so benevolent and farsighted as to bring about a rapprochement between two rival communities."[62] The attitude of a master race towards its subjects is bound to be haughty and snobbish, at best condescending, in most cases, and the Englishmen in India formed no exception to this rule.[63] Furthermore, there was no guarantee that joint electorates, writes K.B. Sayeed, would have necessarily aided the two communities to develop a national outlook in political matters. On the contrary, the joint electorates, in th short run—when Muslim leaders were drifting towards a communal bend—might have deteriorated Hindu-Muslim relations. In the long run joint electorates might have prevailed, but as it turned out Congress leaders were getting impatient of British yoke. They were loath to wait long enough for parliamentary institutions to take firm roots in the Indian soil.[64]

The so-called "communal" problem or the question of the relations between the different religious "communities" had special dimensions in India, and was a serious problem for the national movement. But it was by no means a problem peculiar to India.[65] On the basis of historical experience the conditions under which such problems crop up may be explained.

In Palestine, Arabs and Jews lived peacefully together for centuries. Since British mandate was established, the forcible usherance of Zionism, with the violent conflicts have grown, which are sometimes dubbed as racial or religious conflicts, but represent in reality a national struggle for independence against invasion and alien control.[66]

During the later years of the decline and fall of Tsardom in Russia, Jewish pogroms tarnished its image. From the day power passed to the Russian people in their own country, the pogroms completely stopped.

In Germany during the Weimar Republic, Germans and Jews lived peacefully together. Under Nazi Germany the pogrom regime shifted its base from Tsarist Russia to Central Europe.

Switzerland's diverse peoples have cohabited in a single state for centuries. "There is thus no natural inevitable difficulty." R. Palme Dutt avers, "from the cohabitation of differing races or religions in one country."[67] The difficulties arise from other factors.

The truth is that nation making in India had not been serious and sincere. It had been faulty. "And there lies the source of all our troubles," Chakrabarty says.[68] While India was essentially in a fluid situation, it complacently pretended to claim that it was a nation; and the Indian National Congress embodied that claim, the emptiness of which became more and more poignant till we were caught up with a most shattering irony. "The breaking forth of two Indian nations as a result of India's frenzical struggle to live up with the challenges of modernism and obliterate the odium of default in attaining modern nationhood so long, is one of the stinging ironies in the annals of nation making. An ancient people unified culturally, ethnically, geographically, in a nervous venture to work out a modern political nationality, crashed into two warring nations," Chakrabarty adds.[69]

Indian "nationalism" did not have a set doctrine with a definite import; and was composed of incompatible trends. Nor was there any good effort to blend and solidify them.[70] "The basic problem is the problem of heart unity, which was neither attempted at any time nor reached," Chakrabarty states. If a pact was framed it was to paper the cracks, but the cracks would pierce soon. As the Bible says : There is nothing covered that shall not be revealed.[71] In a way this situation was responsible for the sprouting of Muslim nationalism.

The religious and revivalist movement of the nineteenth century made the Muslims conscious of their cultural and social isolation. It may be said that the idea of Hindu raj almost synchronized with the birth of the Indian National Congress. Hindu nationalism impaired the foundations of the common culture by generating fear and distrust, and finally created separatistic attitudes.[72]

Jinnah, however, did not lose faith in Gandhi who dominated the Congress. He acquiesced in the abolition of separate electorate provided Congress accepted some of the reasonable and rational demands. The Congress rejected his proposals in order to keep up its popularity with the Hindu multitude. In 1931, Jawaharlal Nehru rightly described this attitude as capable of begetting Muslim nationalism in India, Moin Shakir says. "The bania exploitation especially when agriculturists were Muslims, and machine-made goods, which hit the Muslim trader more than the Hindus," continues M. Shakir, "Strengthened Muslim nationalism, which looked to the community rather than to the country." In addition to this, some utterances of Gandhi like "Ram raj" were producing unwholesome effects especially on the educated, radical section of the Muslim community. [73] He had been publicly proclaiming himself a "Sanatanist Hindu."[74] Any moment he could glide from Congress politics to a Hindu reform movement and vice versa, but did not deal with the real question. Thus the chosen leader of the Indian National Congress appeared throughout as the sprightly leader of Hinduism and of Hindu revival.[75] No wonder Congress should be branded a "Hindu movement" even by a sizable body of general opinion, let alone the hostile element. This manner of doing things could not gain a mass Muslim following.[76]

Following the 1937 elections the Muslim leadership made overtures to the leadership of the Congress for an arrangement pertaining to Muslim accommodation in the provincial ministries to be formed and the apportionment of seats therein. The Congress, however, at this stage on a vantage ground spurned the Muslim League bid, repudiated its claim to any political pretension, and asserted that Indian nationalism resided solely in the Congress enclave. From this stage relations between the Congress and the Muslim League took an ugly turn.[77]

An additional reason of the growing alienation of Muslim leaders from the Congress movement was, according to Gunnar Myrdal, "its increasing commitment under the influence of Nehru and other left-wing intellectuals to radical policy declarations."[78] This radicalism of a section of Congress, as the rightism of Gandhi and others, both created misgivings in the heart of the Muslim Community. Jinnah consolidated the dissident Muslim factions and other political organisations of Muslims in India.[79]

This political ferment of the period led to mass awakening and growth in the following of both the major political organizations, the Congress and the Muslim League. The membership of the League which in 1927 had only amounted to 1330 "increased in 1938, according to its claim, to hundreds of thousands."[80] Between 1935-36 and 1938-39 the Congress membership rose ninefold to 4.4 million. "But only a small proportion of these were Muslims," remarks R. P. Dutt. "The overwhelming majority of the newly awakened sections of the Muslims turned to the Muslim League as their political organization."[81]

The enormous growth of the Muslim League and inadequate Muslim representation in the Congress manifested certain political. Organizational and tactical deficiencies in the Congress approach. Non-acceptance of the League coalition offer, to point out one incident, revealed a gross miscalculation of its potentialities on the part of the Congress and provided a lever for the subsequent anti-Congress propaganda of the League. In the tough situation preceding and following the beginning of the war, the amount of confusion, conflicting trends, and staggering moves of the Congress leadership[82] led to political and moral languishment, and weakening the appeal of a united national movement.[83]

The League was strengthened because Jinnah was aided in his mission by the short-sighted policy that the Congress governments and the Congress High Command pursued. He was also probably buttressed by the village mullahs, K.B. Sayeed observes. In the urban areas Jinnah could depend upon his own organising skill, and Muslim students from these areas flocked to the League banner.[84] Jinnah has to be heartily lauded for building up his party machine from scratch.

There were two alternatives for the Muslims on the ideological level—to carve a new destiny for them by embracing Pan-Islamism or adjust with the realities of the Indian situation.

The second alternative did not mean submission to the majority community. After the First World War, Islam had been driven at bay, and Pan-Islamism as a practical proposition had turned out no more than a chimera. A strong tradition of anti-Pan-Islamism nurtured by the Aligarh school was to influence Jinnah and the Muslim intelligentsia. Yet the Muslims were acutely conscious that they belonged to an international community. This factor even if politically of little consequence carried weight in the spiritual and cultural domain. Islam was potentially a volcanic force and intellectuals of the Muslim League including Jinnah cleverly used it with the object of the organization and cosolidation of the community.[85]

These factors were responsible for the invigoration of separatist Muslim nationalism. The notion, existed before but culturally. Now it was asserted in a strident manner. The attitude of many leading Congressmen after the 1937 elections made no bones about deeming the League a factor of no importance.[86] Congress behaved as if it stood for the entire nation, and yet insisted upon cornering the technical advantage of a majority party. Merely to call its Muslim members nationalist Muslims was not good enough nationalism, nor spiritual enough brotherhood, Chakrabarty observes.[87]

The loophole and challenge in the Congress attitude were tempting. The latent Muslim urge of separate nationhood was brought to surface by the Hindu extremist element. The simple thing was now to establish that Muslims were not represented by the Congress, that the Congress was a Hindu body. The democratic goal preached by the Congress implied Hindu raj which would uproot what was most precious in Islam. Jinnah argued that the term Indian nation was a sham, the brain child of some of the Hindu leaders who were doting on that.[88]

An important element of the two nation theory was the historical and spiritual differences existing between the Hindus and the Muslims. Both religions provide definite and dissimilar codes of conduct which regulate man's relation with his neighbour.[89] Jinnah had taken the view that these differences should be recognized as hard realities, and that Hindus and

Muslims should settle down to shape their politics on lines best suited to their respective intellectual endowments and traditions. What was strange and noteworthy was his thesis that Muslims should not be labelled as a minority when they were in a majority in the North-West and Bengal. In the only article he ever wrote, Jinnah waxed eloquent over his thesis and averred that Hindus and Muslims were two separate nations.[90]

Jinnah's two nation theory threw away his earlier concept of liberal democracy. He asserted that the political democracy of the western type was anathema to Indian conditions, and began to counter the logic of democracy with the logic of communal nationalism. His criticism of democracy was tantamount to a blatant pretension for an independent nation state for the Muslims. The demand for a separate homeland constituted henceforth the focal point in Jinnah's schedule. It answered the isolationist tendencies and ambitious cravings of the rising middle class of the community; also it was ardently taken by the commonality as it seemed to be the most plausible solution of all its grievances, real and imaginary.[91]

Communalism was to serve as a phase—a sordidly virile phase—of a search for national identity. The Pakistan programme fired an enthusiasm which the colourless creed of gradualism had failed to evoke. The Muslim question changed its base, from a search for a prescription for Hindu-Muslim accord to the demand for a sovereign Muslim state. A word may be said here about the background of the Muslims, resulting in their distinctive frame of mind.

Muslims, an overwhelming majority of whom hailed from the Hindu stock, could not get absorbed in the mainstream of the country's life, and remained peripheral. They persisted in cherishing the fallacy that they were masters of Hindus and rulers of India before the installation of the British. Far from comprehending the nuances and ramifications of the new dispensation, they viewed it with dismay and sullen hostility. For generations they remained morose, dejected and totally inactive, choosing to fix their gaze towards a past which was as fictitious as it was irretrievable.[92] Once the Indian National Congress was launched, they became somewhat scared.

Subjection to the British was bad enough, but Hindu yoke would be far worse. This mentality may be regarded as reproachable from the higher level of Indian nationality, but it is difficult to say that it was unnatural.[93] It is a paradox of Indian history that those who had sourly withdrawn at the coming of the British later became vehement supporters of the empire.

Muslims were much behind the Hindus in education. They feared joining the latter in the political fight for democracy or nationalism. Dadabhai Naoroji had sagely remarked that because the Mohammedans were backward they would not allow the Hindus to go forward. A community is guided, generally speaking, by considerations of immediate interest involved rather than a remote, if lofty, ideal of which very few have any clear conception. It would indeed have been an act of great sacrifice on the part of the Muslims to collaborate with the Hindus in their political ventures. In social and religious matters a cleavage existed between the two. Historical traditions and memories formed a barrier. What was a source of inspiration to one was held in contempt by the other.[94]

"It may be argued convincingly that in spite of all this a blending of Hindus and Muslims into one nation was not an impossible ideal," R.C. Majumdar writes. However, it must be borne in mind that "what was at best merely a possible ideal"—to be achieved only after herculean labour—should not have been misapprehended for an actual fact, either already accomplished, or nearing fulfilment. But the great Hindu political leaders perpetrated this fatal mistake, Majumdar says. They took for granted what was at best a far off contingency. They never understood, nor cared or bothered to understand, the feelings, impulses and problems of the Muslim community.[95] These men dismissed communalism as an archaic force, and ignored it expecting that it would dry up in the hot winds of nationalism.[96] They failed to discern the plain fact that the Hindus and Muslims were as yet two varied political units. Fired with ambition for democracy and nationalism, the Hindus failed to see that a sizable section of the people for valid reasons, regarded these ideals askance. In the abundant political literature of the period it is futile to look for, Majumdar ruefully states, "a just assessment of the Muslim point of view on the part of the Hindus." They had no patience to listen to the grievances of the Muslims, which might not excuse, but could at least explain their attitude towards the Hindus.[97]

Unable to read the writing on the wall, the Congress leaders satisfied themselves with the illusive notion that the opposition was after all confined to the educated few. But the intelligentsia was the nerve centre of the country, the natural spokesperson of the illiterate masses, the custodian of their interests. Hindus should have known that what they pressed for the country at large applied as truly to a district and strong minority community. They should have had the prescience that ultimately the Muslim masses would inevitably toe the line of their leaders.[98]

Congress seemed to be totally unaware of the drift of the Muslim mind and proceeded as if, observes Moin Shakir, "refusal to recognize reality was the remedy that the situation called for." It was becoming increasingly metaphysical, having lost all touch with hard facts, thereby losing sight of its primary resolve which was meant to be political, Shakir adds.[99]

Nor were the Muslim masses attracted by the strong Hindu religious flavour of the Congress propaganda. The Pakistan scheme was largely the outcome of a communal imbroglio which seemed to have run to a dead end and called for a desperate anti-dote.[100] What had been the role of the British, who occupied the vertex of the triangle, in this respect?

Muslim separatism had for past decades been acknowledge by the British and incorporated in the weightage system as accretional adjustments in the representative government. This move has been depicted as a deliberate attempt on the part of the rulers to set the electorate at variance and thus thwart the growing nationalist upsurge.[101]

"Politics took a heavy toll upon Indian nationalism and projected into it the dissensions and the distrust assiduously fostered among Muslims," says L.M. Singhvi.[102] This process was deepened by the introduction of electoral institutions which were the chief instrument through which the government modified its system of control during the later stages of the empire. These institutions are of supreme importance both to accelerating the pace of political orientation and to the sharpening of communal awareness among the Muslims of various provinces. David Page seeks to provide a structural explanation of Muslim politics and attitudes in the period prior to the crucial year 1937 to complement ideological explanations. The assumption that Islam was in danger was obviously the major factor in the expansion of the Muslim League and mobilization of men to achieve a sovereign Muslim state, yet such a theory was clearly insufficient to explain how disparate Muslim communities throughout India came to look upon Pakistan as a common goal. The theory had to be buttressed by other factors.[103]

It has been suggested that Muslim separatism really started after the British conceded separate electorates to Muslims in 1909.[104] They "helped to entrench separatism and communalism," Singhvi says, and adds that the rise of Muslim communalism implied "the incipient failure of the composite Indian nationalism."[105]

The initiation of electoral institutions ruffled the placid sea of autocracy by providing permanent political links between the different levels of government—district, provincial and national—and helping to the formation of parties. The passing of power step by step to Indian hands, which took place within this electoral framework, by encouraging competition for power, also stimulated political activity, with the result that new classes, castes, communities and interests were hauled around into the vortex of politics.[106] This political awareness was put to good use later.

In north India, in Delhi and the outlying areas which had been the seat of Muslim power, and in the Gangetic expanse eastward where Muslim settlement had been penetrative under the Moghul empire, the Muslim share of land was great and its functional responsibility within the imperial set-up proportionately great. In this region the decline of the Moghul empire did not basically alter the *status quo ante*, and the Muslim landed families largely continued to play a similar role under the British to the one they had played under the Moghuls.[107] The conceding of separate electorates, as in the case of general electorates, had obviously been an endeavour by the raj "to extend and broaden the base of its rule by extending and broadening the support of its traditional allies," remarks David Page.[108] Imperialism seeks to protect all that is culturally backward in the life of the people to obstruct the national demands for reform, and utilises to the utmost the lingering reactionary lines of division.[109] To the British rulers, the importance of a party and a leader was in proportion to their utility in blocking India's constitutional advancement.

The working of the Montford constitution unfolded significant developments for the future of the Muslims. "The crucial point behind the growth of communalism lay in the very logic of participation in the post-1919 political arrangement," Sumit Sarkar remarks.[110] The new constitution had expanded the franchise, but kept up and even enlarged separate electorates. This induced "politicians working within the system to use sectional slogans and gather a following by distributing favours to their own religious, regional and caste groups." A second, related, factor was the spread of education without a corresponding increase in job opportunities. The scramble for limited resources fed communal enmity. Lower down the social scale, social-economic strains could often take an ugly communal twist, particularly now that a suitable ideology was taking shape. [111] Communalism could be defined as a phase of search for a national identity.

This period saw the consolidation of political interests around communal issues, in which the imperial power played an important role, and the shaping of Muslim attitudes both towards the emergence of provincial autonomy and towards the ultimate withdrawal of British domination. "These attitudes, subsequently hardened under the impact of provincial autonomy, continued to govern Muslim thinking to the last," David Page says.[112]

The Hindu Muslim conflict was heightened when more political power was placed on the counter. "Progressive realization of responsible government turned out to be progressive aggravation of relationship of the two communities," observes K.B. Sayeed.[113] This policy was turned into a positive administrative system during the present century.

Concurrent with the progress of the national struggle and the successive stages of constitutional reforms went the process of promoting communal strife through the peculiar electoral system taken in connection with the refroms.[114]

To know the background of this situation, it is necessary to recognize the seeds of social-economic rivalry which affected, particularly, the rising middle class. The expansion of trade, commerce and education took place much earlier in Bombay, Calcutta and Madras, the Hindu majority areas, than in the Muslim areas of the North.[115] With the emergence of the bourgeoisie, conditions of sectional rivalry emerged which could take a communal garb. The Muslim upper classes viewed with displeasure the advance of the trading and industrial bourgeoisie, and regarded that advance as "the menace of the Hindu bania", says R.P. Dutt. Lagging behind the Hindus in education and enterprise, the Muslims found themselves handicapped in every sphere. "This was the soil," writes Dutt, "which made it easy for official policy to play on the latent antagonisms and build upon them a whole political system."[116]

It was argued that such distinctive representation was necessary to prevent the Muslims from being submerged by Hindu majority. The hollowness of this argument was demonstrated in the local government elections in the same period, where these were still carried on the old joint electorate basis.[117]

The intention of forcing the two communities apart was poignantly manifest, not only by the fixation of separate electorates and representation, but by conferring specially privileged representation to the Muslims. An extensive and elaborate system of weightage was conceived.[118] By this measure it was planned to win the support of a privileged minority, and to turn the wrath of the majority against the privileged minority, and not against the government, writes R.P. Dutt.[119]

The system was extended in the subsequent constitutional reforms. The British policy of transferring more power to Indian hands was paying dividends. By treating the Muslims as a separate entity, the imperial power isolated them from other

Indians. By giving them separate electorates, it institutionalized their separation. This was, according to David Page, one of the most crucial factors in the growth of communal politics. Muslim Politicians did not have to call upon the non-Muslims; similarly non-Muslims did not have to call upon the Muslims. This was to prove a big hurdle in the growth of a genuine Indian nationalism.[120]

With the opening of Dyarchy, communal animosity became a permanent feature of provincial politics. The unparalleled growth of both Hindu and Muslim communalism was in fact to a large extent, "the most serious and permanent negative development of these years." Communal bodies proliferated,[121] and the formation of all-India cross communal alliances, which had taken place earlier, now became "first difficult and then impossible,"[122] as Page remarks. The newly emerging questions of regional or national claims to self-determination became entangled with the Hindu-Muslim issue.[123] By the end of 1920s all-India Muslim politics had become virtually the sum total of the politics of Muslim provincialism, and the all-India Muslim politician without a provincial base felt himself to be on flimsy ground. Jinnah's withdrawment to England provides glaring example of the working of these thrusts.[124]

Separate electorates equipped the government with communal auxiliaries enabling it to run the system of control without Congress support. Congress obviously could ill afford their continuance if it wished to retain its all India image. Its efforts to get separate electorates abrogated reflect the working of these factors. As the main opposition party Congress depended for sustenance on those barred from the boons of the prevailing regime, and with political relations in the provinces polarized along communal proclivities, the sources of opposition were also affected, and the Congress came to lean increasingly on communal Hindu support. In these circumstances an all-India communal concord was hardly feasible."[125]

Thus the way was cleared for the renewal of Congress League separation and Hindu Muslim antagonism. The imperialists did not fail to take advantage of this favourable development. Subsequently formidable communal rioting replaced the previous united upsurge for freedom. Communal reaction was on the rise. As a counter to the Muslim League, the Hindu Mahasabha was organized on an all-India basis. Renewed endeavours for arriving at a Congress-League agreement in the All Parties Conference of 1928 could not fructify.[126]

By the end of the 1920s, all India politics had come to a deadlock, and the Congress was left with no option but to broaden its popular appeal, and to challenge the social and economic forces which the constitution was meant to strengthen. It was at this time, Page observes, that the Congress began to work systematically in the rural areas and to group the landlord with the government.[127]

By this stage however, continues Page, Muslim provincialism was in the forefront, and the new twist of Congress policy only exacerbated an already tense communal situation. In the majority province Muslims had little to fear from a sharpening of political mobilization, but for them Congress already signified "Hindu", and a Congress dominated centre could have a menacing effect on their interests and manoeuvring capacity. In the minority provinces, and U.P., in particular, Muslims had a lot to fear because their social and economic status which had carried weight in the system of control was jeopardized. For these reasons, by the early 1930s, for both the majority and minority province Muslims political future depended upon, says Page, on cooperation at the all India level. However, by this stage Muslim politics had taken a distinct centrifugal impress.[128] This politics—as will be discussed presently—first showed its head in Muslim minority provinces.

As Congress took to cutting the ground under the imperial edifice, the Muslims began to slip off. The British response to this situation was the all India federation. If the politically enterprising Hindu community could not countenance the continuance of British control at the Centre, why not have a new Centre as a rallying point for the kindly disposed. If even the solid backing of the Muslims was inadequate for this purpose, it was hoped that by wooing th princes, a stable Centre might be created. But this notion also came a cropper. Because in any case provinces would have exerted big pressure against the Centre. "Politically, even by the beginning of the thirties, the raj had fallen a victim to its own system of control, as stated by David Page. Electoral institutions, howsoever meagre, made a dent in the armour of aristocracy; as they deepened, the raj's capacity for manoeuvre was seriously curtailed. They provided the enemies of the imperial system with an opportunity to procure by organization what they were denied by solicitation. With each set of reforms, friction among the natives intensified, their ambition got whetted. Political realities changed kaleidoscopically till Muslim separatism appeared as a stark reality on the political scenario. Ultimately, even the closest allies of the raj came close only for a purpose.[129] The stage was set for the last act of the play to witness the concurrence of great historical events, devolution and division.

Interestingly, as has been mentioned above, the Muslim nationalist movement did not first grow in the Muslim majority areas of north-west and north-east. It appeared first among middle and upper class conservative Muslims in the United Provinces where they formed a minority. This may not be a matter of surprise, for here Muslims were not a backward community as they were prone to be elsewhere but a comfortably solvent and outstanding minority group, living in the midst of Muslim culture, and cherishing vivid memories of their awesome past. Yet consciousness of past greatness alone would not have nurtured a strong nationalist movement, even though it might have been the cause of an initial discontent. Existent grievances were necessary to fuel and expand such a movement.[130]

The Muslims of the minority areas who earlier became imbued with nationalist ideas, though not a downtrodden community, yet had their misgivings and apprehensions and revolutionary ideas seemed to emanate more from thwarted expectations than from a state of total deprivation. Cognizant of having lost power to the British only a century ago, they were now, as the British retreat became imminent, alarmed at the prospect of losing power permanently to the Hindu majority.

But, observe C.H. Philips and M.D. Wainwright, "the Muslims too very late in the day had been driven to adopt a form of western education, and were beginning to produce an intelligentsia to compete with the Hindus in government and the professional lines in which, however, the Hindus had long acquired a hold." The centre of this new Muslim educational trend and aspirations was the Aligarh Muslim University. Naturally enough, the young western educated men of the Muslim community tended to hold their minority status responsible for any failure in getting employment in accordance with their educational qualifications; rather than to pinpoint the entire faulty set-up. The old might revel in past grandeur and present culture; but the frustration of the young needed a substantial outlet. The Muslim League provided them with such an inducement. "[131]

And it was the minority provinces, as Jinnah affirmed later; who beaconed the majority provinces and led the nationalist upsurge.[132]

NOTES AND REFERENCES

1. Shakir, Moin, *Khilafat to Partition : A Survey of Major Political Trends among Indian Muslims during 1919-1947* (Hereafter referred to as *Khilafat to Partition*), (New Delhi : Kalamkar Prakashan, June 1970), p. 178.
2. Rao, B. Shiva, "India, 1935-1947" In : *The Partition of India : Policies and Perspectives 1935-1947*, Philips C.H. and Wainwright, M.D. (eds.) (Hereafter referred to as *Partition of India*), (London : George Allen and Unwin Ltd. 1970), p. 418.
3. Shourie Arun *"Mohammad Ali Jinnah : The Man Who Break up India"*, The *Illustrated Weekly* of India, October 26, November 2, 1985, pp. 9-10,.
4. Ibid, pp. 12-13.
5. Sayeed Khalid B. *"The Personality of Jinnah and His Political Strategy"* (Hereafter referred to as *"Personality of Jinnah"* In : *Partition of India*, p. 277.
6. Shakir, *Khilafat to Partition*, pp. 178-79.
7. Ibid, p. 185.
8. Sayeed Khalid B. *Pakistan : The Formative Phase : 1857-1948"* (Hereafter referred to as *Pakistan)*, 2nd edn. (London: Oxford University Press, 1968),p. 290.

9. Shakir, *Khilafat to Partition*, pp. 182-83.
10. Ibid, pp. 183-86.
11. Zaidi, Z.H. "*Aspects of the Developments of Muslim League Policy, 1937-47*" (Hereafter referred to as *League Policy)* In : *Partition of India*, pp. 249-50.
12. Chakrabarty, Atulananda, *The Lonesome Pilgrim* (Hereafter referred to as Lonesome Pilgrim) (Bombay: Allied Publishers, 1969) p. 73.
13. Philips, *Partition of India*. p. 419.
14. Kulkarni, V.B. *India and Pakistan : A Historical Survey of Hindu Muslim Relations*." (Hereafter referred to as *India Pakistan*) (Bombay : Jaico Publishing House, 1973), pp. 274-76.
15. Philips, C.H. *The Partition of India 1947* (Hereafter referred to as *Partition 1947*") (Leeds : Leeds University Press, 1967) p. 419.
16. Sayeed, *Pakistan*, p. 290.
17. Tara Chand, "*History of the Freedom Movement of India*", (Hereafter referred to as *History of Freedom*), (New Delhi: Publications Division, Govt. of India, November, 1972), Vol. IV, p. 283.
18. Wallbank, T. Walter, *A Short History of India and Pakistan from Ancient Times to the Present*, (Hereafter referred to as *India Pakistan)* An abridged edn. of India in the New Era, revised and up to date (New York : A Mentor Book, 1965), p. 184.
19. "In December 1928, before the all parties of what he regarded as moderate proposals under which, Muslims would be given one third representation in the central legislature and that 'residuary powers' would be vested in the provinces. These proposals were not only rejected, but Jinnah's representative capacity as a spokesman of the Muslims was questioned. This has been interpreted as another great mistake that the Congress leaders made. It is reported that Jinnah took this to heart. He had tears in his eyes as he said, "Jamshed, this is the parting of the ways", Sayeed *Personality of Jinnah*, p. 279.
20. Pandey, B.N. "*Break up of British India*, (Hereafter referred to as The Break-up)" (London : Macmillan 1969), p. 119.
21. Kidwai, Mohd. Hashim "*Azad on Partition*", *Times of India*, June 1, 1988.
22. Sayeed, "*Personality of Jinnah*" p. 281.
23. Dwarkadas, Kanji, "*India's Fight for Freedom*" 1913-1937 : An

Eye vitness Story, (Hereafter referred to as *India's Fight*) (Bombay : Popular Prakashan, 1966), : pp. 348-51, See Sayeed, *Pakistan*, pp. 290-91.

24. Dwarkadas, *India's Fight*, pp. 351.
25. Spitz, Lewis, W, *The Reformation : Material or Health Company, 1965*, pp, 9-10.
26. Kulkarni, *India Pakistan*, p. 273.
27. Lasswell Harold D., *Power and Personality*, (New York : The Viking Press, 1962), cited by Sayeed, *Pakistan*, p. 292.
28. Hegal, Quoted by *Herald*.
29. Erikson., Erik H. *Young, Young Man Luther : A Study in Psychoanalysis and History*, (New York : W.W. Nortan and Co. Inc.1958, 1962), p. 217.
30. Sayeed, *Pakistan*, p. 292.
31. Ibid, p. 100
32. Shakir, *Khilafat to Partition*, pp. 186 and 194.
33. Sayeed, *Pakistan*, p. 92.
34. Shakir, *Khilafat to Partition*, p. 191.
35. Chakrabarty, *Lonesome Pilgrim*. p. 81.
36. Sayeed, *Pakistan*, p. 82.
37. Chakrabarty, *Lonesome* Pilgrim, p. 78.
38. Shakir, *Khilafat to Pakistan*, p. 190-92.
39. Chakrabarty, *Lonesome Pilgrim*, pp. 81-83.
40. Ibid, p. 82.
41. Ibid, p. 67.
42. Lal Bahadur, *The Muslim League, Its History, Activities and Achievement* (Agra : Agra Book Store, 1954), p. 172.
43. Sood, K.N., *Pakistan's Reluctant Beneficiary" (Hereafter referred to as Pakistan's Beneficiary), The Hindustan Times*, July 23, 1989, p. 5.
44. Chakrabarty, *Lonesome Pilgrim*, p. 76.
45. Sood, *"Pakistan's Beneficiary"*, p. 5.
46. Chakrabarty *Lonesome Pilgrim*, pp. 78-79.
47. Ibid, p. 79.
48. Ibid, p. 72, see, Lal Bahadur, *The Muslim League*, p. 17.
49. Shakir, *Khilafat to Partition*, pp 201, 204 and 205.
50. Sayeed, *Pakistan*, pp. 293-294.
51. Sayeed, *Personality of Jinnah*, pp, 292-93.
52. Ibid, p. 293.
53. Chakrabarty, *Lonesome Pilgrim*, p.92.

54. Ibid, p. 64.
55. Ibid, p. 92 and citation (Coker F.W., Recent Political Thought) therein.
56. Majumdar, R.C. *British Paramouncy and Indian Renaissance, History and Culture of the Indian People,* Majumdar, R.C. (gen. ed) (Bombay: Bharatiya Vidya Bhawan, 1965), Part-III, Vol. X, p. 295.
57. Ibid, pp. 318-319.
58. Zaman, Mukhtar, *Student's Role in the Pakistan Movement* (Karachi : Quad-i-Azam Academy, 1978), pp. 2-5.
59. Panikkar, K. M., *The Foundations of New Delhi* (London: George Allen and Unwin, Ltd, 1963), pp. 56-57.
60. Chakrabarty, *Lonesome Pilgrim, p. 65.*
61. Sayeed, *Pakistan, p. 5.*
62. Majumdar, *British Paramouncy and Indian Renaissance,* p. 337.
63. Sayeed, *Pakistan,* p. 5.
64. Dutt, R. Palme, *India, Today* (New Delhi : Ind. ed. Calcutta : Manisha, 1970, Reprint, July, 1983), p. 453, "Under certain conditions the mingling of diverse races or religious in a single country can give rise to acute difficulties, sometimes even riots and bloodshed. Orangmen and Catholics in Northern Ireland. Arab and Jews in Palestine under the Mandate, Slaves and Jews in Czarist Russia, so-called "Aryan and Jews in Nazi Germany; these are familiar issues of the twentieth century world, without needing to go back to earlier examples. Anti Semitic in Europe is today the shortest expression of this type of racial religious divisions and antagonism", Ibid, p. 471
65. Ibid, pp. 453-54.
66. Ibid, p. 454.
67. Chakrabarty, *Lonesome Pilgrim,* p. 62.
68. Ibid, pp. 62-63.
69. Shakir, *Khilafat to Partition,* p. 186.
70. Chakrabarty, *Lonesome Pilgrim* p. 69.
71. Shakir, *Khilafat to Partition,* p. 186, 194-195.
72. Ibid, pp. 187-88.
73. Religious Obscurantist of an extreme type, see Dutt, *India Today,* p. 471.
74. While the principle 'Crime in this Respect was that of Gandhi, the same attitude was characteristic of a lesser light in the Congress camp, especially those belonging to the Gandhist inspiration and tendency, Ibid, pp. 471-472.

75. Dutt, *India Today,* p. 468.
76. Ibid, p. 468.
77. Myrdal Gunner *Asian Drama,* (Vol. I), quoted Chakrabarty, *Lonesome Pilgrim, p. 80.*
78. Dutt, *India Today,* p. 468.
79. "And by 1944 to an officially claimed figure of some two million," Ibid, p. 468.
80. Ibid, p. 469.
81. "Election of Bose as President and expulsion of Bose, passivity during the imperialist phase of war as policy of neither helping nor opposing the war effort, individual strategies, the ill-starred August Resolution, Ibid, p. 469.
82. Ibid, pp. 469-70.
83. Sayeed, *Pakistan,* p. 90 see chapter-II, "The all India Muslim Students Federation. 1935-40" in Zaman, *Student's Role in the Pakistan Movement,* p. 13-31.
84. Shakir, *Khilafat to Partition,* pp. 188-189.
85. Ibid, p. 189.
86. Chakrabarty, *Lonesome Pilgrim,* p. 85.
87. Shakir, *Khilafat to Partition,* pp. 190-91.
88. Ibid, p. 191.
89. Sayeed, *Pakistan,* p. 101.
90. Shakir, *Khilafat to Partition,* pp. 192-194.
91. Kulkarni, *India and Pakistan,* p. 142.
92. Majumdar, *British Paramouncy and Indian Renaissance,* p. 330.
93. For instance, the name of Shivaji was an inspiration to the Hindus who held Aurangzeb in open contempt. The reverse was the case with the Muslims. Rajput heroes like Rana Pratap were the ideals of the Hindus and enemies of Muslims", Ibid, p. 330.
94. Ibid, p. 331.
95. Pandey, *The Breakup of British India,* p. 119.
96. Majumdar, *British Paramouncy and Indian Renaissance,* pp. 331.
97. Ibid, p. 331.
98. Shakir, *Khilafat to Partition,* p. 198.
99. Ibid, p. 200.
100. Sayeed, *Pakistan,* p. 4.
101. "Only miracle could avert partition", (New Delhi, Nov. 12, 1990), p. 4.
102. Page, David, *Prelude to Partition* : The Indian Muslims and the

Imperial System of Control, 1920-32, (Delhi : Oxford Univ. Press, 1982)

103. Sayeed *Pakistan*, p. 4.
104. Only miracle could avert Partition" (Hereafter referred to as *Prelude to Partition*). p. 4.
105. Page, *Prelude to Partition*, p. 3.
106. Ibid, p. 8.
107. Ibid, p. 74.
108. These are phenomenon (desperate efforts to use reactionary forces) of the break-up of important rule, they represent the calling into play of the last reserves" : Dutt, *India Today*, p. 37.
109. Sarkar, Sumit, *Modern India 1885-47* (Hereafter referred to as *Modern India*, (Delhi : Macmillan India, 1983), p. 234.
110. Ibid, p. 234.
111. Page, *Prelude to Partition*, pp. 259-60 in which the imperial power played an important role.
112. Sayeed, *Pakistan*, p. 7.
113. Dutt, *India Today*, p. 5.
114. *The Hunter Commission Report* in 1882 stated that the number of Muslim students in university education was only 3.65%. To this day, the percentage of literacy is considerably higher among the Hindus than the Muslims" Ibid p. 458.
115. Ibid, pp. 458-59.
116. "Thus in the United Provinces in 1910, the joint electorates with the Muslims, forming one-seventh part of the population, returned 189 Muslims and 445 Hindus to the District Boards, and 310 Muslims and 562 Hindus to the Municipalities," Ibid, p. 460.
117. "Thus to become an elector under the Morley-Minto Reforms, the Muslim had to pay income tax on an income of 3,000 rupees a year, whereas a non-Muslim on an income on 300,000 rupees; or the Muslim graduate was required to have three years standing, and the non-Muslim to have thirty years standing. The values of representation showed a similar method of weighting", Ibid, p. 460.
118. Ibid, pp. 460-61.
119. Page, *Prelude to Partition*, p. 260.
120. Sarkar, *Modern India*, p. 233.
121. Page, *Prelude to Partition*, p. 260.
122. Dutt, *India Today*, p. 464.

123. Page, *Prelude to Partition*, p. 260.
124. Ibid, p. 260.
125. Ibid, p. 261.
126. Dutt, *India Today*, p. 467.
127. Page, *Prelude to Partition*, p. 261.
128. Ibid, pp. 261-62.
129. Ibid, pp. 262-64.
130. Philips and Wainwright, *Partition of India*, p. 27.
131. Ibid, p. 27.
132. Ahmad, Jamiluddin (comp.) *Some Recent Speeches and Writings of Mr. Jinnah*, (Lahore: S.M. Ashraf, 1946), Vol. I, p. 52.

Chapter 4

The Congress Regime and the Muslim League

The discontent of the Muslim League under Congress rule has already been mentioned but in order to appreciate more appropriately the later developments, light has to be thrown on some of the occurrences of these crucial years.

After the great electoral performance, the Congress party found the frenzy of power "a bit-too exhilarating."[1] The triumph at the hustings "had at last made real the potential strength of the Congress and its ability to dominate the political stage." Congress was now more than a mere "nationalist movement or a political party," remarks B.R. Tomlinson; "it became the whole provincial political environment." The status and influence of the Congress and Congressmen was enormously increased.[2]

There was a fly in the ointment, however, for the seats bagged by the Congress were merely "general"—non-Muslim—seats. It had fielded barely 58 candidates out of 482 in the Muslim electorate and captured a meagre 26. Even of these 26 or 5.4 per cent seats, 15 came from the North-West Frontier Province obviously due to the prominent Pakhtun nationalist Khan Abdul Ghaffar Khan and his Khudai Khidmatgars. This showed that the Congress claim to represent the Muslim community was inflated. "There is no doubt whatever that the Congress leadership;" observes Hirendranath Mukerjee, "showed a deplorable vacillation and lack of self-confidence when it forbore from putting up Congress candidates for Muslim constituencies."[3] It could be poor consolation that the Muslim League itself made a pitiful showing at the polls.

Organizationally, the League was far from powerful but signs were discernible "that it was growing fast."[4] After the electoral disaster which had betrayed the total disarray of Muslim politics, desperate efforts were made to consolidate the League organization. When in July 1937, Congress ministries were formed, Jinnah's *amour propre* received another setback,[5] but he was determined to make the best of the adverse circumstances and would not let himself be broken. From this abyss of despair, thanks to the leader's courageous perseverance, the League jumped to strength. The Muslim League Lucknow session of October, 1937 was a remarkable proof of its rapidly growing power.[6] It was there that attempts were made to transform it into a mass organization commanding the allegiance of the community. This awakened mass consciousness also contributed to the growth in League's popularity. "The cold-blooded logician as Jinnah had once described himself," writes K.B. Sayeed, "was moved by the emotional warmth and religious fervour of the Muslim masses."[7] The League had secured less than a quarter of the Muslim seats all over India, having done well neither in seat, nor in vote nor in territorial spread.[8] Particularly its showing in the Muslim majority provinces was dismal. "But at Lucknow it looked," states Sayeed; "as if Jinnah had snatched victory from the jaws of defeat."[9]

In his presidential speech Jinnah showed his indignation and practically equated the Congress with the Hindu Mahasabha only "masquerading under the name of nationalism."[10] He accused the Congress for alienating the Muslims more and more by indulging in exclusive Hinduism. Since their inception the Congress governments had, he affirmed: "by their words and deeds and programme, shown more and more that the Musalmans cannot expect any justice or fair play at their hands."[11]

It is an intriguing irony of history that Jinnah, who some years back was perhaps one of the most religionless leaders of India "became the high priest of communalism and defender of Muslim culture and Muslim practices and rituals which till then he had never observed."[12]

Humayun Kabir puts it thus :

> The irony of the situation lies in the role of Mr. Jinnah who retired from the Congress during the non-cooperation days when that body adopted a programme of direct and if necessary unconstitutional action. His fate pursued him and made him the instrument through which the League was transformed into a body advocating direct and if necessary unconstitutional action just when the Congress seemed to be sliding back to constitutionalism.[13]

Jinnah's Lucknow address marks rupture with the past. He said, "No settlement with the majority is possible, as no Hindu leader speaking with any authority shows any concern or genuine desire for it. An honourable settlement can only be achieved between equals; and unless the two parties learn to respect and fear each other, there is no solid ground for any settlement." He continued, "Offers of peace by the weaker party always mean a confession of weakness : and an invitation to aggression. Appeals to patriotism, justice and fair play and for goodwill fall flat." And further, "All safeguards and settlements would be a scrap of paper unless they are backed up by power. Politics means power and not-relying only on cries of justice or fair play or goodwill." He warned the Muslims of the dangers of turning their faces towards the British or towards the Congress. He wanted them "to believe in themselves and take their destiny in their own hands."[14] He assured the Muslims of all provinces of the cooperation of the League in the social, economic and political betterment of the Musalmans,[15] and exhorted them to develop power and strength till they were fully organized, and had "acquired that power and strength which must come from the solidarity and the unity of people."[16] Referring to the formation of the Congress ministry in U.P., he complained bitterly, "The [Congress] demand was insistent abjure your party, your policy and programme and liquidate the Muslim League."[17]

The speech had an electrifying effect. It signified a vital change in Jinnah's approach to the Indian political gamut. "The

League had been badly mauled," says Z. H. Zaidi, "in the tough political infighting associated with the forming of ministries." Without a strong base and mass support it could not exert any weight at the bargaining table. Goodwill and the eagerness to cooperate, alone were not enough. "From now onwards the Muslim League changed its tactics." Its militancy was taking shape. It must acquire the power to deal with the Congress on terms of equality.[18] The die was cast. Separatism was in the air. Jinnah resolved to strike all the communal chords to win the Muslims for the League.

There should have been some serious thought to anticipate the drift of events in the future. Meanwhile there was no urge for Jawaharlal Nehru to declare, as he did, that there were only two parties in the country—"the Congress as representing the will to freedom of the nation, and the British government of India and its supporters who oppose this urge, to try to suppress it"[19] —and the others "must just line up".[20] Even if the view that the statement was "in the context of India's struggle for freedom" and was "historically well founded," is accepted as V.B. Kulkarni affirms, "it was haughty and uncalled for."[21] And it was not the last, nor the first, of Nehru's casual utterances to have unfortunate repercussions.[22] The "others must simply line up" dictate infuriated the Muslim leader to make the statement, "I refuse to line up with the Congress," and haughtily assert that "there is a third party in this country and that is the Muslims."[23] He added, "we are not going to be camp followers of any party."[24]

Later developments—like negotiations pertaining to the formation of U.P. ministry—"only translated into practice;" argues R.C. Majumdar, "the pithy saying attributed to Nehru."[25] "If the U.P. sample was to be the pattern of Congress's political conduct, then what would be the position of Muslims," wonders Penderal Moon, "when a federal government for all India came to be formed? There would be no room on the throne of India save for Congress and Congress stooges."[26] No sagacious statesman could believe "that the Muslim League would readily give up its own separate identity and merge itself in the Congress." The League could not "commit political *Harakiri* at the bidding of the Congress."[27]

Jinnah declared, "Only one thing can save the Musalmans and energise them to regain their lost ground. They must first recapture their own souls and stand by their lofty positions and principles which form the basis of their great unity and which bind them in one body politic."[28]

Jinnah now emerged as the leader of the united Muslim community. "His clarion call to the Muslims went home," observes Majumdar, "and changed the Muslim political outlook almost overnight." He played on the responsive religious element, a vulnerable factor in Muslim politics.[29] Immediately after Jinnah's presidential address, provincial leaders, who had fought elections on the basis of their splinter parties and had jealously guarded the distinct entity of their respective organizations,—who had been disinclined to merge their parties with the Muslim League—were softened to join this all-India Muslim organization. Muslim members of the Unionist party in the Punjab, under the leadership of the premier Sikandar Hayat Khan, went over *en bloc* to the League. Fazlul Haq, premier of Bengal, declared his allegiance to the Muslim League. Muhammad Saadullah of Assam followed suit. Many Muslim leaders from Sind, Frontier, Madras and Central Provinces came within the League fold. "No better tonic could have invigorated the Muslim League" than these adhesions.[30] The joining of the League by Fazlul Haq and Sikandar Hayat Khan who had not been members of the League, "was a big break-through," remarks A.C. Guha, "for the League's claim to be the sole representative body of the Muslims."[31] The Lucknow session gave a massive push to the League, and the unity which Jinnah yearned for seemed within reach.

Further, the 25th session of the All-India Muslim League directed the working committee to put into effect an economic, social and educational programme to bring the organization into touch with the masses. This included—in line with the Congress programme—amelioration of the condition of factory workers and other labourers, reduction of rural and urban debts and abolition of usury, encouragement of cottage industries, rural uplift and the use of "swadeshi" articles, provision for the relief of unemployment, advancement of compulsory primary education, reorganization of secondary and university education specially scientific and technical, and organization of a volunteer corps for social service.[32] The working committee of the League prepared to tackle almost all the socio-economic problems which the Congress had been dealing with.[33]

As said earlier, Congress leaders do not seem to have apprehended the strong currents that were set free, let alone perceived where they were likely to lead. Nehru seems to have lived in an utopian world of his own creation which had no relation to actual facts.[34] He naively interpreted the Congress victory at the polls "as a deliberate rejection of communalism by the masses." "In this he saw too much;" remarks B. N. Pandey, "where very little existed."[35] Not only Nehru but evidently other Congress leaders also felt, so it seems, that the Muslim League had no great hold over the country. Instead of pacifying the League they deemed it expedient to crush what little influence it still possessed.[36] Nehru honestly believed that communalism—the ominous spell cast on India by the British—had been for the first time wiped out at the polls. Why revivify it with its sinister implications by allying with the League?[37] The crushing defeat of the Muslim League in Muslim provinces—leaving alone Congress failure with the Muslim electorate—led Nehru, as president of the Congress, to announce on 31 March, 1937, "that a separate department would be started to organize Congress contacts with the Muslim masses of India."[38] Congress saw that in spite of its earnest desire to supplicate for the whole nation; inspite of the nationalist Muslims in its fold, there was a vacuum as the Muslim masses had yet to be won over. This was to be achieved through direct political work among the Muslim peasants and workers on the basis of their class urges thus bypassing the middle and upper class communal leaders and "exposing their pro-feudal and pro-capitalist bias."[39]

To the common country folk, the Congress appeal can be delineated thus; "Congress was non-communal, and under its auspices the religious rights of the Muslims would be scrupulously protected. The real issue was social and economic, and the Congress, not the landlords and lawyers of the League, was the champion of the poor. Already it was hard at work at its new agrarian reforms and there were more to come. They were intended for Muslim country folk as much as Hindu, but the former would be wise to make sure of their full share in the blessings of the new regime by joining the Congress party."[40]

The appeal to the upper strata was somewhat squalid. It implied that for a Muslim to stay in the League was tantamount to a lifetime in wilderness. True to its creed, the Congress would not deny a fair share of government jobs to the Muslim minority, but understandably it would not be possible to bestow them only on Congress Muslims.[41]

Jinnah took up the challenge. With odds heavily stocked against him, he rose to his full stature. Playing the crescent card dexterously he completely turned the table on the Congress. The Lucknow address was overwhelming: "The Congress with all its boasts, has done nothing in the past for the Musalmans. It has failed to inspire confidence and to create a sense of security amongst the Musalmans and other minorities. The Congress attempt, under the guise of establishing mass contact with the Musalmans, is calculated to divide and weaken and break the Musalmans, and is an effort to detach them from their accredited leaders. It is a dangerous move but it cannot mislead anyone."[42]

Congress Muslims or Muslim nationalists had little communion with the Muslim masses who were prone to fall in with their communal leaders. "Nehru's mass contact with the Muslim population aroused," says A. Chakrabarty : "these communal stalwarts who called Jinnah to their leadership. Grossly disesteemed by the Congress, Jinnah reacted with alacrity, and speedily mastered the communal craft which he had so long religiously eschewed. Handling artfully, he soon transformed the communal into a national cause. Gandhi said later that in Khilafat days no one talked of dividing India. Well, no one thought of dividing India before he started the Khilafat venture. "Division was," asserts Chakrabarty, "directly the reaction to 'Mass Contact',"[43] This contact business provoked the Muslim League that the Congress launched upon the campaign for capturing Muslim votes. Thus the League saw the mass contact as a challenge, and it took up the challenge with enormous success. Nehru felt that he could charm the Muslim lower classes and this eventually turned out to be a fatally fond fallacy. Gandhi had to appeal to the masses by the use of religious terms. This alienated the Muslims for religious appeals were heavily spiced with Hindu imagery. Muslim attitude stiffened as the old fantasy of Khilafat fraternity gave way to the new nonsense of Mass Contact.[44] Jinnah's call was heeded to. In order to neutralize its effect the AICC made a frantic appeal to the Muslim masses, but to no avail.[45]

Far from "seeking to bridge the gulf that had been created between them and the League—grown suddenly much more formidable"—the Congress leaders aggravated the situation by engendering this move among the rural Muslim folk. "This was a signal to the League," observes Penderel Moon, "to be stir itself and also gave it its cue." Hitherto it had concentrated mainly on middle and upper class Muslims, but the Congress (a preponderantly Hindu organization) attempted to woo Muslim peasants and artisans on a mass scale was deemed an outrage which the League could not bear.[46] A departure from League's earlier attitude, states Lal Bahadur; "was the enunciation of a dogma that Muslim masses should be approached only through its own leaders." The Congress movement "was derided as an attempt to win over the Muslims to the Congress ideology and programme."[47] And before it had much advanced, the League itself turned towards the masses. Prominent Leaguers were also getting perturbed at the radical agrarian programme of the Congress which might tear up their feudal roots. They feared that the growth of anti-imperialist feelings among the Muslims would lead to the retraction of the official backing of the communal leaders. They riveted their attention on the common folk. The League gained the support of Muslim middle class and through it filtered into the masses. As the educated community was the legitimate spokesperson of the illiterate masses, the natural custodian of their interests, the Hindu political leaders "should have foreseen that ultimately the Muslim masses were bound to fall in line with the views of their leaders."[48] The Muslim mass contact programme of the Congress fizzled out. Congress lost, observes Bipan Chandra, "flexibility at the top without gaining any new ground among the Muslim masses."[49]

Like the Congress of an earlier days, steps were taken to reorganize the League. Provincial and district branches were to be remoulded. Even the remotest villages were covered in the network. "Paid workers were employed," states B.N. Pandey, "and speakers were trained to carry the message of Muslim unity." To popularize the League, the membership fee was reduced to two annas which poor Muslims could also afford.[50] "The council of the Muslim League," writes Z.H. Zaidi, "was to consist of 465 members elected by provincial branches and no one was to be elected on the said council without being a member of the primary league, district or tehsil.[51] Thus the Leaguers strained every nerve to set their house in order to start an active programme of political expansion.

The establishment of Congress government in various provinces and the exclusion of the Muslim League made the Muslims generally sour. The utter hopelessness of their situation engineered a reaction among the bulk of politically minded Muslims against the Congress rule, which was presently to make the League a more powerful force in every Muslim Indian, then it had ever been before.[52] Unscrupulous propaganda was carried on to rouse Muslims of all dominations of the danger of Hindu raj. To quote Penderal Moon "this was an appeal to essentially the same basic nationalist sentiment as the Congress had been playing upon in its long struggle against British Rule and it is strange that the Congress leaders did not foresee that by embarking on a 'mass contact movement' among the Muslim they would impel the League to invoke powerful sentiment against themselves". "As a means of appealing to the Muslim masses", add Moon "it was far more effective than the Congress programme of social and agrarian reforms"[53]. The *Mullahs* of the countryside were soon up in arms against the sacrilegious Congress propagandists. "It was blasphemy, they told their blocks to say that politics was purely secular affair," argues R. C. Majumdar "bare logic and sheer instinct of self preservation demanded a similar citadel" for the Muslim minority.[54]

Those members of the League who were also members of the Congress were now regarded askance. It was felt necessary to debar them from the League, though till then there was no restriction against such double membership. Important men like Wazir Hasan and Yaqub Khan, Lal Bahadur points out, "were thus sacrificed and the council took disciplinary action against both". Wazir Hasan moaned his ouster regretting "the ruinous path of disunity and separation which is being shown to our people to follow now". He remained confident "that the true interests of the Muslims of India lay not that way but in the closest unity with the Indian National Congress". "The militant character of Muslim League", remarks Lal Bahadur "was taking shape and effect party discipline was greatly stressed, even at the cost of losing important personalities."[55]

The next important step in the Muslim League programme was the inculcation of the Congress ministries and it spared no efforts to discredit the Congress among Muslims. Nor did it find it difficult, says Humayun Kabir, "for many of the Congress ministers were inexperienced and in any case they were human."[56] They handled some of the sensitive communal problems in a bungling manner.[57]

Kabir enumerates the charges of the Muslim League against Congress ministers under four heads; 1. Interference with religious rights, 2. Tampering with cultural traditions, 3. Discrimination towards Muslims in services and representation, 4. Social snobbery. Congress ministers have refuted all these charges but, holds Kabir "the agitation in the minority provinces could not continue unless there was real discontent or sense of injury behind it". "The ground may have been imaginary but the discontent", he affirms, "was real".[58]

As for interference with religious rights, the practice of the playing of music before mosques and the slaughter of cows turned out to be the most obnoxious. "Juridically, Hindus have as much right to play music on the public road as Muslims have the right to kill cows on their own grounds."[59] Rightly or wrongly, the Muslim enjoys eating the cow and rightly or wrongly, the Hindu holds it in reverence entitled to protection. The Hindu is fond of music, which is a concomitant of his prayers and consecrates rites. The Muslims may admire music but he shuns it when at prayer. History is replete with sanguinary incidents over cow slaughter and music before mosques.[60] The Congress attitude on these questions was not sufficiently firm and determinate, but was supine and vacillating.[61] Congress failed "to organise a consistent and principled fight against communalism in particular".[62] On the other hand "legislation permitting songs and dances in front of mosques, which outraged Muslim religious feelings and prohibiting the killing of cows under pain of criminal prosecution", writes Gankovsky and Gordon-Polon-skaya, "was introduced in provinces where the Congress formed its governments."[63] The use of the criminal law for the prevention of cow slaughter was a mistake as this was an encroachment on the civil liberties of a community. The same thing holds good to the question of music before mosques. "If the criminal law were to be used at all it should have been used to restrict those who sought to curtail the civil liberties of others."[64]

Another source of Muslim discontent was the Wardha Scheme of basic education sponsored by the Congress governments. A new experiment, in primary education initiated by Gandhi,—who sought to solve the problem of finances as well as that of adjusting eduction to social needs,[65]—there was nothing basically wrong in the scheme. It had been thrashed out by two outstanding Muslim educationists, Zakir Hussain and K. G. Saiydain, "to substitute a coordinated training in the use of the hand and the eye for a notoriously bookish and volatile learning which village children unlearned after leaving school."[66] As such the scheme pointed the way to a much needed educational reform. However, some Hindu protagonists tried to give the scheme a religious tinge and this made the Muslims resentful. Even if certain features of the scheme, for example, the emphasis on the manual work were fundamentally sound, "these were overshadowed", as the Raja of Mahmudabad points out, "by its general spirit of indoctrination." Any scheme based on the ideology of one political party is viewed by the minorities and peripheral groups with disfavour as a device to impose the peculiarities in the culture of one community on members of the other. In a variegated country like India it was absolutely essential to keep public education free from the religious tone of any community.[67]

The uncertain future of Urdu also added to Muslim disquiet. Even if Hindustani was made a compulsory subject, it soon became obvious that Hindustani, at least to Gandhi, who had coined the term *Hindi athva Hindustani* (Hindi that is Hindustani), was something quite different from Urdu. It may be pointed out that for the Muslim, Urdu was not merely a medium of expression or thinking, it was a vital part of their culture, a language which had been one of the common bonds between the Hindus and the Muslims.[68] The most mischievous feature of Congress rule according to Pirpur Committee[69] was an attempt to impose Hindi to the detriment of Urdu. Jinnah snarled, "Is there any doubt now in the mind of any one that the whole scheme of Hind-Hindustani is intended to stifle and suppress Urdu?[70].

Muslim intellectuals and the intelligentsia recalled that in the third quarter of the nineteenth century, a movement had grown aimed at the substitution of the Hindi language and Devanagri script for Urdu and Persian script. This had pained Sir Syed Ahmad Khan so much that he was led to make the portentous statement. "Now I am convinced that the two communities will not be able to cooperate sincerely in any matter. It is only the beginning. In future 1 envisage mutual opposition and conflict increasing day by day on account of those who are called educated people. He who lives will see."[71]

Urdu and Hindi are intrinsically the same language, the difference being only in their scripts. Many Congressmen in fact stood for the adoption of a neutral script, the Roman, but the traditional element in the Congress would not however agree to such a modernist solution and the Congress dilly dallied between the two scripts.[72] But the hesitation itself disconcerted the Musalmans. Muslim Congressmen deplored that the conceding of equal status to the two scripts generally remained a pious resolution. The official Congress policy of Hindustani written both in Devnagari and Persian scripts was not adhered to. The Muslim leaders clinging to a Persianized Urdu and the Congress ministries trying to propagate Hindi.[73]

Language stirs complex psychic emotions in a human being and associated with religion, it is a source of communion with God. The economic status of an individual is dependent on his mastery of the language. Muslim talent had sought outlet in government service. Muslims were alarmed at the ominous attributes of Hindi extremism, feared that Hindi would be forced on them and felt that their political future was in jeopardy.[74] The conviction was growing that Muslim education and culture so long safe under the neutral British government were in danger and bound to suffer under the Hindu regime of the Congress.

The social exclusiveness of the Hindus pertaining to all non Hindus in general and the Muslims in particular, was one of the most potent causes of Hindu-Muslim discord. A good Hindu would not let a Muslim touch his eating utensils or his drinking glass. Such social and moral disabilities corroded the Muslim ego more fatally than economic or even political ones, though social disabilities themselves ultimately tend to manifest morbidity, which is a concomitant of eco-political iniquities. Therefore, Muslim annoyance at Hindu orthodoxy, which was tantamount to snobbery, was understandable. Forces of modernism were no doubt asserting to rend as under the barriers of caste and untouchability. But till that was actually achieved, they were bound to be gnawing.[75]

The main source of dissension between the two communities was however the disparity of ratio in services and representation. It was alleged that in the Muslim share of public appointments, due regard was not paid to the size and importance of the Muslim community.[76] The question had become acute once Congress ministries had taken office as the provincial Muslim politicians chafed at their ouster from the government.[77] Since the establishment of British power in India, Hindus had achieved an economic and governmental preponderance which Muslims started challenging ever since they concentrated on English education. The de-industrialization of the country had further heightened the value of services. Greater strength in the legislatures was sought to gain power to control ratios in service and influence political and economic policy. So that communal tussle has to be viewed in the ultimate analysis as a tussle "between the middle classes of the two communities to share in the good things of life", and mass energy was used for that end.[78] In the light of the above survey, one can comprehend the Muslim League tendency to intensify trivial neglects and give a communal colouring to incidents, which were originally neutral and innovous[79]. The period 1937-38 saw a dangerous development, which was an outcome of the working of the reforms. Most of the normal things, which had been going on for decades, were now labelled as anti Islamic.[80] On the Congress side the tendency was to let matters drift.[81] At the same time it launched the intensive campaign to recruit more Muslims into its fold. It was fully entitled to do this but the action was ill-timed.[82] In fact the Muslims' mass contact campaign maligned the Congress ministries. Conducted by Congress workers while the party was in office, it naturally gave the impression that it was being organised not at the behest of the Congress party but that of the provincial governments. The Congress workers bore the stigma of belonging to the ruling party and this proved to be one of the factors responsible for the failure of the venture and aggravated the situation, "as perhaps, the Congress did not perceive, as, the Raja of Mahmudabad observes that office has its own drawbacks." The party in power is naturally more exposed to criticism of every kind by those who are in opposition, without always being able to justify its policies. In this respect the League worked from a point of vantage[83]. In a big country like India there should inevitably be occasional cases of nepotism. Muslim League could conveniently depict them as cases of rank communal discrimination since the majority of Congress ministers were Hindu.[84] Many Hindus in Muslim majority provinces might have had similar grievances but their all-India status made them less insecure. The upshot was "to leave the Muslims convinced that their position under Hindu rule would be hopeless," and it was from the belief that the Hindu would be dominant in any form of central government of a united India that the demand for a separate homeland sprouted.[85]

Therefore, in the late 1930s, India's struggle for freedom had reached the crucial stage of crystallization of political concepts and social ideology. Provincial autonomy had bestowed some power on ministers. Even unsparing critics of the Congress admitted that the record of work of Congress governments in the span of twenty-seven months was not devoid of credit.[86] "The old contention that Indian self government was a necessity for any really radical attack on the social backwardness of India was thus confirmed." Samuel Hoare paid tribute to "the great constitutional success of provincial autonomy in India", in Parliament.[87] It appeared to many that full power or substantial power was just round the corner. So there was a natural proclivity of bipolarisation of the tension between the two big blocs regarding the future posture of things as also differentiation of political and social ideals and objectives. What had been lying somewhat dormant below the surface came out in the open.[88] The Muslims concocted bitter animosity towards Congress. The League was pitch forked by the government into the position of the sole representative organ of the Muslim community. Catching a leaf out of the Congress propaganda against British Rule, it started a venomous campaign of slander against Congress producing atrocity reports—the Pirpur Report in the U.P., the Sharif Report in Bihar and propagandist literature by Muslim intellectuals like Shafat Ahmed Khan—as a plank of their new politics of hatred.[89] Even Fazlul Haq sang the same tune in December 1939, ad his pamphlets, entitled, "Muslim Sufferings under Congress Rule." In this propaganda the League was being "indirectly encouraged," asserts Guha, "by the services or the bureaucracy."[90]

The exposition by the League on the failings of the Congress rule through stigmatising reports served to fortify its hold on the Muslims. These reports were at once the effect and the cause of the bad blood between the two parties. A vicious circle of mutual calumniation was perpetrated. "Whether the complaints were genuine or false or exaggerated, was besides the point". There was no denying their explosive possibilities by sedulously poisoning the Muslim mind against the Congress and the Hindu community in general.[91]

"The important practical point", as Griffiths, says "was that Muslims genuinely believed them." Vainly did the Congress leaders appeal to Jinnah to agree to an impartial inquiry."[92] "The League was not trying to convince the British or the Hindus," remarks B. R. Nanda, "its propaganda was meant for home consumption', for the Muslim community; in this aim it attained a remarkable success."[93] The dread of Hindu raj raised its ugly head; religious emotion was ruffled to a high pitch. A religio-political duststorm as forceful and raging as the duststorms in the Gangetic plain overwhelmed the land.

Jinnah had realised that a new slogan and organizational reforms—resorted to in October 1937 Muslim League session—were essential to attract and unite the various provincial Muslim groups and to win the masses.[94] He "planned his strategy carefully, executed it ruthlessly, and achieved in a short period between August 1937 and December 1939", observes B. N. Pandey, "what had been denied him at the poll in 1937. His position in 1938 was similar to that of the Congress in 1937 after the great electoral victory. He purposed to all Muslims and various Muslim organisations under the League banner and for this he took inspiration from propaganda techniques reminiscent of those, which the Germans had recently employed in Czechoslovakia."[95] The League proclaimed that a fascist Hindu had been installed and that Muslims had been shabbily discarded.[96] Gandhi machinated, said Jinnah, to "sabotage and vassalize the Muslims under the Hindu raj."[97]

The propaganda method of the League, thus, was similar to that of the Nazis in Germany : "The League leaders had begun to echo the fascists' tirade against democracy..... The Nazis raised the cry of hatred against the Jews and the League, against the Hindus."[98] Notwithstanding the discomfiture of his party members, Jinnah demanded that the League be acknowledged by both the Congress and the government as the sole representative of the Muslims of India, and himself being its sole spokesman. This amounted to the repudiation of the Congress claim to be an all-pervasive organisation. It implied that Indian politics were to be bifurcated on religious ground, the League representing the Muslims and Congress, the Hindus.[99] Clearly, the Congress could not accept all this without stultifying its glorious past as a national organisation embracing Indian of every creed, caste and community. Says Majumdar, "The Congress demand in 1937 that the Muslims must liquidate the Muslim League if they wanted to share powers with Congress was bad enough, but it was far worse to demand that the Indian National Congress, with its proud records of more than half a century's service as a national organisation, should voluntarily degrade itself into a communal Hindu organisation only to serve as a counterpart to the Muslim League."[100]

Obviously Jinnah knew that the Congress would not accept this demand. Similarly he could see that his appraisal of the Congress governments, which remained in office for a short duration, was motivated. This was too brief a span for the rectifying of chronic maladies. Jinnah certainly had the sense to appreciate it, "but", says Ram Gopal, "the choice for him was difficult; it was the choice between this appreciation and the injury caused to the League's rising campaign for Muslim solidarity under the green crescent flag."[101]

The League now fanned up Muslim apprehension that Hindu raj had arrived and that "the vast majority of those who counted in the hierarchy were Mahasabhaies at heart"[102]. "But for the Congress, secularism was an article of faith". It fondly cherished the hope that it could provide flesh to this creed by its Muslim mass contact programme. In the communal atmosphere that was thickening and not thinning, thanks to the British, it was a cold hope.[103]

The Congress had been in office only three months when the League, assembled for its annual session at Lucknow inveighed against the Congress governments saying : "Any individual Musalman member who was willing to unconditionally surrender and sign their pledge was offered a job as a minister,... These men are allowed to move about and pass of as Muslim ministers for the loyal services they have rendered to the Congress by surrendering and signing the pledge unconditionally and the degree of their reward is the extent of their perfidy."[104]

In one of its resolutions, the League brought its sentimental complaint against the hoisting of *Bande Mataram* as a national anthem upon the country. It may be recalled that the song was adopted in the distant days of the anti-partition movement in Bengal and had come to be regarded by the British as a symbol of sedition. From 1905 to 1920 it "had been sung at innumerable meetings", writes Nanda, "at some of which Jinnah himself was present"[105]. During the long and hard struggle for freedom from 1905 to 1947, *Bande Mataram* was the rallying cry of the patriots and thousands braved the baton charges, the firing of the alien police or met the hangman's noose with *Bande Mataram* on their lips.[106] It was inseparably linked with nationalism, and was for many years, the hymn of nationalism.[107] "Such was *Bande Mataram* to which Congressmen clung as a supreme national sentiment, and to which the League was taking exception."[108]

In order to understand properly Muslim feelings pertaining to *Bande Mataram*, it would be worthwhile to examine the historical background of the song. The song occurs in the great Bengali novelist Bankim Chandra Chatterji's *Anandmath* (Abbey of Bliss) as a battle cry against the foreigner. The central theme turns around a band of Sanyasis (Hindu ascetics) "who left their hearth and home and dedicated their lives to the cause of their motherland."[109] They rebelled against Muslim rule in Bengal in the seventies of the eighteenth century.[110] They worshipped their motherland, says Majumdar, "as the Goddess Kali; they knew no other deity save the land of their birth and no other religion except the service of motherland". The novel was an emotional protest at least ostensibly, against the Muslim rule. "This aspect of the *Anandmath* and the imagery of Goddess Kali leave no doubt that Bankim Chandra's nationalism was Hindu rather than Indian" affirms Majumdar.[111]

During the freedom struggle, those who suggested that this song should be adopted as the national anthem argued that Bankim wished to inspire the people with revolutionary fervour and that the Muslim rulers were chosen as the target of the fury of the sanyasis evidently to avoid British wrath. The song was invoked to arouse patriotic sentiments and became as dear as the motherland itself. "But Muslims had nothing common with this sentiment."[112] Hindu nationalists could be impersonal and detach the song from its context, but for Muslims it was extremely difficult especially when communal mischief was rampant.

There was also opposition to the Congress flag which, said Jinnah, was "to be obeyed and revered by all and sundry."[113] The Congress tricolour was started, observes Nanda "during the days of the Khilafat movement and its colours had been determined to represent the various communities: Saffron for Hindus, Green for Muslims and white for other minorities."[114] Maulana Muhammad Ali, the great Khilafat leader, delivered scores of stirring speeches under this banner as a symbol of India's unity and national solidarity against foreign rule."[115] Jinnah himself had saluted it for a number of years.[116] It was never deemed un-Islamic. But in the prevailing tense atmosphere these seemingly innocuous things became jarring.

Gandhi described Jinnah's presidential speech at Lucknow as a declaration of war "against the Congress and indirectly against Hindus also."[117] Jinnah had reprimanded the Congress for saying one thing and doing quite another and held it responsible for the loss of Muslim interest in the body."[118] His opposition to the party was augmenting. If he compromised he might lose his credibility with his community. As champion of Muslim culture and practices for which till then he had never bothered, he drew up his indictment of the Congress complaining that Hindi was to be the national language of all India. He opposed basic education and the Vidya Mandir scheme associated with that.[119] Besides *Bande Mataram* and the Congress flag he opposed the appointment of Congress Muslims as ministers although they did not enjoy the confidence of the Muslim representatives or the public outside. At the same time he upbraided the British authorities for default to use their power towards special responsibility to protect and shield the minorities through incurring censure of the calamity.[120] In the Bombay Assembly, a Muslim Leaguer moved as a counter missive, "that the reading of Koran and Surah must be made compulsory for Muslim boys and girls in schools and colleges as this knowledge was essential for every Muslim in his daily life."[121]

From the beginning of 1938, there started a correspondence between Jinnah and Jawaharlal Nehru, which continued till December 1939. Jinnah was in correspondence with other leaders most illustrative pertaining, to the basic Hindu-Muslim contrarieties. Besides Jinnah's Fourteen Points, a number of other important problems were discussed like the issue of *Bande Mataram,* the alleged imposition of Hindi by Congress governments, the issues of cow slaughter, as well as Jinnah's stubborn claim for the Muslim League to be the sole representative of the Muslim community.

On the issues of *Bande Mataram,* the Marscillaise of the nationalist movement, it was argued that the two stanzas approved by the working committee to be used as national anthem were not likely to affront anybody's susceptibilities. The Congress could not conveniently discard what crowds of people had come to cherish so fondly and for so long. At the same time Muslims would find it difficult to acquiesce in an official national song taken from a novel, which contained passionate anti Muslim comments.

Regarding the language question, Nehru and Azad put forward the official Congress viewpoint that the common—national and inter provincial—language was Hindustani, written as said before, both in Devanagri and Persian scripts. But the language controversy could not be resolved. On the other hand, it hardened stands on both sides with Muslim leaders sticking to Urdu and the Congress ministries favouring Hindi.[122]

Throughout the correspondence, Jinnah continued to insist on the point that before any dialogue, the Muslim League must be recognised as the sole authoritative organisation of Muslims of India. This was a novel demand and had been raised earlier.[122] Nehru's accedence to it would, as said earlier, reduce the Congress to a purely Hindu organisation. This very thought was an anathema to Nehru and other Congressmen. If the Congress was to accept Jinnah's demand, what was it to do with the hundred thousand Muslim members on its rolls.[123] Jinnah on his part was not keen for a final settlement at this juncture.[124] He wanted to gain time, to build up his own organisation and make it strong enough to peremptorily demand complete equality.

He avoided negotiations. Almost all the political demands of the Muslim community had been implemented in the constitution which was installed in 1937, and, remarks B. R. Nanda, "Jinnah had no concrete demands to make."[125] The Congress coterie was also probably marking time and certainly was optimistic about the success of its Muslim mass contact programme.[126]

It has been discussed previously that Wardha Scheme of basic education was regarded by the League with disfavour. It was taken to be an ingenious device to undermine the culture and education of the Muslims "and promote the revival and supremacy of the primitive Hindu culture of Vedic times."[127] As if to justify Muslim opposition, the basic schools started in the Central Province were given a name which was revolting to the Muslim mind. The name was Vidya Mandir (temple of learning). Mandir means a home, at the most a sacred home, and implies no affront to any religion; it is, not a religious expression. But in common parlance, as Ram Gopal observes, "it means almost always the abode of a Hindu God."[128] "For Muslims a Hindu temple was a place," says Khalid B. Sayeed, "where idols were worshipped" and this they regarded as purposed outrage to Islam's denunciation of idolatry.[129] Except for a literature, no Hindu would take Mandir for a common home. "Any thoughtful and perceptive person would have avoided wounding Muslim sentiments and adopted a neutral term."[130] Muslims were also incensed that no arrangement was made for separate Muslim schools, that Muslim school boys were obliged to sing *Bande Mataram* with folded hands and offer reverence to Gandhi's portrait.[131] To the Muslim League, these were clear indications "of the tyranny of Hindu brute majority over the helpless Muslim minority."[132] The Vidya Mandir scheme was bitterly resented by "the three per cent Muslim minority but their protests were disregarded." Even if the League was magnifying Congress injustices, there is no denying of the fact that the Congress governments during 1937-39 tended to look at social and educational problems from a Hindu point of view.[133]

The Congress' attitude towards the minorities was shown by a resolution of the Working Committee passed in November, 1937 which assured that "there would be no interface in matters of conscience, religion or culture and the minority would be entitled to keep its personal laws". It condemned the communal award but nevertheless declared that there should not be any unilateral attempt to change or modify it. Showing concern for the proclivities of the minorities, it expressed its wish to proceed in all matters affecting them with their cooperation and goodwill. But Jinnah or the League would have none of it and intensified their crusade against the Congress.[134]

Jawaharlal Nehru now called upon the Congress to energise the mass contact move which would invigorate the Congress to magnetise the growing awareness and ferment among the masses.[135] But Jinnah threatened the Congress with dire consequences if it meddled with Muslim affairs.[136]

The Muslim League launched a systematic onslaught on the Congress indicting it for trying to deprive the Muslim minority of its distinct entity and integrity. Full scope was given to League's imagination to hunt for "imaginary" grievances of a discriminatory treatment towards the minority community. The Pirpur and Sharif Reports listed these charges in highly coloured phraseology. The former report which was published in December, 1938 (after a one-sided enquiry) contained a severe and distorted appraisal of the Congress rule. It assailed the Congress "closed door" policy and cited it was proof that there was a basic difference between the body politic of this country and that of Britain.[137] The report pointed out that unlike the situation in Britain where parties in power are challenges, in India there was a permanent Hindu majority and the rest were minorities which are not within any thinkable span of time to be transformed into majorities.[138] The Muslims felt that no tyranny could equal the tyranny of the majority. The Pirpur Committee accused the Congress for trying to dismantle the Muslims politically by the "Divide and Rule" stratagem.[139] It complained of the preferential treatment of the majority community in the services, the Congress flag being flown on government buildings, of Muslim children being forced to sing the obnoxious anthem and worship the portrait of Gandhi. The Committee deplored that Muslims were cowed for eating cow and barred from local bodies, that the Urdu language and scripts were discouraged, and that the police was partial to Hindus in communal riots.

The Pirpur "Report, perhaps, does not now seem," observes Richard Symond, "very shocking by comparison with the events of 1947". But it was just such irritants and the turning of them to account "which for the first time obtained for the Muslim League the overwhelming support of Muslim lower middle and working classes."[140]

According to the Sharif Report, the parliamentary system established in the provinces after the enforcement of the new Act was even worse than the system it replaced.[141] The spectra that the Muslims would be permanently relegated to the position of second-rate citizens yoked to a majority rule raised its head. Subsequently, League's approach to the constitutional problems suffered a change. Weightages and safeguards by the constitution were no longer deemed satisfactory.[142]

Coming to economic affairs, the Congress governments were accused of devising and scheming measures to threaten the well being of the Muslims. According to the official version: "The Muslims were generally subjected to trade boycott by the Hindu. They were largely excluded from the benefits of social welfare schemes." And further: "the execution of beneficent schemes was in the hands of Hindu officials who saw to it that the Muslims did not get their due share in the benefits. Most departments and services of the governments were almost entirely manned and officered by the Hindus". Thus "Muslims were gradually squeezed out of key positions."[143]

In the words of A.F. Salahuddin Ahmed, a Bangladeshi historian, who has made a reasoned appraisal of the repercussions of this state of affairs, "The movement which led to the creation of Pakistan was not a religious movement", he says that, "fear of Hindu political domination which would adversely affect that community's political, economic and cultural interest seemed to have been an important factor which influenced the movement. In traditional Islam, politics and religion may be intertwined, but this does not hold good for the present day Muslim society. Despite the opposition of some orthodox Muslim theologians who maintained that the League's leadership was not quite Islamic, the Muslim League gained plebeian following because of it. "Pakistan offered an opportunity for many sided developments without fear of competition."[144]

As Muslim separatism began to be crystallized, "Muslim capitalists, bankers, merchants, all looked forward to the time", writes Sayeed, "when competition would be less fierce and the prospects of making high profits infinitely brighter." The contest was perhaps the most biting in the domain of government jobs. Nor was it surprising because in the "subcontinent so many citizen's interests were determined by the decisions of provincial and central servants." The Muslim share in the subordinate public services in provinces like the United Provinces and Bengal, was lopsided and likely to cause friction.

Was there a way out of this muddle? Gandhi competently hoped that all these problems could be solved once the long hand of the British was removed and India was left to herself. But "it was obvious from the very beginning", Sayeed aptly remarks, "that Gandhi could never hope to exercise any profound hold over the Muslim." After the Khilafat venture, as years rolled on, he was becoming increasingly aware of his will-o-the-wisp hold over the Muslim. It was not only the incompatible culture and interests of the Muslims that hindered his smooth sailing, but also his own Hindu approach to politics.[145] "It is embarrassing," states H. Mukerjee, "to find Gandhiji speaking as 'we' and Muslims as 'they'."[146] During the non-cooperation movement, Gandhi had stated for "me there are not politics but religion, they sub serve religion." To remove Hindu disquiet engendered by his fraternization with the Muslims, he said; "It has been whispered that by being so much with the Musalman friends, I make myself unfit to know the Hindu mind. The Hindu mind is myself. Surely I do not live amidst Hindus to know the Hindu mind, when every fibre of my being is Hindu."[147] "Even some of Gandhiji's phrases," Nehru confessed, "Sometimes jarred upon me—thus his frequent reference to "Ram Raj" as a golden age which was to return. But I was powerless to intervene."[148] But Congressmen were aware that in order to make Congressism increasingly broad based and attractive a man from the grassroots had to address his appeals in symbols and forms which would stir the Hindu of the lower rung.[149] As a corollary, Gandhi's role, if unwitting, in estranging the other community may not be insignificant.

The League, as has been earlier discussed was on the warpath with vituperative campaign twisting facts against Congress atrocity charges. Meanwhile, the upper class urbanised Hindus who partook with the Muslims the composite Hindu-Muslim culture knew little of the emergence of Hindi extremism as an appendage to politics, so they were perplexed as to what was bothering their Muslim brethren.[150]

It has to be noted that the Election had brought forth its men from the countryside. No doubt many Congressmen still entertained a romantic picture of themselves as members of the knightly order soaring on a high moral altitude dedicated to the cause of freedom and to the cherished ideals of the Congress.[151] But the Congress movement with its earth bred support under the lead of Gandhiji who had galvanized grovelling masses into tough fighters of the battles for freedom produced new kinds of leaders whose cultural ties were tucked up with the same broad Hindu masses.[152]

A new type of Hindu political worker had emerged to respond to the post-election challenges, the type hitherto familiar to the officialdom was an English-disciplined middle class person of a superior caste. The emergent type largely belongs to the non English speaking middle and lower-class, entrained in ruralism barely affected by urban influence, 'clinging to traditional *"Hinduaization"* and devoted to *"Sanskritization"*[153], no caring a brass farthing for westernisation.[154] Nor did it entertain pleasing memories of Muslim rule. It frowned upon both English and Urdu.[155] Although the common language recognized by the Congress was Hindustani, "the language used besides English in the administration and the schools was Hindi."[156] The Hindi enthusiasts in their zeal to *sanskritize* the language, proceeded to deter hundreds of words taken from Persian and Arabic. Nor were they disappointed with the reaction of the Hindu government on their doings.[157]

However, between 1937 and 1939, the Congress and the

government were linked together inextricably and Congressmen dominated the whole gamut of political activity in most provinces. The political life of the Congress was transformed into the political life of the provinces. This situation vastly enhanced the power and status of the Congress and Congressmen.[158]

The top Congress leaders had created a High Command, a central controlling authority to direct the provincial ministries in their administrative work. "This move by making Congress Cabinets," observes Kanji Dwarkadas, "responsible to an outside clique and not to their respective legislatures and the electorate struck at the very root of democratic government depriving them largely of initiative and self-reliance,[159] to say nothing of intensifying Muslim resentment." Nehru openly stated that "the ministers were the spokespersons of a mighty national movement of India and were under the discipline of their party and directly controlled by the Congress Working Committee." "It looked as though," says Walter Wallbank, "in the United States the National Committee of the Republican Party laid down all the policies to be followed by all state government who were Democrats." To Muslims Congress' policy was authoritarian, rendering provincial autonomy fallacious.[160] That a "Congress raj" had been established in their provinces was betrayed, writes, Reginald Coupland, "by the conduct and bearing of Congressmen", many of whom behaved as if they were a ruling caste, as if they owned the country.[161]

Provincial autonomy was worked as far as it could be, but in default of a responsible government at the centre, it could at best be a truncated state. Also lure of office brought internal clashes and dissensions among the Congressmen. But the most frightening feature from Gandhi's viewpoint was the growing corruption and ostentation[162] in the Congress circles and the tendency to exploit political power for private ends[163] "to work off their personal grudges."[164]

The Congress party men frowned upon the favourable positions that Muslims occupied in the subordinate public services of the United Provinces. At the same time the Congress High Command planned to use their power and prestige to procure Muslim support through the far-reaching Muslim mass contact programme, discussed above. They could not see the discrepancy "in the two pronged offensive of their party." Any diminution in authority and influence of Muslim subordinate officials was bound to cause resentment among Muslims which might boomerang at the Congress in the defeat of Muslim mass contact, to say nothing of the propaganda against the Congress launched by the wheels of the League, which were rapidly acquiring strength, speed and efficiency.[165]

During the two years of Congress rule, the abyss of misunderstanding and acrimony between the Congress and the League continued to deepen. From the Muslim standpoint, the period represented a nightmare of harassment in various fields. Exception was taken to the distinct impress of the Gandhi cult, for the creed of non-violence and the craft of spinning and weaving, howsoever genuine and idealistic were certainly tainted by Hindu rather than by Muslim thought.

The advent of the Congress Ministries signalised, states Ispahani, "an alarming increase in the number of Hindu-Muslim riots."[166] To quote Fazlul Haq (Speaking on April 17, 1938), "In Congress Provinces, riots have laid the countryside waste, Muslim life, limb and property have been lost and blood has freely flowed;" And: "The sufferings of Muslims are, to the Congress, matters for mockery and laughter.[167] In an atmosphere surcharged with communal feelings, communal riots were not unusual. The Muslim community was in a highly wrought-up state by the stories of wrongs committed by the Congress governments. Jinnah, the astute politician, gave his own interpretation to the Muslim voice, which had by now gone sharp and grating. All the time he was clamouring from the housetops that the rights of the minorities were being trampled under foot by the Congress ministries. His entire outlook had undergone a drastic change, "We cannot surrender, submerge or submit", declared Jinnah, "to the dictates or the ukase of the Congress High Command which is developing into a totalitarian and authoritarian caucus functioning under the name of the working committee and aspiring to the position of a shadow cabinet in a future republic.[168]

A few months later in December 1938, Jinnah said, "It is the misfortune of our country, indeed it is a tragedy that the High Command of the Congress is determined, absolutely determined, to crush all other communities and cultures in this country, and to establish Hindu raj. They talk of national Government; but they mean only Hindu Government." But the bubble had been pricked too soon.[169] Jinnah's charges were couched in provocative and insolent terms, and there was no dearth of eagerly listening ears, but who could guess the Hindu-Muslim antipathy had plunged into the rapids on the partition, which still lay blurred in the mist of time.

Before 1937, there was little serious urge to create a separate Muslim state in India. So what were the pressures working in the three years following the 1937 election that gave such gusto to the Pakistan movement? For an exposition of this intriguing phenomenon one must focus the United Provinces, "a key province so far as Hindu-Muslim relations were concerned".[170] Congress on assuming office "initiated three movements", remarks Venkatachar, "which brought to the surface the latent forces of Muslim separatism". If the Congress spurning the idea of coalition with the League was unfortunate, the programming of Muslim mass contact was no less so.[171] The core of this programme was the U.P. It put the Muslim communalists on a vantage ground, enabling them to raise the cry of religion in danger, on condemning the Congress governments on numerous counts. Seized with despair that the Congress was out to annihilate them, the Muslims rallied to the League. The third move—now clearly seen in the light of after time—"was the attack, emanating from deep Gangetic earth, on Muslim culture". Jinnah never failed to exploit these moves even if Congress regarded them without much malice, the League did response to such one sided cruelty charges.[172]

Hindu-Muslim relations, in the United Provinces, which had been somewhat cordial until the general elections, were fast deteriorating. It was in the United Provinces that the Muslim nationalist movement—the political ideals of nationalism in contrast to the sense of Islamic fraternity—had first germinated, although Muslims here were in a minority. Nor is this surprising, for the U.P. Muslims were not a retrogressive body lay elsewhere, but rather a well to do assertive distinct entity living in the metropolis of Muslim culture,[173] where Mughal traditions still lingered, and where they succeeded in retaining a political importance at variance with their inferior numbers.[174] "Yet," as Philips and Wainwright point out, "consciousness of past glories and culture would not alone have been sufficient to provide the motive power to sustain an effective nationalist movement," even though the sterile awareness of a magnificent past, might have done the groundwork for an initial discontent. Such a movement had to be constantly nurtured by existing grievances.

Muslims of the minority areas had their own worries and apprehensions. Hindus throughout the country enjoyed an overall upper hand. Muslims were prone to blame their minority status in the country for any ill success that attended them in obtaining suitable jobs.[175] As a matter of fact, as has been earlier, the U.P. Muslims had occupied a favoured position in the subordinate services.

Now the Muslim League could point out that under the Congress regime, Hindus were determined to eject them, from their advantageous positions,[176] ill-will deepened and powerful springs of separatism sprouted. The old might be content to revel in past greatness and present culture, but the disappointment of the young needed a substantive outlet. The League satisfied this craving.[177]

The worsening communal situation in U.P. attracted outside attention. The strength of the Congress, it was felt, could be challenged gainfully on the communal front. The Pirpur Report served a good advertising stunt for the Muslim League.[178] The story that it had begun was carried forward "with even more lurid and gruesome details of Congress oppression."[179] Before long, the U.P. "a weak spot among the Congress-governed provinces," became a focal point of every-one with a grievance against the Congress. Congress must be attacked where it appeared to be vulnerable.[180] And so, it was the minority provinces, as Jinnah vouched later, "who spread the light when there was darkness in the majority provinces." It was they who spear-headed the move.[181]

The attitude of the native states to the Congress and Muslim League may be noted. Till the passing of the Act of

1935, Congress had kept a somewhat neutral attitude towards ferment in the Indian states. However, it became difficult to maintain this posture for long as democratic unrest was gathering momentum in the states.[182] Nehru had been chafing at the weak and vacillating policy of the Congress in this respect. In 1935, the AICC resolved that the interests of the people of the states were as much the concern of the Congress as were those of the people of British India.[183] In February 1938, the working committee decided to set up Congress committees in the princely states. This was a significant departure from the earlier stand.[184] Nehru denounced "the state governments as out of date and their treaties with the British rulers moth-eaten documents not binding on the people."[185] The princes had sensed that the good old days of personal rule were coming to an end.[186] Tradition-ridden, they were loath to revolutionary changes which might impair their power and hold, whereas democratic agitation therein was responsible for introducing a new dimension to the concept of India's unity.

Princes, even Hindu princes, filled with presentiments, resentful of "trouble-mongers" within their domains, grew conspicuously favourable to the Muslim League, thanks to Jinnah's overtures. To quote Shiva Rao :

> On one occasion the Jam Sahab of Nawanagar (at that time the chancellor of the chamber of princes) told me, in discussing an alliance between the Muslim League and the chamber for the federal elections : "Why should I not support the League? Mr. Jinnah is willing to tolerate our existence, but Mr. Nehru wants the extinction of the Princes."

While probing the genesis of the concept of the vivisection of India it is necessary, says Majumdar, to mention "one important factor which was responsible to a very large extent for the emergence of the idea of partition" of the country on communal lines. "This was the Hindu Mahasabha,"[187] which was playing a significant role "in poisoning the stream of Indian politics."[188] Its slogan implied that "India belongs to the Hindus and is nobody else's patrimony."[189] The Mahasabha accused the Congress of encouraging Muslim communalism, and preached "Hinduism, Hindutva and Hindudom."[190] To counter the Muslim communal theory of two nations the equally fantastic theory "that India was a Hindu *rashtra*, or state, and that Muslims would have to adopt Hindu ways of life if they wished to stay on in India,"[191] was propounded. Some of the leading Hindus in the Congress party upbraided the Mahasabha for its intemperateness, but the harm was done.

The "latest" high priest of Hindu communalism was Vinayak Damodar Savarkar, a renowned revolutionary leader of Maharashtra. A.C. Guha says, "He was for full Hindu domination." The burden of his outpourings was : "Hindustan is for the Hindus." He talked of the Hindu nation, of its past glory, its bright future; he was bitterly anti-Congress.[192]

Under the leadership of Savarkar, the Mahasabha was developed into a political and communal organization of the Muslim League stamp. But, as Majumdar points out, there was one vital difference between the two. Neither theoretically nor practically could the Hindu Mahasabha claim to represent the Hindus in the sense in which the Muslim League represented the Muslims in 1938 and subsequently. For the large majority of the politically conscious Hindus were associated with the Congress which condemned the Muslim League and Hindu Mahasabha alike for narrow communalism. "The fact of the matter is that the Mahasabha," continues Majumdar, "as fiercely attacked the Congress as anti-Hindu, as the Muslim League did on the ground that it was anti-Muslim."[193] Nevertheless, the Muslim League took serious umbrage at the speeches of Savarkar (the permanent president of the Hindu Mahasabha) who preached rabid Hinduisation in Hindustan, where Muslims, "only territorially Indians", would have "to live as a minority, in the position of subordinate cooperation with the Hindu nation."[194]

However, deplorable might be the attitude of the Hindu Mahasabha from a national point of view, "it had no large following," affirms Majumdar, "among the Hindus and did not represent the Hindu community in any sense of the term." Thus logically the Mahasabha, with its adverse utterances ought not to have carried much weight for the high minded Muslims. But men are often swayed by sentiments rather than logic. "There are two special reasons," observes Majumdar, "why the Muslims got nervous over the views so frankly expressed by Savarkar." First, he aspired to establish (and minced no words about it) Hindu raj in India, a contingency which was a horrifying apparition for the Muslims and never ceased to obsess them. Secondly, the Muslim League was fully aware of the effect produced by impassioned appeals to communal urges. Might not the same weapon, by which the League acquired preponderance notwithstanding nationalist Muslims and other Muslim organizations, also enable the Hindu Mahasabha to secure predominance in the Hindu community inspite of the Congress.[195] The League's call to the Muslims to come under its fold egged on the Hindu Mahasabha to start a counter campaign among Hindus; the Mahasabha's aggressive politics made the League's task of rallying Muslims facile. Savarkar affirmed a Jinnahian idea that the Hindus and Muslims could never be forged into a single Indian nation for the mere wish to do so.[196] Speaking at the Annual Hindu Mahasabha Session of 1937, Savarkar said: Several infantile politicians committed the serious mistake in supposing that India was already welded into a harmonious nation. These men out of naivety took their dreams for realities. That is why they were impatient of communal tangles. "But the solid fact is that the so-called communal questions are but a legacy handed down to us by centuries of cultural, religious and national antagonism between the Hindus and the Muslims. When the time is ripe you can solve them; but you cannot suppress them by merely refusing recognition of them." And further : "Let us bravely face unpleasant facts as they are. India cannot be assumed today to be a unitarian and homogeneous nation, but on the contrary there are two nations in the main, the Hindus and the Muslims."[197]

"But," says Ram Gopal, "Savarkar's solution was not the division of the country into a Hindu India and a Muslim India: he would have a dominant position for the Hindus who constituted the majority."[198]

Nor did the Pirpur Report, "which had undisguised British support,"[199] fan religious feelings of the Muslims any less when it stated that "the conduct of the Congress governments seems to substantiate the theory that there is something like identity of purpose between the Congress and the Hindu Mahasabha."[200] Suspicion breeds mistrust and general Muslim feeling was that with the exception of "some sincere leaders among the top echelons of the Congress, who wished to give a square deal to the Muslims, and who were for a genuine national integration on secular lines,"[201] "a vast majority of the Congress members are Hindus who look forward, after many centuries of British and Muslim rule, to the re-establishment of a purely Hindu raj."[202] E.W.R. Lumby—in *The Transfer of Power in India*—takes the same view. Now that the Hindus had recovered something of their ancient power, they automatically, observes Lumby, "began to mould everything to their own way of life, so that it seemed to Muslims that unless the process was checked the whole structure of their own religion and culture would be undermined."[203]

Like the Nazi propaganda in Germany, the League propaganda was grossly biased. Masses came under its spell readily, and those who ought to have known better swallowed it, because it served their purpose.[204] The art of propaganda as perfected during the second world war has taught us how credulous even an educated and critical audience can become.[205] If the highly educated Germans could be carried away by the propaganda of Hitler and Goebbels, it is not surprising that the unsophisticated Muslims gulped down League's travesty of truth as truth,[206] let alone the effect of the Hindu Mahasabha's audacious utterances. Communal chasm was widening, to the grief of the saner elements of the two communities and to the relief of the British.

The Congress leadership was dejected and disappointed over the political climate in the country. It felt that if the goal of "complete independence" was to be achieved it was essential that the people presented a united front to the obstructionist forces. Leading Congressmen particularly noticed the new strength of the League and felt that a fresh effort for rapprochement should be made.[207] In May 1937, Jinnah himself had approached Gandhi for Hindu-Muslim settlement. But things changed totally in 1938.[208] Jinnah steadily succeeded in attaining his objective of making the League the most powerful organization of the Muslims. He would offer his own terms now. His demand was simple—"recognize that the Muslim League is the only representative organization of the Muslims and also that the Congress could speak only on behalf of the Hindus." "Later he limited the scope of the Congress," observes Guha, "only to the caste Hindus."[209] Acceding to Jinnah's demand, as has been discussed earlier, would have been for the Congress suicidal as a national organization. The demand was too heavy, and it was probably made so purposely that it might never be conceded and the Congress leaders be held responsible for the failure of talks.[210]

As if this was not enough, Jinnah specified[211] "that the Committee appointed by the Congress to discuss Hindu-Muslim questions should not include any Musalman."[212] Gandhi wanted to have Abul Kalam Azad with him in his talks with Jinnah knowing fully well that between Azad and Jinnah there was no love lost. This was not a propitious way of pursuing a trying dialogue, but perhaps at that time, observe Mukerjee, Gandhi was too preoccupied confounding the Left to have time left even for inter-communal appeasement.[213]

Jinnah had strained every nerve to organize and vitalize the League; if however, in the very process of doing so he jeopardized all chances of striking a peaceable settlement with the Congress that was another matter. "The more he tried," writes S.R. Mehrotra, "to rally the Muslims under the banner of the League by appealing to their communal hopes and fears, the more he had to succumb to and identify himself with those communal hopes and fears."[214] He became enmeshed in the communal web from which it was not possible to wriggle out except at the cost of loss of face. Willy-nilly he had to yield to his new destiny—as the high priest of new Muslim nationalism, the protagonist of Muslim separatism. Psychoanalysts would call this destiny part of a negative identity; an identity which he was not to become, but which he nevertheless found himself compelled to become, protesting his wholeheartedness." Tremendous indeed had been the distance traversed from his original stand as "the Ambassador of Hindu-Muslim unity."[215]

Nehru and Gandhi watched the developing situation from different angles. Nehru had little realistic conception of the gravity of the Hindu Muslim problem. Nor did he make a correct appraisement of the power and potentialities of the Muslim League. He seems to have lived in a utopia of his own creation;[216] dwelt tamely on his favourite theme that the logic of events would lead the Congress to socialism as a sure cure for India's malady. Nehru's freedom from communal bigotry was crystal clear, and never doubted even by his enemies. His personal qualities of head and heart seemed to make Jinnah relent a bit and correspondence was pursued in 1939. "In retrospect, it appears strangely thoughtless," remarks H. Mukerjee, "that Jawaharlal virtually threw away unequalled opportunities of an approach at least to an understanding." He harped on a so-called "psychological barriers", so much so that he was rather sceptical of the utility of mutual discussion. It is disappointing that Nehru, Mukerjee notes ruefully, "normally so conscious of his own personality and its diverse and complicated pulls, was insensible of analogous, if dissimilar, intricacies in the mental make-up of the older man."[217] On October 18, 1939, Nehru wrote to Jinnah that he was ashamed of himself that he had not been able to do much to the amicable adjustment of the communal problem, that most of his interests lay in other directions; and that, "I feel as if I was an outsider and an alien in spirit." Futile romanticism hardly becoming a functioning, pragmatic nation builder. Nehru failed deplorably in surmounting the slope from "abstraction to realities."[218]

Gandhi occupied a singular position. Realizing that he was now wanted by the leaders more as a symbol than as a leader to lay down the rules, he had decided to withdraw from the Congress altogether.[219] Yet, "it was well known that," states Majumdar, "the Congress leaders took no decision in vital matters without consulting him." Nehru called Gandhi the "permanent super-president of the Congress."[220] No doubt earlier his traditional and intrepid role had done much to bolster up the freedom struggle. But once Congress got involved in administrative imbroglio, and had begun to realize how greatly the span of political issues had been stretched by the fast changing international situation, "Gandhi's role," as Philips and Wainwright observe, "became an irritant, and a source of perplexity." Once communal trend was in the ascendant, "Gandhi's bewildering fertility of ideas and arguments had disrupting effects on Congressmen, confusing their sense of strategy" and debilitating their initiative.[221] Right upto the beginning of the war, and even in its early stages, Gandhi's concern was not to embarrass Britain. During this period he leaned more to Rajagopalachari and Gobind Ballabh Pant than to Nehru and the left wing element in the Congress.[222] The younger section was losing faith both in the non violent programme which had yielded but poor dividends, and in its exponent.[223] In communal overtures Gandhi's attitude was sometimes queer. He had written to Jinnah (22 May, 1937) that he felt utterly helpless, and cried out to God for light.[224]

The Viceroy Linlithgow was at his wit's end at the diminishing prospects of federation "which was conceived partly as a method," so says Percival Griffiths, "....to weld the provinces of British India and the states."[225] Held in a whirl of diverse pressures—Congress, League and the Princes—he found it increasingly difficult to bring about the smooth implementation of the federal part of the Act.[226] Moods, thrusts were changing; earlier commitments were being thrown to the wind. It was the political naivety of the Congress party, in showing open hostility to the state governments, that was responsible to a considerable extent for their recalcitrance. In the opinion of Griffiths : "Just as the Congress mass campaign against the Muslims at this time was one of the ultimate causes of the demand for partition, in the same way, the militant Congress campaign in the states resulted in a definite hardening of the attitude of the princes" vis-a-vis a federation in which the Congress, in its new militant mood, would be predominant. "It is no exaggeration to say," continuous Griffiths, "that, by its unhappy timing of these campaigns, the Congress helped to kill the federal scheme and perhaps destroyed the last chance of preserving a united India."[227]

It has been pointed out by some politicians [228] who were instrumental in the making of the 1935 Act that if its federal provisions had been carried into effect before the war the partition of the country could have been averted.[229] India might have joined voluntarily in the war against the fascist forces and the pressure of joint war effort might have cemented the federation to surmount Hindu-Muslim antagonism without partition and integrated the states, so opines Conrad Corfield, "without eliminating their value." However, it was put into the cold storage and never revived,[230] and writers of history and whole generations were led tantalizingly to speculate as to what would have happened if the federal part of the Act had been enforced before the war.

It remained a paper work: As Tara Chand remarks, "No one seemed really to want it." The diehard imperialists were absolutely opposed to it, because they were not prepared to concede even the constricted transfer of power at the centre which it entailed. As such they had applied brakes making it immobile, two of these being the vetoes of the Muslims and the princes.[231]

But, the reluctance of the princes had already become of secondary importance; "far more serious and significant was the growing opposition of the Muslims."[232]

Zetland, the Secretary of State, certainly restrained the effort to expedite the creation of the federation for fear of a conservative revolt; he felt the process required some years to consummate. Linlithgow who had taken up the task of inducing the princes to join the federation was halter-hung to pursue the matter vigorously. He was less blameworthy than the British statesmen suggest.[233]

The federation scheme fizzled out not because of the failing of the Viceroy's implementation of the Act, nor because of the arch diehardism of an influential section of the Conservative party which had procrastinated its passing, "but because," as R. J. Moore points out, "it was flawed in essential respects."[234] However, Linlithgow failed to handle the situation with imaginative dexterity. Perhaps a Viceroy with something of the brilliance of a Mountbatten might have succeeded in mastering the communal and separatist forces that were portentously surfacing, but it was quite beyond the horizon of the more pedestrian talents of the man on the spot.

And time was running out.

In the words of Percival Spear :

The years 1937-39 were notable for a great success, a great failure, and a great mistake. The success was the Congress ministries, for which both government and Congress must share credit.[235] The failure was the inability of the government to persuade the

> princes to join the federation..... The great mistake was the Congress attitude toward the Muslims.[236]

To Congress it might have appeared good tactic to nip the League regenerative trend in the bud by approaching Muslim masses. But, as Spear says, this was a severe blow to Jinnah. Turning desperate, "From the classes he went to the masses with the cry of 'Islam in danger' .... The magic worked." Writes Spear, "The present writer can testify to the changed atmosphere which greeted him on a return to Delhi in 1939 after an absence of two years. Pakistan was in the air."[237] I.H. Qureshi was also away during the two crucial years. He expressed similar feelings. To quote him: "The writer of this paper was away from the subcontinent from June 1937 to September, 1939 when considerable intensification of ill will took place." He was astonished "at the change that he witnessed on his return. The atmosphere was now surcharged with emotion." Profound estrangement between the two communities had taken place which was manifest even in social gatherings. "The idea of Pakistan," states Qureshi, "had caught the imagination of the Muslims like wild fire."[238] The belief was instilled into their mind that they could not share destiny with the majority community.

When the Congress ministries resigned there was sentimentalism on government and Congress sides, but Jinnah proclaimed a day of thanksgiving at relief from Hindu tyranny. It was the end of a terrible dream, as it were. Nehru looked upon the League's decision to celebrate "deliverance day" as a "psychological barrier" which blocked the way to mutual rapport. The sure success of this occasion evinced that anti-Congress feeling among Muslims was stronger than Congress leaders were inclined to acknowledge. "A political storm cone had been hoisted in the national sky and its colour was green."[239]

As for the villager, the cultivator and the artisan, who constituted the bulk of India's population, he lived in the 1930s much as he had lived for a 100 years. Hindus and Muslims lived in the same village, but in different *mohallas*. The Muslims did not inter-marry or inter-dine with the Hindus. His eating habits, dress and name had a distinct Muslim impress. When he died he was buried, but the Hindu was cremated. Politics meant little to him. Ever since he could remember, notwithstanding politicians' harangues, the British conducted the day to day administration. But in 1937, something novel happened. Congress ministers clad in *khadi*, occupying government offices, controlled and directed the British officials. The Congress flag with its spinning wheel blazed proudly forth on government buildings. And Congress was evidently predominantly Hindu. So when he was told by League workers of the grievous injustices which his co-religionists were undergoing under the Congress rule, he readily believed them. A spectre grew in his mind; in an Independent India—in the land his Moghul forbears had once ruled—he would be submerged by Hindu majority raj. The idea was revolting. Once he had heard that his religion was at stake, he was stung to the quick, and no talk of communal safeguards could impress him. Congress's thoughtful, ameliorative socio-economic reforms signified nothing to him. If the British were going there would be either Hindu raj or Muslim raj. Islam was in danger; and the only leader he would adhere to was one who promised to protect it. Naturally, it was the Muslim League leaders, in political wilderness and resentful, intrepid on that count, who first raised the slogan, but once it was raised it could not be silenced.[240]

"No power on earth can prevent Pakistan," declared Jinnah in 1940.[241] He spoke shrewdly. "In this period," observes Guha, "perhaps the most important aspect of the nation's life was a near-complete cleavage between the two important communities," as well as between the Congress and the Muslim League.[242] The historical importance of the period of the Congress governments lies not so much in the question of whether the Muslim grievances were real or whether they were fabrications or exaggerations, but in fact that the great majority of Muslims believed them to be true.[243] The Indian Muslims were made to feel that they were Muslims first and Indians only second, that they were a distinct entity. "The allegations inflamed," writes Majumdar, "the passions of the Muslims to such an extent that the view was entertained by some that the whole thing was conceived as an ingenious propaganda to rally the Muslim masses round the

League."[244] For Nehru and others there was no meeting ground for a settlement. The war extinguished whatever urge the League leader might have had for a reasonable arrangement with the Congress. Having no compromise formula, staking inflated claims and working at cross purposes in an incrassating climate, the Congress and the League steadily polarized as two incompatible absolutes.

The greater was the likelihood of a Congress dominated centre, the stronger was the Muslim resistance to the envisaged federation. Nor did the Muslim League hesitate to play on the aversion of some of the princes such as the Nizam to help fix a Hindu raj upon their Muslim brethren. How could the Congress demand for a true democratic set-up and League's pressing requirement of safeguards for Muslim interests be harmonized? Towards the end of 1937, Zetland had scented Muslim stubbornness. He was aware, he wrote in 1938, "of the almost irresistible centripetal force of Islam as such"; and grew convinced that the dominant factor in determining the future form of the Government of India would.prove to be the All-India Muslim League." During 1939, he pointed out that leading Muslims were thinking in terms of clustering provinces into communal blocs which might combine under a weak centre. The separatist tendencies fruited in a definite scheme.[245] Zetland hinted to his opposite number for a tactful handling of the situation and discussing the matter with representatives of the Congress, the League and the princes. "The Viceroy's insensate, and a thorough going optimist, remained apathetic. He did not presage;" says Moore, "serious trouble from the Muslim side." Belatedly, Linlithgow did admit that he had failed to discern the gradual hardening of the outlines of the Indian problem during the two foregoing years;[246] which brought into sharp relief, the League and Congress requirements.

NOTES AND REFERENCES

1. Sayeed, Khalid B. *Pakistan : The Formative Phase 1857-1948*, 2nd, edn. (London : Oxford University Press, 1968), p. 88
2. Tomlinson, B.R. *The Indian National Congress and the Raj, 1929-*

1942 : The Penultimate Phase, (London : The Macmillan Press. Ltd., 1976), pp. 85-86.
3. Mukerjee, Hirendranath *India's Struggle for Freedom.* 3rd rev. edn, (Calcutta : NBA, Nov. 1962), pp. 200-01.
4. Mukerjee, Hiren, *Recalling India's Struggle for Freedom,* (Delhi : Seema Publications, 1983), p. 125.
5. Guha, Arun Chandra, *India's Struggle—Quarter of a Century 1921-46,* (New Delhi : Publications Division, Govt. of India, June 1982), Part I, p. 402.
6. Zaidi, Z.H. "Aspects of the Development of Muslim League Policy, 1937-47", In: *Partition of India; Policies and Perspectives 1935-1947,* Philips C.H. and Wainwright, M.D. (eds), (London: George Allen and Unwin, 1970), p. 259.
7. Sayeed, *Pakistan,* p. 87.
8. Chandra, Bipan, *Nationalism and Colonialism in Modern India,* (New Delhi: Orient Longman Ltd., 1979), p. 261.
9. Sayeed, *Pakistan,* p. 87.
10. Guha, *India's Struggle,* p. 402.
11. Zaidi, A.M. (chief ed.), *Evolution of Muslim Political Thought in India, The Demand for Pakistan,* (New Delhi: S. Chand and Company Ltd., 1978), Vol. VI, p. 37.
12. Guha, *India's Struggle,* p. 402.
13. Kabir, Humayun, *Muslim Politics 1906-47 and Other Essays.* (Calcutta: Firma K. L. Mukhopadhyay, 1969), p. 32.
14. Zaidi, *Demand for Pakistan,* p. 39.
15. Tara Chand, *History of the Freedom Movement in India,* (New Delhi: Publications Division, Govt. of India, Nov. 1972), Vol. IV, p. 239.
16. Zaidi, *Demand for Pakistan,* p. 39.
17. Ibid. p. 37; Guha, *India's Struggle,* p. 402.
18. Zaidi, "League Policy," pp. 258-59.
19. Pandey, B.N. *The Break up of British India,* (London : Macmillan, Press, Ltd., 1969), p. 142.
20. Mukerjee, *Recalling India's Struggle,* pp. 125-26.
21. Kulkarni, V. B., *India and Pakistan; 'A Historical Survey of Hindu—Muslim Relations,* (Bombay: Jaico Publishing House, 1973), p. 316.
22. To mention two such Nehruvian 'casual' utterances: (1) Nehru's alleged remark that Jinnah had been "finished" infuriated the latter to return to India in January 1935 as Tinker Hugh has suggested (*South Asia: A Short history, London, 1966, p. 219);* (2) Nehru's 10 July, 1946 statement at a Press Conference in

Bombay after the Congress and the Muslim League acceptance of the Cabinet Mission Plan "that Congress would enter the Constituent Assembly completely unfettered by agreements and free to meet all situations as they arise"—made Jinnah take umbrage and issue a counter-statement leading to the subversion of the whole scheme; Azad, Abul Kalam. *India Wins Freedom: An Autobiographical Narrative*, (Bombay: Orient Longman, 1959), pp. 154-56.

23. Kulkarni, *India and Pakistan*, p. 316.
24. Bolitho, Hector. *Jinnah: Creator of Pakistan* (London : J. Murray, 1954), pp. 113-14.
25. Majumdar, R. C. *History of the Freedom Movement in India*, (Calcutta; Firma K.L. Mukhopadyay, 1963), Vol. III, p. 563.
26. Moon, Penderel. *Divide and Quit*, (London: Chatto and Windus, 1962), p. 17.
27. Majumdar, *Freedom Movement*, p. 563.
28. Zaidi, *Demand for Pakistan*, p. 40.
29. Majumdar, *Freedom Movement*, pp. 567-68.
30. Sayeed, *Pakistan*, pp. 87-88; Zaidi, "League Policy", p. 259.
31. Guha, *India's Struggle*, p. 405.
32. Zaidi, *Demand for Pakistan*, p. 54; Padmasha, *Indian National Congress and the Muslims 1928–1947* (New Delhi: Rajesh Publications, 1980), pp. 165-66.
33. Ibid, p. 166.
34. Majumdar, *Freedom Movement*, p. 564.
35. Pandey, *The Break-up*, p. 147.
36. Majumdar, *Freedom Movement*, p. 565.
37. Pandey, *The Break-up*, p. 145.
38. Majumdar, *Freedom Movement*, p. 565.
39. Chandra, *Nationalism and Colonialism in Modern India*, p. 271.
40. Majumdar, *Freedom Movement*, pp. 565-66.
41. Ibid. p. 566.
42. Zaidi, *Demand for Pakistan*, p. 41.
43. Majumdar, *Freedom Movement*, p. 568.
44. Moon, *Divide and Quit*, pp. 17-18.
45. Bahadur, Lal, *The Muslim League: Its History, Activities and Achievements* (Agra: Agra Book Store, 1954), p. 245.
46. Moon, *Divide and Quit*, pp. 17-18.
47. Majumdar, R.C. "Muslim Community," In : *History and Culture of the Indian People, British Paramouncey and Indian Renaissance*, Majumdar, R.C. (gen. ed) and Majumdar A.K., and Ghose D.K. (Asst. eds.), (Bombay : Bharatiya Vidya Bhavan, 1965), Part

II, vol. X, p. 331.

48. Chandra, *Nationalism and Colonialism in Modern India,* p. 272.
49. The 35th session of the Congress held at Nagpur in 1920.
50. Pandey, *The Break-up,* p. 148.
51. Zaidi, Z.H. "League Policy," p. 259.
52. Coupland, R., *Report on the Constitutional Problem in India, Indian Politics* (1943), cited by Ibid, p. 260, (London : Oxford Univ. Press, 1944) Part II, p. 112.
53. Moon, *Divide and Quit,* p. 18
54. Majumdar, *Freedom Movement* p. 568.
55. Bahadur, *The Muslim League,* p. 246.
56. Kabir, *Muslim Politics,* p. 27 "The most alarming feature, from Gandhi's angle, was the growing corruption in the Congress organisation manifesting falsehood and indiscipline as also the tendency to exploit political power for vested ends. Violence was also there in the atmosphere and Hindu militancy was raising its head as a counterpoise to Muslim obduracy and bellicosity.
57. Prasad, Bahadur, *Changing Modes of Indian National Movement* (New Delhi: People's Publishing House), p. 131.
58. Kabir, *Muslim Politics,* p. 27.
59. Ibid, pp. 27-28.
60. Hasan, Mumtaz, "The Background of the Partition of the Indo-Pakistan Subcontinent" In : *Partition of India,* Philips, (ed.), p. 58.
61. Kabir, *Muslim Politics,* p. 28.
62. Chandra, *Nationalism and Colonialism in Modern India,* p. 262.
63. Gankovsky, Y.V. and Palonskaya Gordon L.R., *A History of Pakistan* (Moscow: Nauka Publishing House, 1964), p. 68.
64. Kabir, *Muslim Politics,* p. 28.
65. Tara Chand, *History of the Freedom Movement in India,* Vol. V. (New Delhi : Publications Division, Govt. of India, Nov. 1972), Vol. V, p. 253.
66. Nanda, B.R. "Nehru, The Indian National Congress and the Partition of India, 1935-47" In : *Partition of India,* Philips, (ed.), p. 161.
67. Raja of Mahmudabad. *Some Memories,* Ibid, p. 387.
68. Ibid. p. 388.
69. Committee appointed by the League "under the presidentship of Raja Mohammad Mehdi of Pirpur to investigate Muslim complaints against Congress governments and Hindus". The report of the Committee was published at the end of 1938,

Gopal Ram, *Indian Muslim : A Political History* 1858-1947, (Bombay: Asia Publishing House, 1958), pp. 258-59.

70. Zaidi, *Demand for Pakistan*, p. 92, "Things apparently of no significance sometimes matter deeply, and it is strange that Jawaharlal Nehru was a party—and Abdul Ghaffar Khan also to the ceremonial opening in the late "thirties of a temple to Mother India, the Bharat Mata Mandir in Varanasi and on the walls of which are engraved, along with a relief map of India, the alphabets of all major Indian languages with the exception only of Urdu on account of the foreign origin of its script. How this kind of thoughtless affront to an important element of our own people could pass muster seems nearly inexplicable", Mukerjee, *"Recalling India's Struggle,"* p. 130.
71. Venkatachar, C.S. "1937-47 in Retrospect : A Civil Servant's View" In: *Partition of India*, Philips, (ed.), p. 471, see Altaf Husain Hali, *Hayyat-i-Javed, Urdu Eternal Life*, p. 138.
72. Kabir, *Muslim Politics*, p. 29.
73. Sayeed, *Pakistan*, pp. 91-92 "Although the Congress recognised that the Hindustani language had two literacy forms—Urdu and Hindi, the language used besides English in the administration and the schools was Hindi. Muslim demands that Urdu be placed on par with Hindi were ignored. The compulsory study of Hindi in schools and the refusal to introduce the Urdu language and Arabic and Persian literature as the ground work of the "Traditional Muslim Education' incensed 'the Muslim intellectuals," Gankovsky, *A History of Pakistan*, p. 68.
74. Venkatachar, "1937-47 in Retrospect," Liaqat Ali, reportedly said "that the Muslim in U.P. feared (sic) that Hindi would be imposed on them, that was one of the factors in the creation of Pakistan," Geoffery Tyson, In : *Nehru : Years of Power*, 1966, Ibid, p. 471-72.
75. Kabir, *Muslim Politics*, p. 30.
76. Khan, Abdul Qayyum. Member of the Indian National Congress until 1945 when he joined the Muslim League writes "what I saw and heard in fact was an eye opener. The Muslim constituted seventy five per cent of the population, but they were mainly occupied in menial and low paid jobs. Hindu landlords were extorting rack rents from the Muslim peasantry while the Muslim landlords were under Hindu banias. Caste Hindus dominated all the higher services, monopolised trade and commerce and also whatever industry there was in Sindh.

The provincial Congress committee and the local Hindu Mahasabha were presided over by two Hindu brothers who lived under the same roof. In my report to the Congress Working Committee which had deputed him to go to Sakkur and to submit a report after an on-the-spot enquiry. I strongly recommended radical change in Congress policy in Sindh. I told them that the Sindh Congress and the local Mahasabha were interchangeable and that unless the Congress took up the cause of the Muslim majority and rescued them from their economic slavery to the Hindus, the future of the Congress in Sindh was dark indeed. I suggested that the soil was fertile enough for the Muslim League to dominate Sindh. Nothing was along by the Congress, and Sindh was one of the first provinces to stand out for Pakistan." Khan, Abdul Qayyum, "Reflections of some on the Causes of Partition of the Indo-Pakistan subcontinent, In : *Partition of India,* Philips, (ed.), p. 37.

77. Tomlinson, *Congress and the Raj,* p. 104.
78. Kabir, *Muslim Politics,* p. 30-31.
79. Ibid. p. 31.
80. "The crest of Calcutta University—perhaps devised long before the university had any popular control—was taken up as a fighting point. The crest had a lotus with the word Sree and that was considered a symbol of idolatry and as such anti Islamic" Guha, *India's Struggle,* pp. 394-95.
81. Kabir, *Muslim Politics,* p. 31.
82. Griffiths, Percival. *Modern India,* 3rd edn. (London : Earnest Benn Ltd. 1962), p. 91.
83. Raja of Mahmudabad, *'Some Memories,'* pp. 387-88.
84. Kabir, *Muslim Politics,* p. 31.
85. Griffiths, *Modern India,* p. 91.
86. Guha, *India's Struggle,* p. 396, see Prasad, *Changing Modes,* p. 130.
87. Coupland, Reginald, *Report on the Constitutional Problem in India,* (New York : Oxford University Press, 1945) Part II, pp. 156-57.
88. Guha, *India's Struggle,* p. 396.
89. *Venkatachar,* "1937-47 in Retrospect", pp. 470-71.
90. Guha, *India's Struggle,* p. 395.
91. Chand, *Freedom Movement,* p. 283, see also Ibid, p. 270.
92. Griffiths, *Modern India,* p. 91.
93. Nanda. *"Nehru Congress and Partition"*, p. 162.

94. Gankovsky, *A History of Pakistan*, p. 66.
95. Pandey, *The Break-up*, p. 147.
96. Gopal, *Indian Muslims*, p. 255.
97. Ahmad, Jamiluddin, (ed.), *Some Recent Speeches and writings of Mr. Jinnah*, (Lahore : S.M. Ashraf, 1946) p. 154.
98. Norman, Dorothy. *Nehru : The First Sixty Years.* London : MacDonald), Vol. II.
99. Pandey, *The Break-up*, pp. 147-48.
100. Majumdar, *Freedom Movement*, p. 570.
101. Gopal, *Indian Muslims*, p. 262-63.
102. Khan, Qayyum, *"Partition of the Subcontinent"*, p. 375.
103. Gopal, *Indian Muslims*, p. 254.
104. Zaidi, *Demand for Pakistan*, p. 37.
105. Nanda *"Nehru Congress and Partition,"* p. 161.
106. Majumdar, R.C. "Birth of Nationalism, In : *British Paramouncey and Indian Renaissance*, Majumdar, R.C. (gen. ed.). Part-II, p. 478.
107. Mukerjee, *Recalling India's Struggle.*, p. 74.
108. Gopal, *Indian Muslims*, p. 256.
109. Majumdar, *Birth of Nationalism* p. 478.
110. Ispahani, M.A.S. "Factors leading to the Partition of British India" In : *Partition of India*, Philips, (ed.), p. 333.
111. Majumdar *Birth of Nationalism.* pp. 478-79; "this is made crystal clear from his other writings, which contain passionate outbursts against the subjugation of India by the Muslims from the day the sun set on our glory—that is the refrain of his essays and novels which not often, contain adverse, and sometimes even irreverent remarks against the Muslims," Ibid, p. 479.
112. Gopal. *Indian Muslims*, p. 256.
113. Zaidi. *Demand for Pakistan*, p. 38.
114. Nanda. *Nehru Congress and Partition*, p. 161.
115. Kulkarni, *India Partition*, p. 324.
116. Pandey, *The Break-up*, p. 148.
117. Guha. *India's Struggle*, p. 402.
118. Chand. *Freedom Movement*, p. 265.
119. Guha. *India's Struggle*, p. 402, for the Vidya Mandir Scheme.
120. Zaidi. *Demand for Pakistan*. p. 38.
121. Guha. India's Struggle, p. 402.
122. Sayeed. *Pakistan*, pp. 91-92 See p. 21. It was raised "when Jinnah, discussed the communal award with Rajendra Prasad, who was Congress President in 1935. At that time he had

insisted that the agreement with the Congress should also be endorsed by the Hindu Mahasabha" Rajendra Prasad, *India Divided,* 1946, p. 155, cited by Nanda, *"Nehru Congress and Partition"* p. 163.

123. Ibid. p. 163
124. Sayeed. *Pakistan,* p. 92.
125. Nanda. *"Nehru Congress and Partition,"* p. 163.
126. The *Statesman* (weekly, overseas edn,), Calcutta, April, 21, 1938, cited by Sayeed in *Pakistan,* p. 92.
127. Ispahani. *Partition of British India* p. 343.
128. Gopal. *Indian Muslims,* p. 261.
129. Sayeed. *Pakistan,* p. 97.
130. Gopal. *Indian Muslims,* p. 261.
131. Sayeed. *Pakistan,* p. 97, see also Khan, *Abdul Qayyum, Partition of the Subcontinent,* p. 375.
132. Sayeed. *Pakistan,* p. 97.
133. Guha, *India's Struggle,* pp. 402-403, and Chand, *Freedom Movement,* p. 267.
134. Guha, *India's Struggle,* p. 403.
135. Chand, *Freedom Movement,* p. 267.
136. Hasan, Saiyed, Matlubul, *Muhammad Ali Jinnah (A Political Study)* (Lahore : S. M. Ashraf, 1945), p. 558.
137. Gopal, *Indian Muslims,* p. 259.
138. Zaidi, Z.H. "Aspects of the Development of Muslim League Policy," In : *Partition of India,* Philips, (ed.) p. 260.
139. Gopal, *Indian Muslims,* p. 259.
140. Symonds, Richard, *The Making of Pakistan* (London : Faber and Faber) pp. 54-55, The Pirpur Report, concluded, that the British Rule, sent a wave of horror in the Congress circles. The Congress offer to submit the case for investigation to the Chief Justice of India, an Englishman, was rejected by the League leader, and the latter's proposal that a Royal Commission be appointed for the purpose was pooh poohed by the Viceroy who was sure that the League's allegations were nothing but an irresponsible figment, and let the matter drop. Chopra, *Advanced Study in the Modern India* (1920-1947), (New Delhi: Sterling Publishing Pvt. Ltd., 1977), Vol. III, p. 118.
141. Ibid. p. 118.
142. Zaidi : "Development of Muslim Policy," p. 260.
143. Pakistan Historical Society Publication, Haq, S. Moinul, Gen. Sec. (Karachi, 1970), pp. 43-44.
144. Chandra, Bipan, Tripathi, Amul and Barun, De. *Freedom*

Struggle, 3rd, reprint, (New Delhi : National Book Trust, 1977), pp. 209-10.

145. Sayeed, *Pakistan*, pp. 95-96.
146. Mukerjee, *India's Struggle for Freedom* p. 202.
147. Ispahani, *Pattern of British India*, p. 337.
148. Nehru, Jawaharlal : *An Autobiography* (London : The Bodle Head, 1958) p. 72.
149. Sayeed, *Pakistan*, p.287.
150. Venkatachar, 1937-47 in Retrospect, p. 471.
151. Tomlinson, *Congress and the Raj*, p. 84.
152. Sayeed, *Pakistan*, pp. 287-88.
153. Sociologically, adoption of Brahmanical ways of life; or upward mobility; M.N. Srinivas "The Cohesive Role of Sanskritization", pp. 1-45 In: *Social Change in Modern India* (Berkeley : California Univ. Press, 1971), in plain language, Indianization or Hinduization.
154. For details, see "Westernization," in Ibid, pp. 46-88.
155. Venkatachar 1937-47 in Retrospect, p. 471.
156. Gangovsky, *History of Pakistan*, pp. 21 and 72.
157. Venkatachar 1937-47 in Retrospect, p. 471.
158. But at the time, it adversely affected the solidarity and unity of the Congress; Tomlinson, *Congress and the Raj*, pp. 85-86.
159. For example, Vallabhbhai Patel took Bala Saheb Kher, Chief Minister designate of Bombay, to task "for approaching Jinnah for his cooperation; Kanji Dwarkadas, *India's Fight for Freedom 1913-1937: An Eyewitness Story*" (Bombay : Popular Prakashan, 1966) p. 469.
160. Wallbook, T. Walter, *A Short History of India and Pakistan* (abr. edn.), India in the New Era, (rev. edn.), (London : A Mentor Book, 1965), p. 187.
161. Ispahani, *Partition of British India*, p. 343.
162. "On Gandhi's advice, the working committee directed that Ministers should take a salary up to Rs. 500 and councillor, Rs. 70 per month. In view of this direction.... The cabinet put the cash salary of Ministers at Rs. 500 a month but in addition, allotted to Ministers a free furnished house, free water, electricity and garden maintenance and free transport for private and public use. These requisites ran into a couple of thousand rupees per month. The British Governors also allowed Ministers to have their own choice of houses, furniture and cars, partly to expose the working committee to further public ridicule, and partly to win defectors. All Chief Ministers

and Ministers alike made an undignified scramble for the largest and the largest most spacious bungalows. Lakhs were spent in equipping them with air conditioners, refrigerators and expensive furniture. Several thousand were further spent to pander to ministerial hypocrisy : putting up Khadi, curtains and covering expensive silk upholstery with drab, badly soon begun to show patches of hair oil, betel nut stains and dripping of quink in between a milky way of roses, jasmines and lotuses. They neither indicated simplicity nor the artistic. This mockery of Rs. 500 shocked Gandhi, Sahni, J.N. , *Fifty years of Politics—1921-1971,* (Bombay : Allied Publishers, 1971), p. 116-17.

163. Bisheshwar Prasad, *Changing Modes of Indian National Movement,* (New Delhi : People's Publishing House, 1966), pp. 130-31.
164. Sehaster George and Guy Wint, *India and Democracy* (London : Macmillan Press, Ltd., 1941), p. 179.
165. Sayeed, *Pakistan,* pp. 88-89.
166. Ispahani, *Partition of British India,* p. 344.
167. Zaidi, *Demand for Pakistan,* p. 69.
168. Presidential Address of M.A. Jinnah, All-India Muslim League, Special Session, Calcutta, April 17-18, 1938, Ibid, pp. 77-78 and Saiyed, *Jinnah,* p. 605.
169. Zaidi, *Demand for Pakistan,* p. 91.
170. Rao, Shiva, India, 1935-47, In : *Partition of India,* Philips, (ed.) p. 71.

    "Nehru launched this scheme in the U.P. to establish direct contact with the Muslim masses without the mediation of nationalist Muslim organizations. There was opposition to this within the Congress itself. Venkatachar, "1937-47 in Retrospect," Ibid, pp. 469-70.
171. Ibid. pp. 470-71.
172. Philips C.H. and Wainwright, M.D. "Introduction," Ibid. p. 27.
173. The U.P. Muslims formed only 14 per cent of the population of the province: Venkatachar, "1937-47 in Retrospect," Ibid p. 486; "according to the 1941 census the Muslim percentage in the United Provinces was 15.3, Wyle, Francis, "*Federal Negotiations in India, 1935-39,* and After" Ibid p. 517.
174. "Rather than to put the responsibility on the system itself, with its over production of graduates," Philips and Wainwright, "Introduction," p. 27.
175. Sayeed, *Pakistan,* p. 96

176. Philips and Wainwright, "Introduction", p. 27.
177. Rao, India, 1935-47, p. 420.
178. Sayeed, *Pakistan*, p. 27.
179. Rao, India, 1935-47, p. 420.
180. Philips and Wainwright, "Introduction", p. 27.
181. Guha, *India's Struggle*, p. 397.
182. Ibid. p. 414.
183. Ibid, p. 397.
184. Chand, *History of Freedom Movement*, p. 260.
185. Guha, *India's Struggle*, *p.* 424.
186. Rao, *India, 1935-47*, p. 420.
187. Majumdar, R.C. (Gen. ed.) *Struggle for Freedom, History and Culture of the Indian National Movement*, (Bombay : Bharatiya Vidya Bhavan, 1969), Vol. IX, p. 612.
188. Gupta, D.C. *Indian National Movement*, (Delhi : Vikas Publications, 1970), p. 182.
189. Durrani, F.K. Khan, *The Meaning of Pakistan*, (Lahore : S.M. Ashraf, 1944), p. 93.
190. Gupta, *National Movement*, p. 182.
191. Khan, Abdul Qayyum, *Partition of the Subcontinent*, p. 375.
192. Guha, *India's Struggle*, pp. 405-06.
193. Majumdar, *Struggle for Freedom*, p. 612.
194. Mukerjee, *India's Struggle*, p. 219, with reference therein; "Savarkar's Speech at the Calcutta Session of the Hindu Mahasabha, Dec. 1939, was printed as a pamphlet." Ibid p. 9.
195. Majumdar, *Struggle for Freedom*, p. 612.
196. Gopal, *Indian Muslims*, p. 264.
197. Ibid. p. 265.
198. Ibid. p. 265.
199. Gankovsky, *History of Pakistan*, p. 69.
200. Coupland, Reginald, *Report on the Constitutional Problem in India* (New York: Oxford University Press, 1945), Part-II, p. 194.
201. Khan, Abdul Qayyum, *Partition of the Subcontinent*, p. 375.
202. Coupland, *Report on the Constitutional Problem in India*, p. 194.
203. Lumby, Esmond Walter Rawson, *The Transfer of Power in India—1945-47*. (London : George Allen and Unwin Ltd. 1954), p. 23.
204. Chand, *Freedom Movement*, pp. 546-47.
205. Steiberg, S.H. *The Thirty Years War and the Conflict for European Hegemony 1600-1660* (London : Edward Arnold, 1966), p. 91.
206. Chand, *Freedom Movement*, p. 547.
207. Gupta, *National Movement*, p. 184.
208. Majumdar, *Freedom Movement*, p. 569.

209. Guha, *India's Struggle*, p. 405.
210. Gupta, *National Movement*, p. 185.
211. In his letter to Subhash Bose, dated August 2, 1938; Majumdar, *History of Freedom Movement*, p. 569.
212. Ibid. p. 569.
213. Mukerjee, *Recalling India's Struggle for Freedom*, p. 126.
214. Mehrotra, S.R. *Towards India's Freedom and Partition* (New Delhi : Vikas Publishing House Pvt. Ltd., 1979), pp. 195-96.
215. Majumdar, *History of Freedom Movement*, p. 564.
216. Rao, India, 1935-47, p. 420.
217. Mukerjee, *Recalling India's Struggle for Freedom*, pp. 130-31.
218. Ibid. p. 131.
219. Sahni, *The Lid off*, p. 112.
220. Majumdar, *History of Freedom Movement*, p. 578.
221. Philips C.H. and Wainwright, M.D. "Introduction", Ibid. p. 25.
222. Rao, India, 1935-47, p. 421.
223. Majumdar, *History of Freedom Movement*, p. 578.
224. Mukerjee, *Recalling India's Struggle for Freedom*, p. 126.
225. Griffiths, Percival, *Modern India*, 3rd edn., (London : Earnest Benn Ltd., 1962), p. 85.
226. Rao, India 1935-47, p. 421.
227. Although it is by no means certain that the princes "could in any case have survived as islands of autocracy in a sea of popular government," yet "by their refusal to join the federation, they made their own destruction inevitable." "They failed to understand that they could never hope for a recurrence of such favourable terms and threw away their last chance (if at all it was a chance) of effective survival," Griffiths, *Modern India*, pp. 86-87.
228. Lord Templewood, Secretary of State as Sir Samuel Hoare, August 26, 1931—June 7, 1935; and Lord Halifax, Viceroy, as Lord Irwin, April 3, 1926—April 18, 1931; see Moore, R. J. *The Making of India Paper Federation, 1927-35*, Philips, (ed.), p. 54.
229. Moore, *India Paper Federation*, pp. 54-55; and Pandey, *The Break-up*, pp. 137-38.
230. Corfield, Conrad, "Some Thoughts on British Policy and the Indian States, 1935-47", In : *Partition of India*, Philips, (ed.), p. 528.
231. Chand, *History of Freedom Movement*. p. 254.
232. Moon, *Divide and Quit*, pp. 18-19.
233. Moore, *India Paper Federation*,p. 76.

234. "It was not the viable alternative to partition that Templewood and Halifax suggest," Ibid, p.78.
235. "In the provinces in which it had taken office, Congress, ... proceeded to show a capacity for firm, progressive government, comfortably maintaining law and order, and initiating new economic measures.... its viewpoint was continental, (it) gave an impression of strength, unity, and single-mindedness of purpose"; Philips, *Partition of India,* p. 24.
236. Spear, Percival, India, (Ann Arbor : The University of Michigan Press, 1961), pp. 393-94.
237. Ibid. p. 394.
238. Qureshi, I. H. "A Case Study of the Social Relations Between the Muslims and the Hindus, 1935-47," In : *Partition of India,* Philips, (ed.), p. 363.
239. Spear, *India,* p. 402.
240. Symonds, Richard. *The Making of Pakistan,* (London : Faber and Faber), pp. 59-60.
241. Ibid. p. 60.
242. Guha, *India's Struggle,* p. 401.
243. Symonds, *Making of Pakistan,* p. 60.
244. Majumdar, *History of Freedom Movement,* p. 572.
245. To be discussed in other chapters.
246. Moore, R. J. "British Policy and the Indian Problem, 1936-40," In : *Partition of India,* Philips, (ed.), p. 83-84.

Chapter 5

And Then Came The War

The outbreak of war added a new issue; perhaps dimension, to the Indian scenario, for every one could see that vital changes were in store after the war. It brought India into the full spate of international politics. The war of 1914 had fermented India's political problems; that of 1939 threw the primary issue of India's freedom into prominence. With its enormously improved techniques of destruction; the second world war was bound to prove disastrous to empires that had braved the earlier global deluge. One of the great aims of Hitler was to dismantle the British empire, and he was aware of the value of India to it. He felt that the chief source of Englishman's pride was India. Nor were Britain's allies anxious to keep the British empire intact. They were interested in "the liberation of the subject peoples as a cardinal item in post-war settlement." Once the war opened India's future and freedom "ceased to be Britain's exclusive concern." The fate of British hegemony in this country was sealed.

Whitehall did not, however, feel the same way.[1] It still hoped to give a new lease of life to the empire. On the other hand India, generally speaking, "was far more detached in attitude than it had been in 1914." She was deemed "no longer a country aspiring for recognition, but an adult country still deprived of the right to manage its own affairs," states Percival Spear; "the war was therefore none of her business."[2] The Congress ministers were directed to give no aid in preparations for war.[3] April 23 had been observed as the anti-war day.

The confidence of the Indian national movement is evidenced by the fact that contrary to the state of affairs in 1914 when not only the native rulers but also the great leaders had rallied to the buttress of the empire, the tussle between the nationalist forces and the alien government was overt and poignant during the very early phase of the war.[4] Indian attitude to the global combat would have been much more positive and helpful if the political situation had been lucid. This, however, steadily grew thicker.[5]

Yet the British were sanguine in their anticipation that their empire would endure indefinitely. With only eight short years for the raj to run, the illusion of durability was as robust as ever—at Whitehall and Delhi. "The illusion of British permanence in India," observes Francis Hutchins, "was a significant component in the consciousness of the British nation; for the Englishman in India it was everything." Like other dominant communities who have felt their privileges defined, "the British in India reacted by holding all the more tenaciously to their pretensions and by drawing sharp lines of distinction between those who were known to be sympathetic and those who were not."[6] To the British rulers a party or individual was valued according to its ability in obstructing India's constitutional progress. Their concept of the minorities was all pervasive, and no single reactionary group could assert as "being the sole ally of British diehardism."[7] That there should be any general impression that the British seriously contemplated evacuation in any computable period of time, wrote Linlithgow to Zetland; "seems to me astonishing." He had "every hope of a satisfactory development on constitutional lines of the relations between the two countries on the basis set out in the Act."[8]

Reviewing the British position in India, his opposite number pointed out the dynamic significance of the Congress factor but contentedly averred the inability of India to defend herself without British aid, and the worsening relationship of the Congress and the Muslim League which "would brake any rapid progress by India towards the full Dominion Status envisaged by the 1935 Act."[9] This discussion took place in January 1939. To both men, the crucial problem of defence, Britain's chief bargaining counter in an increasingly hostile world, seemed good reason for the British staying in India.[10]

The armed hustle-bustle which prologued the war had been

manifest for sometime, and India's national movement, aware of the impending international confrontation, had warned against the dreaded catastrophe. During 1938 in the full flow of the Chamberlain appeasement when the British government was giving practical and diplomatic succour to fascist aggression, Congress leaders, Nehru in particular; had flayed British foreign policy as a betrayal of democracy. As the war clouds began to deepen, Congress affirmed that it would not fight in other people's wars.[11] In spite of imperialists' euphemistic utterances "that they were fighting against Hitlerism, for freedom and democracy," "in reality, they were doing nothing of the sort." It was on both sides a combat for supremacy, for imperialist possessions; vested interests, economic exploitation and privilege.[12] Indian national movement, whatever its failing, kept itself abreast of the machinations of imperialist power politics.

When war began, it placed the Indian leaders in an embarrassing situation. Congress party's political strategy was disturbed by international contour which crystallized into a pattern in which, on the whole, "Britain and the majority of Congress were taking the same side."[13] Congress was strongly opposed to the fascist philosophy with its widespread ramifications like brutal totalitarianism, racialist bigotry, power famishment. It sympathised with the victims of fascist onslaughts, the people of Spain, Ethiopia and Czechoslovakia. It regarded the Nazis and the Fascists as the enemies of freedom and progress. On the other hand, it held in high esteem "the British democratic and parliamentary institutions; and admired British culture, literature, philosophy, science, manners and mores and industry." However, although Indians were prepossessed in favour of Britain and the allies, they looked askance at the British in general. British statesmen appeared unscrupulous, whose professions and doings did not tally and whose ability to meet the challenge of the dictators was dubious. Their dealings with India—arrogant and callous—during the years immediately preceding the war had not endeared them to the people of the subcontinent. The foreign government had taken a strong aversion to the Congress with its emphasis on India's freedom.[14]

Thus while, on the one hand, India wished no harm to the British people, on the other, she craved for emancipation from alien tutelage. Long before India was unceremoniously dragged into the war, in the sombre background of impending peril, the Congress had explicitly warned the government what its attitude would be. It had firmly dissociated itself from British foreign policy. Abul Kalam Azad said, "The Congress is opposed to imperialism and fascism alike and is convinced that world peace and progress required the ending of both of these."[15] Congress leaders were as inimical to imperialism as to fascism. If it was going to be a fight between the old imperial powers solicitous to preserve their colonial hold over Afro-Asian nations and the new imperialists—the so-called fascists—who themselves were out to grab colonial chunks as their share, India would wash her hands of the entire sordid business. But if it was going to be a real fight "to save the world for democracy", there should be full cooperation with those who stood for freedom and the breaking of political and social bonds, for Indians would feel one with them in their struggle against imperialism and fascist reaction. There must however be concrete evidence to testify to the verity of the British professions in the form of substantial devolution of authority to the representatives of the people from whom immense sacrifices were required, which bring us to the British response and measures.

The Government had been informed unequivocally by the Congress that a declaration of war on behalf of India without her concurrence would make for trouble. "Forewarned the Government forearmed itself."[16] Ever since India became an appendage of British imperialism she played a major role in the imperial strategy and proved an unfailing source of manpower and raw materials.[17] The great imperialist powers of the world—Russia in the nineteenth and Germany in the twentieth century—had always cast their longing looks towards her, but the British had managed to keep the war away from her borders. With the lengthening of the shadows of war in 1939, Britain naturally grew anxious to utilize India's plenteous resources for the prosecution of war. Later, the proximity of the theatres of war increased India's strategic importance. The urge to keep the structure of the raj intact was intensified due to strategic need overstepping the borders of the Indian subcontinent. With the emergence of aggressive powers ambitious to carve new empires, Britain had to make a hard reappraisal of her imperial attitudes. The arguments of those who were thinking in terms of arranging for a fair quantum of self-government were obscured by those who wished to keep India under bondage; the 'die-hard' imperialists complacently gloating over the military and strategic needs gained the upper hand. "The raj, a relic of an 'old imperialism,' " writes Johannes H. Voigt, "was destined to contribute to warding off the challenge of the 'new imperialism," disturbing the power equilibrium of Europe and the mutually recognized colonial systems in Asia which were already internally challenged by the forces of nationalism. "This new strategic role of the raj," Voigt adds, "was to influence British attitudes towards India till the end of the Second World War."[18]

India situated at the head of the Indian ocean with the Middle East and Africa on the west flank, Burma, Malaya, Guiana and Australia on the east, was a pivotal point of defence of this region—preponderantly an area of British influence. "As the external danger became graver," states S. C. Bartarya, "India's involvement became greater and her internal condition worse."[19] In April 1939, Britain began to undertake provident military measures; a contingent of Indian troops was sent to reinforce the garrison at Aden, and the British parliament passed a bill granting the Viceroy and the central government in India complete emergency powers over the provincial administrations. Congress indictment was that a war dictatorship was in the making. Such charges, however, fell on deaf ears and a second despatch of troops was carried on in August when two contingents were sent to Egypt and Singapore. Thus Indian soldiers were sent out to guard the outer defences of the empire. Congress retaliated by admonishing its members not to attend the central legislature.[20]

Events moved fast from the day that the second world war opened in the European theatre. On September 3, 1939, the Viceroy proclaimed that war had broken out between His Majesty's Government and Germany; and without their consent India's millions found themselves in the lap of war. The Viceroy's action of declaring India a belligerent on his own without even the formality of consulting the central legislature—let alone the popular provincial governments, the well organized political parties or outstanding leaders of the people—"proved afresh, if further proof was necessary," so says Azad, "that the British Government looked on India as a creature of its will and was not willing to recognize India's right to decide her course for herself even in a matter like war.[21] The Viceroy's action, which was after all constitutionally valid did "underline the fact that in spite of the 1935 Act," to quote Michael Edwardes, "effective power still lay with the British, and that Indians themselves even in matters concerning their life and death ... did not count very much and had no right to be consulted."[22] A Government of India Amending Act was rushed through parliament in the record time of eleven minutes granting the Viceroy special wartime powers, warranting him to override the provisions of the Constitution even pertaining to provincial autonomy. The Viceroy also promulgated the Defence of India Ordinance giving wide powers to the Government and curtailing the civil liberties of the people on the plea of defence of India.[23] Suspension of the preparations for Federation was announced. All this implied "a sharp reversal of the process of decentralization which had reached its climax in 1939. The centre was resuming its unitary grip on British India," observes R. G. Coupland, the eminent constitutional historian.[24] The functioning of autonomous provincial governments was severely curtailed. Complexion of politics changed; while federation was in abeyance, immediate constitutional change could be deferred. In the words of R. P. Dutt : "Autocratic government was to continue in India, without any constitutional fig leaf and reinforced by the most far-reaching Extraordinary Powers." Once again, as in the previous war, "the Indian people were to be dragged at the heels of the British Government into a war in whose making they had no choice," and concerning which they had firmly protested at the policy which had made it inevitable.[25]

With the start of war Linlithgow, a man of pedestrian talents, found himself in an unenviable position. As the supreme of the British Indian empire his responsibility was immense. If due to some action or lack of it on his part, Britain or the Empire suffered, his country would not forgive him. His initial loyalty was with Britain. "He had not consulted Indian leaders before declaring war, " Philips and Wainwright aptly remark, "because he knew that they were intent on driving a political bargain, and he was uncertain what his course ought to be in the event of their refusal to participate."[26] Possibly a Viceroy with something of the brilliance of a Mountbatten might have procured the willing participation of Indians. It was quite beyond the scope of the lesser man. He was not keen to face the nation knowing fully well that such a gesture might come a cropper.

Declaring India's belligerence after the people's verdict to the contrary would have been worse. Convinced "that in India, time was on Britain's side," and that if it came to rebellion, the Indian parties would be effectively dealt with (as was done in 1942), he had no qualmishness that the right British approach in India was to keep intact the political *status quo* certainly through the period when the future of Britain herself was in jeopardy.[27]

As a dependency India was automatically legally involved in the war, but the blunt manner of doing so touched "the now well established Indian pride" and brought forth a wave of resentment. There was an immediate crisis. "Some British observers." remarks P. Spear, "have found it difficult to understand the depth of feeling aroused by Lord Linlithgow's clumsiness."[28] The reaction of the Congress was sharp. It felt slighted and its sympathy for Britain began to dwindle.

As such the differences of opinion within the Congress were great. Subhash Bose welcomed the conflict because a dash to Britain in Europe would undoubtedly loosen her grip on India. To him: "The task of the Indian people is the revolutionary utilization of the war crisis for the achievement of national freedom. The capture of power is an immediately realizable goal."[29] "Other Congress leaders had no clear cut vision of the future."[30] They were "divided on such polemical issues as to whether their participation in the war should be non-violent and moral, or violent but defensive. Whether, if imperialism was bad, Nazism and totalitarianism were worse."[31] Opinion oscillated between democratic disapproval of Hitlerism and nationalist suspicion of British and French imperialism. Left wing Congressmen, trailing behind Nehru, if denunciatory of Germany were mistrustful of Britain.[32] As for Gandhi, "he would offer the British moral support during the war, but on a non-violent basis."[33] He told Linlithgow of his personal sympathy for Britain and said that he stood for unconditional support for the allies, but this was only an individual view point, not the Congress policy, he specified. "The whole of his political philosophy was conceived," says Edwardes, "not in terms of defeating the conquerors of India, but of converting them; without the British, everything that Gandhi stood for was bereft of meaning." If Britain were to lose, India might well find herself under another master, one who would have little sufferance for the Gandhian way to politics.[34] Nehru with his usual casuistry had said that Congress was not out to bargain, but he did set a price for its support.[35] States Voigt, "Jawaharlal Nehru wanted an immediate declaration of independence as a pre-condition for a support of the war by Congress."[36]

This viewpoint was shared by the majority including such stalwarts as Abul Kalam Azad and Rajagopalachari.[37] They strongly felt that now that war had started India must not shrink from "aligning herself with the democratic powers." "If the British Government made an immediate declaration of India's independence," things would become smooth. Pertinently India could not fight for others' freedom when she was herself in bondage.[38] The majority of the Congress Working Committee, led by Nehru and Azad, pressed for a resolution expressing their readiness to support Britain but reiterating an earlier demand for Britain to clarify her war aims in regard to imperialism and democracy, warning that the Congress could not take long upbraiding Britain's use of India's resources in a war to which she was not a party.[39] Bose continued to favour direct action that opportunity should not be lost for the establishment of India's freedom. The members of the Forward Bloc declared openly that they did not want Britain to win because only after the defeat and collapse of the British empire could India be free.[40] Bose's audacious stand impressed the Congress. The left wing groups and the Forward Bloc were anxious for an all-out campaign against the Raj but the events of March to September, 1939 had disrupted the unity and circumscribed the appeal of left wing organizations. They were in no position to force their demands on the national leaders and "were unable to attract much support."[41]

It may be relevant here to make some reference to other parties and groups. The non-Congress governments of the Punjab, Bengal and Sindh pledged their full support to Britain, and their action was endorsed by the legislatures. The native princes to be sure were solidly with the British.[42] The landlords too, as could be expected, decided to support the war measures of the government. Among the political parties, the Indian Liberal Federation appealed to other political parties to take a broad view so that the country was left in no doubt to range itself on the side of Britain. "It also demanded," states A. C. Guha, "Dominion Status, Indianization of the Army and some such things. But their appeal for support was not conditional on the fulfilment of those demands." "The All India Hindu Mahasabha offered 'responsive cooperation' in the war,"[43] while the Congress refused to cooperate with the government in any way. "Between these two extremes stood the Muslim League" with its ambivalent attitude. While its High Command did not offer to support Britain, it had done nothing to thwart the ministries of Bengal and Punjab from doing so.[44] The Muslim League would customarily hanker for the fulfilment of Muslim requirements as the stipulation to giving its definite views on any matter. "The overall position in the country was that the Congress alone was opposed to cooperation in the war preparations or help the government in that direction," A. C. Guha says.[45]

Two days after the announcement of the war, the Viceroy called Gandhi for a conference. The latter told the Viceroy, as mentioned above, that he could not commit the Congress but as a devotee of non-violence he denounced Hitler's doing.[46] To Gandhi, non-violence was a creed, the breath of his life.[47] He could not as a pacifist support the war, he wrote in his news paper *Harijan*, but his sympathies were with England and France "from the purely humanitarian viewpoint."[48]

Nehru had revised his idea of fighting for power at the centre on the political reckoning of 1937-39. He was happy to state to an English friend Edward Thompson, "that Britain's cause was just." "We now know," says C. S. Venkatachar, "that he had given Desmond Young, editor of *The Pioneer* reasonable and moderate terms on which he and the Congress would have been prepared to cooperate with the British Government."[49]

We have seen the war had found the Congress leaders split over what policy they should follow. The task was rendered more complicated by the increasingly difficult dual role of the Congress as a governmental party in the majority of provinces and an opposition party at the centre. This division of roles and attitudes could be managed somehow or the other in times of peace. In the war situation it became obnoxiously cumbersome. With the opening of war, "Congress had a simple, yet difficult choice: it had to choose between cooperation or no cooperation, which might turn eventually into non-cooperation and confrontation."[50]

Congress did not issue any statement of policy immediately after the war, and evidently took time to brood over the situation. But its two leaders, Gandhi and Nehru, who were often led by emotion rather than by reason, expressed deep sympathy for Britain in her hour of trial. Gandhi wrote in *Harijan:* "I am not just now thinking of India's deliverance. It will come, but what will it be worth if England and France fall, or if they come out victorious over Germany ruined and humbled?" He would benevolently offer the British moral support during the war—non-violent support. Nehru went a step further and argued that "India should offer not only sympathy but unconditional support to Britain"; that the Indian people should not think of taking advantage of Britain's difficulties; they must sympathise with democracies and "throw all their resources into the struggle for a new order."[51]

This hyperbolic sympathy and support for Britain appears odd in view of the earlier Congress declarations. At Haripura (February, 1938) and Tripuri (March; 1939) Congress had passed resolutions condemning British foreign policy as one of purpose betrayal of democracy and refusing to permit India's resources to be manipulated to cater to Britain's imperialistic ambitions. Only one leader, Subhash Bose, stood up boldly in vindication of the

Congress policy.[52] Bose asserts that his "uncompromising attitude had its effect and the Gandhi wing gave up altogether the idea of cooperation with the British Government."[53] Whether it was due to the influence of Subhash Bose or not, something unusual happened. For once, the Congress high command refused to trail behind the emotional lead of the doyens. Not surprisingly, however, Nehru's emotions, after the first flash of enthusiasm was over, gave way to cold reasoning. He and others took a more pragmatic view and broke away from Gandhi on this vital point.[54] Gandhi's emotionalism, tinged with mysticism, persisted throughout the war; he had to plough a lonely furrow, because even his devotees could not go along with him beyond a certain point.

The war endeavour, by its very nature, required strict coordination of policy at all layers—central, provincial and local. "In war there could be either full cooperation at all levels, or none at any"; lopsidedness of roles would not work. The Working Committee majority might have been aware of this.[55]

With Bose's plan being too bald and outspoken and Gandhi's approach quixotic and dreamy, the Congress working committee tended to converge on Nehru. Led by him, midway in September, it adopted a resolution in which it was stressed that the declared wishes of the Indian people had been deliberately ignored by the British Government. The statement sums up the attitude of Indian nationalism towards the war. It expressed its entire disapproval of the ideology and practice of Fascism and Nazism, unhesitatingly condemning the latest Nazi aggression against Poland, but at the same time, on the other hand, took the "gravest view" of the Viceroy's proclamation of war on behalf of India, the decreeing of the amending Bill, and the promulgation of the most stringent war Ordinances—all without India's consent. The Congress further laid down that "the issue of peace and war must be decided by the Indian people"; they could not "permit their resources to be exploited for imperialist ends." If cooperation was sought, it "must be between equals by mutual consent for a cause which both consider worthy." India's sympathy was on the side of democracy and freedom, but she could not associate herself with a war said to be for democratic freedom when that very freedom was denied to her, and such limited freedom as she possessed taken away from her. "If the war is to defend the *status quo* of imperialist possessions, colonies, vested interests and privileges, then India can have nothing to do with it." On the other hand if Great Britain was fighting "for the maintenance and extension of democracy then she must necessarily end imperialism in her own possessions and establish full democracy in India, and the Indian people must have the right of self determination by framing their own constitution through a Constituent Assembly" without external interference. The crisis that had encompassed Europe was not of Europe alone but of humanity and was "the inevitable consequence of social and political conflicts and contradictions which have grown alarmingly since the last Great War and it will not finally be resolved till those conflicts and contradictions are removed" without external interference. In the struggle for that new world order, the committee was eager and desirous to help in every way, but could not associate themselves or offer any cooperation in a war which was meant to consolidate imperialism in India and elsewhere. The working committee therefore invited "the British Government to declare in unequivocal terms what their war aims are in regard to democracy and imperialism and the order that is envisaged, in particular, how these aims are going to apply to India and to be given effect to in the present."[56]

These demands and arguments appear cogent, said feelingly and convincingly. The demand for clarifying war aims was a legitimate one. So was India's claim for democracy and freedom so that she might participate in reshaping the world on a new pattern. The upshot was the ending of imperialism and exploitation. But that was an odd phraseology for the Tory diehards who having failed to read the writing on the wall still hoped to give a new lease of life to the empire. As such imperialism was on a death dance and capitalism under the pressure of its inner contradictions was tottering."[57] The final contest between British imperialism and Indian nationalism was to be in full swing during the Second World War.

"Both Nehru's and Gandhi's policies" Voigt points out, "would have thwarted political cooperation as envisaged by the British". Gandhi, if he was indulgent in the political field, would not hesitate impeding the war effort if it crossed the moral barrier. Nehru, with his sophistry, though willing to give full support to the war effort put such a telling price as to ruin Britain's objective. "Governed by Indians", to quote the same author, "India's resources would not then be easily available for the war as under British rule. India could not then be commandeered into a mobilisation of her power but would have to be asked for it.[58]"

It may appear strange that the opening and early stages of war failed to bring forth meaningful political concessions to win Indian adhesion. There were good reasons for that. Firstly, the Congress party's earlier indifference towards defence, let alone Gandhi's clinging to non-violence, had made the British sceptical. Secondly even if concurrence pertaining to war venture with Congress under Nehru's leadership could have been achieved, there would still have remained threats of peripheral challenges from the 'right' by Gandhi, and from the 'left' by Bose. And thirdly, the administrative set-up in the provinces under Section 93 of the Government of India Act of 1935 was considered more effective during war than the democratic system of responsible Congress governments.[59]

The British problem was that any wartime confrontation with Congress would not only mean trouble in India but would have propaganda repercussions in neutral countries, especially in the U.S.A. (which was to be amorously wooed by Britain), as well as in hostile lands. On the other hand, any significant concessions to Congress would imply a meddling with the 1935 Act leading to obvious complications. "Indian control of defence and finance, desired by Congress," the Secretary of State felt, "would lead to endless controversies."[60]

The Muslim League had evidently been on the watch as to the Congress reaction before formulating its own policy. "The outbreak of Hitler's war," says Venkatachar, "paved the way for the decisive break-through of Jinnah's leadership and the ultimate resolution of the age-long dilemma of the Indian Muslims in the manner he wished."[61] In 1939, he was believed to be "in a reasonable frame of mind," but the war and its possible impact on Indian politics extinguished what flicker he might have had for an amenable settlement with Congress.[62]

"The beginning of the war saw," observes Humayun Kabir, "a complete reversal in the roles of the League and the Congress." The Congress adopted a militant and somewhat revolutionary programme, while the League tended to go astern to constitutional grooves. "The old constitutionalism could not however be revived." Jinnah was still too deeply steeped in Congressism to fit into the rut of moderate liberalism that could entice the bureaucrats. Moreover two decades of nationalist sermonizing had created in the people a toughness of soul that could not be easily obliterated.[63] Most of the Muslim youth and petty bourgeoisie recalled that specific trend in the national movement, "when the Muslims had acted as a religio-political entity," and were wheedled by the League's impassioned and exaggerated statements.[64] Like Congress, the League also came to entertain diverse political ideologies though the dominance of vested interests made the League much less radical in its programme.

Interestingly, since the outbreak of the war, the League, "at every step followed the Congress in its programme and decisions, though generally with a time lag and for apparently different reasons." But while the Congress was equipped to force issues and, if necessary, resort to direct action for achieving its goal, the League chose to sit complacently on the fence and await developments, wishfully anticipating that out of the clash of forces so created, would emerge a favourable situation, and it would be able to attain its objective without effort or sacrifice.[65] "The brunt of the struggle for the liberation of India," says B.R. Nanda, "was borne by the Congress. The Muslim League had no lot or part in this struggle, of which the establishment of Pakistan was a by-product. Others forced open the doors through which Jinnah walked to his goal."[66] The build of the League with an upper hand of vested interests was mainly responsible for this inertness. With big stakes involved, the propertied classes were prone to stand for the *status quo.* Jinnah's personal proclivities were also partially responsible for this. A lawyer to the core, he preferred the nuances of diplomacy than the manifestation of brute force.[67]

If such sluggishness did "a permanent injury to the Indian Muslims," that is another matter. Constant harping on their numerical inferiority produced in many, a tendency to lean on the alien power. The great indictment against Jinnah, according to H. Kabir, ought to be that he tried to inculcate "into the minds of ninety millions of Muslims, a weakness and inferiority" in competition to other communities and groups.[68]

It has been discussed above that the Muslim League was bitterly against Congress rule in eight out of eleven provinces. Four days after the Congress working committee, it passed its resolution on the situation created by the war. The League Resolution (of September 18) contained repeated reference to the term 'Muslim India' which "occupies a special and peculiar position in the polity of India," and which for several decades had worked, the resolution reads, "for a free India with free and independent Islam in which they [Muslims] could play an equal part with the major community with a complete sense of security," but the developments that had taken place, had nullified all hope. The resolution repeated the usual charge against the Congress ministries tyrannizing over the Muslim minorities.

It was further stated :

> While Muslim India stands against exploitation of the people of India and has repeatedly declared in favour of a free India it is equally opposed to the domination of the Hindu majority over Musalmans and other minorities and vassalization of Muslim India, and is irrevocably opposed to any 'Federal objective' which must necessarily result in a majority community rule under the guise of democracy and a parliamentary system of government. Such a constitution is totally unsuited to the genius of the peoples of the country which is composed of various nationalities and does not constitute a national state.[69]

The opposition of the Muslim League was not merely to the 'details' of the Federal plans embodied in the Act, rather it strongly urged upon the British government "to review and revise the entire problem of India's future constitution' *de novo*" in the light of recent experiences and developments.[70] The League further urged upon the British authorities to give an assurance that "no declaration regarding the question of constitutional advance for

India should be made without the consent and approval of the All India Muslim League nor any constitution be framed and finally adopted by .... the British parliament without such consent and approval."

While expressing deep sympathy for Poland, England and France, the Committee however felt "that real and solid Muslim cooperation and support to Great Britain in this hour of her trial cannot be secured successfully if His Majesty's government and the Viceroy are unable to secure to the Musalmans justice and fair play in the Congress governed provinces....."

If full, effective and honourable cooperation of the Musalmans was solicited in the grave crisis that was encompassing the world at that time, the Muslim League courteously informed the government, "it must create a sense of security and satisfaction amongst the Musalmans and take into its confidence the Muslim League which is," the resolution categorically stated, "the only organization that can speak on behalf of Muslim India."[71]

Interestingly enough, the Muslim League, "made its promise of support contingent upon Britain's guaranteeing the Muslims 'justice and fair treatment in the Congress provinces' and promising not to make any constitutional changes in India without the consent of the League."[72] On the other hand, use of pungent phrases like 'vassalization of Muslim India' was bound to give to the Muslim mind a suggestive jolt. Doom of the federal scheme put the League at a coign of vantage to ask for a thorough reappraisal of the entire constitutional problem.

Thus within a fortnight of the outbreak of war, the working committees of both the Congress and the League had passed resolutions on the crisis offering at best only conditional cooperation. But London was not going to give many concessions. Both the big parties were demanding assurances "about India's post war constitution as the price of their support,"[73] yet "the British stuck to their tradition of no change during a war; whatever you want, after the war provided you are good."[74] They were careful to make no commitments during the war which might restrict their freedom of action after the war; they must retain the leverage. The British policy makers were disinclined to repeat what they regarded "as the greatest mistake in India policy of the 1914-18 war—the tactic of buying short term Indian support by the announcement of definite plans for long term constitutional advance."[75] On the other hand, India's dependence on Britain's support was well emphasized. Lord Hailey impressed that in case British power was subverted, the whole system of progressive thought preaching political liberties to the Indians and others would be thrown overboard. The Commander-in-Chief laid open the potential dangers hovering about India from strategic point of view.[76] Britain's doings were an act of piety—imperial piety. The statements on behalf of the government were prevarications to avoid the real ssue. The circuitous method of non-commitment however, could not satiate national urges.

The demand of the Muslim League that the Congress should be given no assurance without its consent "suggested a way to the Viceroy Lord Linlithgow" who in order to hit the Congress with the old weapon of "divide and rule"—having already taken the crucial decisions—started a spate of interviews with the spokespersons of every conceivable class, interest and community as if to make up for his earlier default by securing their endorsement and support on what he had already done, and at the same time to show "a bitter lack of unity among the Indians."[77] He, however, had precious little to tell the Indian leaders. This attitude provoked Clement Attlee, the leader of the Opposition in the Commons, to criticize the Viceroy's lack of tact in not caring to bring India into the war "on a level with us", and as being out of touch with realities in India.[78]

What was called for in the autumn of 1939, remarks B. R. Nanda, "was a little imagination and a little courage; these qualities were not forthcoming from the government of India headed by Lord Linlithgow and the British government headed by Neville Chamberlain."[79] Linlithgow resorted to the old policy of boosting communal and special interests against Congress. He glowed to watch the growth of Muslim communalism. Then there were other communities and special interests whose leaders did not regard the Congress as the representative of all interests. The Viceroy was confident that "Britain's hold on India was safe so long as the discords between the communities and classes remained." Congress demand was therefore not given serious thought.[80] In the October 18, statement, the Viceroy explained nothing and gave no assurances to Congress. "All Britain was prepared to offer anybody was a promise that, at the end of the war, she would be prepared to regard the scheme of the Act as open to modification in the light of Indian views."[81]

The government had been forewarned, as has been hinted above, by the Congress that declaring India a belligerent without contacting Indian opinion would portend trouble. The Viceroy was already accosting the provincial Governors on possible repercussions when the Ministers would resign and Section 93 of the Government of India Act would be enforced so that drastic action might be taken against any organization which might in any way impede the efficient prosecution of the war. "At the same time alternative avenues," observes Tara Chand, "were explored to avert a clash—argument, appeal, and yielding to demands which involved no real transfer of power."[82]

The Viceroy had been conversing with all the important Indian leaders,[83] some fifty in number, with the purpose of rallying public opinion to the side of Britain. The statements that surfaced, all side-tracked the Congress demands of war aims and Indian independence. Zetland in the House of Lords, reprimanded the Congress leaders saying that "the time should have been ill-chosen by them for a reiteration of their claims" (September 26, 1939).[84] "The Cabinet in London needed three meetings," to quote J. H. Voigt, "to decide on a policy towards India after the Viceroy had declared her to be in a state of war with Germany."

Mindful of the mistake, discussed above, in the India policy of the 1914 war, Zetland, Secretary of State for India, was ill-prepared to pledge India Dominion Status for the post war period and suggested that a body of non-official Indians "be associated in a consultative capacity with the central government". His colleagues objected to this proposal arguing that Indian "advice as to the conduct of affairs in India in relation to the war opened up dangerous possibilities." It would be harmful if Congress was allowed to dominate the new body. On the other hand, in support of the proposal, it was said that such an arrangement would be "preventing too much attention from being directed to questions of defence, which was, and would continue to be, a reserved subject". In its first meeting, the Cabinet countenanced the creation of a "War Advisory Board" of "representative Indians" which would be so framed as to gratify Indian urge for cooperation and at the same time soothe British apprehensions of an Indian upper hand in defence matters.

At the second Cabinet meeting on October 2, 1939, Winston Churchill insisted that the "War Advisory Board" should be purely consultative. Zetland assured the Cabinet that confidential military information would in no case be given to this board as "the public and leaders in India were extremely ignorant on questions of defence."[85] Linlithgow too had to convince the hesitant Cabinet that a consultative committee would get no chance to blend itself irrevocably in the machinary of the government, and that "it would be dissolved the moment it looked like getting out of hand."[86] Eventually on October 14, the Cabinet acquiesced in Linlithgow's draft statement declaring for a consultative body but putting off any constitutional change till the end of the War, [87] which brought home that there was going to be no break in Britain's traditional policy towards India.

On October 18, came Linlithgow's package to the Indian people. In this White Paper, the Viceroy reiterated British aims of ultimate Dominion Status for India "in an indefinite and presumably distant future;" but pointed out that for the present, the Act of 1935 held good. The only hope that was held out was the promise of post war "consultations with representatives of the several communities" (and not any democratically elected constituent assembly) to modify the 1935 Act. Transfer of substantial power to the Indians was deemed impracticable during the war but when this was done the advice and assistance of all the parties would be taken, full weight being given to the opinions and interests of the minorities. Clearly the Congress claim to represent the whole of India was cold-shouldered. And as for the immediate present, a purely consultative group consisting of the representatives of the important communities and interests, "with no real executive power whatsoever," would be set up to help the Viceroy in the conduct of war.[88] On Britain's war aims, Linlithgow made no commitments.[89]

It seems probable that Linlithgow was hopeful that his offer would win Congress support. He thought too much perhaps of his luring the Congress in 1937. "He may also have overestimated." Says R. J. Moore, "the influence that Gandhi, who had initially and emotionally pledged his personal and unconditional support for the war effort, exercised in the Congress of 1939." He made Zetland understand, continues Moore, that the Congress wouldn't mind if its September 14, statements were "taken at a good deal less than its face value"; whereas the British Labour Party apprised Zetland that the Congress was in earnest and that the situation was "grave". Attlee "saw slipping past the last chance of bringing India freely into the British Commonwealth."[90]

The October 18, declaration obviously was a machination baiting the Indians with the consultative group associating them with the conduct of war. An attempt at dividing the Indians, it referred to "marked differences of outlook, markedly different demands and different solutions for the problems that lie before us.[91] Nor did the carrot of Dominionhood, dangled at a safe chronological distance, produce any salutary effect on the cruelly disappointed nation. There was a general feeling that the British would cling to the empire to the last throwing a sop to Cerberus.

The Working Committee of the Congress regarded the Viceroy's statement as unfortunate in every way. Congress antagonism to fascist encroachments had doubtless been "more forthright and consistent than Britain's own record so far." Yet Linlithgow had turned down Congress "offers of full cooperation in the war effort," remarks Sumit Sarkar, "provided some minimum conditions were met: a promise of a post-war constituent assembly to determine the political structure of a free India, and the immediate formation of something like a genuine responsible government in the centre." "Such conditions," says Sarkar, "the Congress argued with considerable justice, were essential if Indian opinion was to be really mobilized for a war which in 1939, ...was still a very distant one," for else the Allied indoctrination from the housetops for "democracy and the principle of self determination of nations against tyranny and aggression" would appear unabashedly hypocritical.[92]

The Congress leaders could not concede that "no constitutional advance in India was possible without the agreement of all sections of British Indian and Princely opinion."[93] Yet Linlithgow seemed unmoved. He wrote to Zetland, "I do not think that either you or I, or for that matter the Cabinet, can feel that there is anything which we have left undone which we ought to have done." The fact of the matter is that "the price has been put up a good deal by the other side."[94] "Linlithgow's attitude," as Sarkar has pointed out, "was not an aberration, but part of a general British policy to take advantage of the war to regain for the white dominated central government and bureaucracy the ground lost to the Congress from 1937 or earlier." It is easy to see that, as in 1931, the situation envisaged by a goodly section of British officialdom was a confrontation with the Congress at a time when the government had thorough going powers.[95]

As Linlithgow's 18 October offer was not acceptable to the Congress, the working committee rejected it outright, and called for the resignation of Congress provincial ministries. Accordingly the eight Congress governments gave up their authority. Rajendra Prasad made it clear to the Viceroy that the Congress leadership resented the communal question being dragged in this connections. "It has clouded the issue," he said.[96] Congress ministries relinquished office, but the door was left slightly ajar so that if Britain should relent and change her attitude, adjustment and cooperation were still possible.

There had been an immediate crisis over the unilateral association of India with Britain's declaration of war on Germany. On the other hand, the resignation of Congress ministries was deemed a damp political squib and aroused no zealous interest in the average Indian. There would seem to have been competition as to which side should err more grievously. At the start of war, the Viceroy began with his clumsy bungling. Even if legalistic, he announced the fact so baldly as to give general offence. The Congress on its part without appraising the consequences, heedlessly ordered the provincial ministries to withdraw; which they did by mid-November.[97] The Viceroy, promptly, promulgated in the Congress provinces executive rule through the Advisors' regime under Section 93 of the Act.

Congress abandonment of provincial office evinced, observe Philips and Wainwright, "a fundamental lack of appreciation of the realities of powers, or at least of the extent to which those realities were bound to change in India which had moved from peace into war."[98] By this move it took its "hands off the levers of provincial power at a critical moment." Holding them during the war would have exerted a restraining influence on the League which could not have waxed strong as it did, for the Viceroy would have had to look to the Congress for prop instead of fostering the League.[99] Doubtless, Congress had its valid reasons and there were extenuating circumstances. It may be argued that Congress had only taken office recently after lot of dilly-dallying; and by a narrow margin, with strong opposition from the left wing, and that it could not honourably commit itself to war on behalf of an India which was under surveillance.[100] The very idea, that India should fight for the freedom of others while she herself was not free, was revolting against human nature itself. Said Nehru, "Freedom can have no meaning for us if we ourselves do not possess it."[101] "But these were considerations," as Philips and Wainwright remark, "born of domestic and peace time politics." The fact was that at a time when Britain was embroiled in the deadliest global contest which threatened her very existence, Congress naively "sacrificed the gains of twenty years," sullenly abandoned "the political initiative and position of authority for little apparent gain," and at the same time loosed to its adversaries, especially Jinnah and the Muslim League, the avenues hitherto blocked.[102] Congress had the mystique of being the nation building body of five and a half decades standing. Its official retreat set the stage for others. No wonder Jinnah was exultant. And he was a man equal to the situation.

If the acceptance of office was an epochal event, its abandonment twenty-seven months later, was a big setback.

So long as it occupied seats of authority, Congress could hopefully influence British policy, at least to some extent, since the government, engaged in a total war, would not antagonize a great national organization wantonly. At any rate a Congress in power would have thwarted a manoeuvring rapport between British diehardism and Muslim communalism with disrupting repercussions to the country's integrity. Perhaps, "excessive preoccupation with the present deprived the Congress leadership of the vision of the future."[103]

The suspension of the provincial part of the Act was a serious matter, but to the British it could not have been unwelcome. The British bureaucracy, as hinted above, never stomached Congress accepting office, and would have given anything to see it in wilderness during the war years. Congress blunder furthered its desire.[104] Unencumbered "by the politicians, they [the British] could now concentrate upon beating the Germans."[105] Linlithgow would make India Britain's most pliant tool in supplying the sinews of war.

Opponents of Axis totalitarianism all over the world, observes Walter Wallbank, "were deeply disappointed that the parties to the controversy, the British government and the Congress, had been unable to accommodate their different views." The Congress leaders continued to aver that the only solution was a constituent assembly, without external interference, called to frame a constitution for an independent India, and that the mention of minority interests in Linlithgow's October statement "was completely irrelevant."[106] Diplomatic dialogue between the Viceroy and the leaders of the Congress ensued but led to no more than offers of concessions conceived in miserly spirit which altered nothing in substance. Imperialism, at bay, in Europe, was firmly resolved to retain its hold on India.

The Muslim League on its part was not willing either to follow the lead of the Congress or to sanction the policy of unconditional support taken by the Muslim Premiers of the Punjab, Sind and Bengal. Before accepting or rejecting the Viceroy's statement, it required further discussion and clarification. It condemned the proposed amendment of the federal part of the Act. The scheme, it opined, had to be discarded as junk and the entire constitutional problem to l e considered afresh. As for the constituent assembly demanded by Congress, Jinnah referred to it as "a packed body, manoeuvred and managed by a Congress caucus."[107]

In order to understand the League's reaction to the resignation of the Congress governments, it would be helpful to examine its changing attitude to war and to the British government. Jinnah and his following, as has been discussed above, regarded Congress rule with antipathy and defamed it to the utmost. According to him, democracy was unsuited to Indian conditions. In connection with the Viceroy's October 18 declaration, "the Muslim League passed," states Lal Bahadur, "a lengthy resolution of satisfaction with certain parts of the viceregal statement."[108] "In the assembly of every Congress majority province," writes A.C. Guha, the Muslim League put forward a resolution as an amendment denouncing the ruthless methods of the fascists, and assuring "the Government of India full cooperation in the successful prosecution of the war." The resolution asked the government to convey to his Majesty's government that in conformity with the cherished ideal of the British empire, "Dominion Status of the Westminster type" should be conceded to India immediately after the war, and with definite assurance of the rights and interests of the recognized minorities. "It should be noted," Guha points out, "that this resolution was not in line with the policy of the League as embodied in its resolution on war passed on September 18." In that resolution, the League had put certain conditions for "full, effective and honourable cooperation of the Musalmans."[109] It had stated: "If full, effective and honourable cooperation of the Musalmans is desired by the British government in the grave crisis which is facing the world today.... it must create a sense of security and satisfaction amongst the Musalmans and take into its confidence the Muslim League."[110] Here the tone is somewhat sour. It should also be noted that if the Premiers of the Punjab and Bengal offered cooperation in the war effort, that was in violation of the League directive.[111]

In the months following the outbreak of war, the Muslim League under Jinnah "became more aggressive," as Wallbank puts it, "more the single representative of Muslim public opinion, and more determined to challenge the claims of the Indian National Congress to speak for all elements and creeds in India."[112] In particular, it was at this time that Mohammad Ali Jinnah had come to be regarded "the living symbol of Muslim unity," and Muslim politics was getting "so completely centred round him that he had become almost an institution in himself." Muslims were pleased with his leadership and people were learning to repose confidence in the League.[113]

But with all this, the Congress did not abandon hope of squaring up differences with the Muslim League. Nehru was in touch with Jinnah. But while the country was in an expectant state looking forward to renewed parleys between Nehru and Jinnah, "the latter sprung a surprise on the country in the shape of 'Deliverance Day' to be observed by the Musalmans of India on Friday, December 22, 1939". This day was to be celebrated in connection with the Congress governments quitting official power. All entreaties of Gandhi to call off the "Deliverance Day" proved ineffectual. Jinnah's attitude, undeniably, created an intractable situation for efforts pertaining to Hindu-Muslim rapprochement. The general Muslim reaction to Congress resignation, observes Lal Bahadur, "was one of unbounded joy and felicitation." A great demonstration marked the occasion with the Congress atrocity propaganda played its full part.[114] The Congress stood aghast at these frightening developments.

Meanwhile, Linlithgow had been feeling somewhat uneasy. He could not remain totally oblivious of the popular demands. After the Congress rejection of his October offer and the resignation of ministries, he through Zetland secured the Cabinet's approval for a fresh overture. He now purposed to expand his executive to include representative Indians, and early in November contacted the presidents of the two organizations, Rajendra Prasad and Jinnah, together with Gandhi; and started discussions on this score.[115] "But *ab initio*, the discussion was," feels Guha, "irrelevant and out of context."[116]

The Viceroy said : As an *ad hoc* wartime arrangement, the representatives of the Congress and the League, together with one or possibly more representatives of other important groups, could be included in the Viceroy's executive council.[117] The position of anyone appointed to the Viceroy's council "as a member of a political party would be identical, in privileges and obligations, with that of the existing members" of the said body, and "the arrangements would be within the general scheme of the existing law."[118]

This could however be done only if the Congress and League leaders reached a basis of agreement between themselves "in the provincial field," said Linlithgow, "consequent on which you could let me have proposals which would result in representatives of your two organizations immediately participating in the central government as members of my executive council."[119] He thus "threw upon the Congress and the League," writes Moore, "the onus of reaching agreement about the reconstruction of the provincial governments as a preliminary to their framing proposals for representatives of their parties to join the central executive."[120] Prasad replied to the Viceroy on November 3, stating "at the outset that both he and Gandhi missed at the interview any reference to the 'main and moral issue' raised by the Congress about clarification of war aims, without which it was impossible for the Congress to consider any subsidiary proposal."[121] Prasad further said that they were anxious to settle the communal question but that should not be made to come in the way of the declaration of Indian freedom. The discussion was bound to fail as the Muslim League was tacitly recognized the sole representative organization of the Muslims. The Viceroy gave a communal start to the discussion from the beginning and Jinnah was satisfied.[122] To Congress, this approach was not palatable; its demand that Britain grant India's right to frame her own constitution at the end of the war had still been left out in the cold. Jinnah's reply on the other hand had different import. In his letter dated 5 November, Jinnah insisted that no declaration should, either in principle or otherwise, be made or any constitution be enacted "without the approval and the consent of the two major communities of India, viz., the Musalmans and the Hindus."[123] "Linlithgow had little difficulty in making the desired promise."[124]

Jinnah entered into a prolonged and secret correspondence with the British supremo; the fate and future of India was to be decided between the two.[125] In his reply dated December 23 (Just the day after Jinnah's 'Deliverance Day'), to Jinnah's letter of November 5, Linlithgow gave assurance that the government was "not under any misapprehension as to the importance of the contentment of the Muslim community to the stability and success of any constitutional development in India." He told him to feel confident "that the weight which your community's position in India necessarily gives their [the Muslims] views, will be understood."[126]

The Muslim League working committee meeting in the first week of February, 1940, was of the opinion that the Viceroy's reply was "not satisfactory as certain important points still required further clarification and elucidation." The statement was not reassuring and emphatic enough; doubts and apprehensions still lurked in the mind of "Muslim India".[127] In his letter of February 23, Jinnah asked from the Viceroy "a definite assurance that no commitments will be made with regard to the future constitution of India or any interim settlement with any other party without our approval and consent." The Viceroy replied to him after meeting him on March 12 and April 19, when the latter explained to him fully his party's requirements. The Viceroy's letter of April 19, if in chronological disarray, would pay perusal. He called Jinnah's attention to the Secretary of State's speech in the House of Lords the day before, in which he pointed out that a "substantial measure of agreement amongst the communities in India" was necessary if the vision of a united India, which had been the dream of so many Indians and Englishmen, was "to become a reality". And further : "I cannot believe that any government or parliament in this country would attempt to impose by force upon, for example, 80 million Muslim subjects of His Majesty in India, a form of constitution under which they would not live peacefully and contentedly." The Viceroy told the League leader that such a categorical statement should be enough to remove all "possible doubts on this point".[128]

This amounts to a patronizing pat-on-the-back after the Lahore Resolution. It reminds one of a Muslim deputation, years ago, waiting on the Viceroy, Lord Minto, who gave the 'line clear' signal to Muslim separatism.

Clearly, the Viceroy and the Congress pulled towards different directions. "While the former's effort was to give a communal turn to what was purely political, the latter insisted on keeping communalism and politics apart."[129] Congress British relations had, thus, reached a stalemate.

While the early November discussions were taking place between the Viceroy and the Congress-Muslim League leaders, Jinnah offered terms for an interim arrangement with the Congress for the duration of war.[130] These terms were :

I. Formation of a Congress-League coalition "not only at the centre but in the provinces too."[131]
II. Congress concurrence of the stipulation "that no legislation affecting Muslims would be passed by a provincial lower house if two-thirds of the Muslim representatives in that house were opposed to it."
III. An undertaking from the Congress not to fly its flag on public buildings.
IV. An assurance against the singing of *Bande Mataram.*
V. A Congress undertaking to desist from maligning the League.[132]

Evidently the Congress leaders could not accept all this. Rather they revived the demand for an elected Indian body to work out a future constitution as a contrivance to set aside the benefits that the League might acquire by appealing to the British soft corner for minorities. The negotiations fizzled out.[133] Jinnah claimed to have tried to induce the Congress leaders to agree to the Viceroy's proposal of throwing his executive open to representative Indians "subject to a settlement with the League in the provincial field." "But the Congress," it was stated, "was adamant."[134]

The Secretary of State declared that the government could not oblige the Congress on the plea that it had responsibilities which it could not disregard. He asserted that no constitution could work successfully which did not meet with the general assent of the minorities. Muslims, he said, enjoyed peculiar status; they were much more than just a minority.[135]

The Viceroy made a broadcast on November 5, expressing his profound regret that the conversations between the representatives of the Congress and the Muslim League had not achieved what he had hoped. He accused the Congress for having rejected his offer of a consultative committee, and tried to impress that the consultative group "holds out great possibilities for the future—possibilities, I feel sure, greater than are commonly realized." On the other hand, Gandhi censured the government for having made it impossible for the Congress to cooperate with them.[136]

Soon after his November discussion with the Viceroy and Jinnah, Gandhi wrote an article, The *Congressman,* in which he preached non violence and communal amity. He ruefully observed "that the Muslims generally regarded the Congress as anti-Muslim." Referring to the Congress factionlism, he pointed out that each faction might be anxious to seize power and consequently centrifugal forces might be rampant. So he exhorted Congressmen to be cautious and alert as "one false step by the Congress will retard the country's progress." He wanted the country to beware of the ominous implications of "the British government in alliance with the so-called minorities arrayed against Congress single-handed." A stage had been reached when there was no going back for the Congress. Gandhi warned Congressmen against divided counsels, vacillation or lukewarm obedience to instructions. Even in the highest echelon of the Congress , there was a split opinion in the matter of shaping its attitude towards the war, let alone the subject of non violence.[137] As grim realities were crystallizing, Gandhi was losing his grip. He already seemed an anachronism.

Britain's professed reason for declining the Congress demand was that it did not agree with the League's requirement of a veto pertaining to any constitutional change whatsoever. Linlithgow had found Jinnah firm; says Moore, that the League be acknowledged as the sole Muslim spokesman in future discussions; and he was hostile to the much harped on Congress scheme for a constituent assembly. On the other hand, Congress was profoundly distrustful of Britain's motives.[138] Yet Linlithgow was not inclined, observes Tomlinson, "to gamble too heavily on the League as a source of loyal support to the raj during the war." It seemed too anti-democratic and anti-nationalist to be reckoned with an enduring political factor, and Jinnah's claim for veto power on any constitutional advance was found too hard a pill to swallow. But he was still anxious to give the League some say in India's future, and to boost its morale; it was a good weapon to be used as a counter to the Congress ambition for a voice in the conduct of the war.[139]

Nor were the feelings of most of the cabinet members any different. As a matter of fact they looked to the communal rift as the most effective trap to arrest the forces of nationalism. They sought "to divide and minimize the Indian response to the new situation so that they could carry on as if nothing had happened." Churchill was not more inimical to India's nationalist aspirations than most when "he condemned the Viceroy's attempts to get an agreement between the Congress and the League as suicidal."[140] Such agreement, he affirmed, was "almost out of the realm of practical politics, while, if it were to be brought about," he had the effrontery to say, "the immediate result would be that the united communities would join in showing us the door." To him the Hindu Muslim feud was an effective bastion of British rule in India. Linlithgow was no less uncompromising notwithstanding his resumption of discussions with Indian leaders.[141] His resolve not to yield to the Congress demands that would be distasteful to the Muslims or the princes, brought British policy to a blind alley.

But not for long. He was ruffled into action by his opposite number. Zetland had started weighing in mind the Congress proposal for a constituent assembly.[142] He discussed it with Stafford Cripps, "who proposed the idea of a constitution making body representative of all parties and groups and princes, and stipulated that if an agreed constitution were to emerge, Britain should agree to it and its relations with India could be regulated by a treaty."[143] Zetland was much impressed with Cripps' proposals and sounded the Prime Minister, Neville Chamberlain, on them in the beginning of December.[144] Amba Prasad holds that the latter expressed his readiness [145] to consider "what not so long ago would have been regarded as a revolutionary proposal". Zetland then worked the scheme out in a letter to Linlithgow dispatching him "a draft of a restatement policy." He argued that Britain "should call upon the major parties in India to agree the composition of an all-India body to determine a constitution for a self-governing India." She should be able to express her readiness to legislate in accordance with the plan chalked out by the body at the end of the war.

Linlithgow did not quite relish the idea. He remained unconvinced that there were reasonable grounds for a "radical" move on the Indian scene. Afterall, Congress had been "unresponsive to his earlier overtures" and unprepared to smooth its contrarieties with the Muslims. Why go after the recalcitrant body? The existent dissonance between the main communities could fortify Britain's hold on India for many long years. If, on the other hand, Britain accepted the Congress demand for a constituent assembly, then the Congress would be established securely, and would go hard with the minorities and with such things as Britain's commercial involvements in a self-governing India. Linlithgow advised that Congress be given time to cool, so that it might "welcome a government move to settle the communal difficulty in the provinces."[146]

Yet Linlithgow did conjecture an alternative plan, that "he should extract from Jinnah minimum terms for the accommodation of the Muslims," and then have Gandhi's approval for them. The details of the scheme would be ratified by prominent Indian leaders. He would then declare "Britain's intention to introduce a scheme of federation as soon as possible" in order to enter with minimum delay, if possible before the end of the war, "into the Dominion Status stage."[147] Good, if unconvincing, phraseology, to while away the time.

The Congress working committee, meeting from November 19 to 23 to study the situation though there was not much new to study, affirmed that the issue involved was a moral one, and not of political bargaining. Reiterating its old demand—for a constituent assembly and declaration of India's independence —it stated that the declarations made on behalf of the British government being dissatisfactory had "compelled the Congress to dissociate itself from the British policy and war effort." In the meantime, pressure had been mounting for starting civil disobedience.[148] The committee while complimenting Congressmen on their eagerness for it, told them to keep restraint and discipline. Throughout 1939, Gandhi and his associates had warned Congressmen that time was not ripe yet for civil disobedience. Now Gandhi said that it was impossible since indiscipline and factionalism were rife and might lead to violence and infighting with the Muslim League. The Congressmen, he wrote, "were now less prepared for civil disobedience than they had been in 1930," and urged them to prepare for future action by promoting constructive work—*khadi, charkha* and communal amity etc.—as the only suitable programme at the time.[149]

The working committee, meeting in mid-December, declared that the British were still resorting to the old stratagem of "divide and rule", and that the communal problem could not be solved unless the Indians stopped looking to the British for arbitrament.[150] It called upon "the people to observe Independence Day on December 26."[151] The Congress's main thrust was on India's post war status, but the British were unprepared to give any assurance "acceptable to the Congress and go beyond an offer of immediate changes of an interim character."[152]

Linlithgow was now satisfied that Congress was "incorrigible". He did little to thaw it out of the stalemate since he supposed it was overbidding its hand, and had calculated that if it could but hold out for a little longer "we shall be prepared to offer them a better bargain."[153] In this deadlock, was Muslim League's chance. The Viceroy now leaned more on its support. In January 1940, he received League's terms for an arrangement with the Congress. The League leader again asked for "a Congress-League coalition government in all the provinces and refused to accept any form of democratically elected central government." Not surprisingly, this proposal was rejected by Gandhi. From the failure of this last bid until June 1940, Linlithgow importuned the Secretary of State that Britain should "lie back and not move," "refrain from action," "wait upon events" and "avoid running after the Congress."[154]

The Congress had perceived early that the war flame could shoot up any time and engulf India. The old issues had become anachronistic. The crisis deepened and demanded fresh moves. It was this urge which had prompted Nehru to approach Jinnah having learnt from a common friend that the League leader had spoken in affectionate terms about him; that he seemed to be in a conciliatory frame of mind. He implored Jinnah to join the Congress in protesting against Britain's approach. He appealed to Jinnah's patriotism. For once Jinnah seemed thawed, "but he did not commit himself to any course of action,"[155] and "the expected rapprochement between the Congress and the Muslim League never took place." Many times it seemed within grip, but it always in the end proved elusive. The war carved out a new destiny for the man.[156] The Congress and the government were drifting asunder but there was still an off-chance of a *modus vivendi* between them. It was only when government-Congress negotiations failed that he audaciously showed his colours.[157] The British were to gain nothing by their intransigence; the war had in any case doomed their Indian sway, but Jinnah was to reap a rich harvest out of it. Had Congress retained provincial hold he would probably, making a virtue of circumstances, have adjusted relationship with it.[158] Once the Congress was out, Jinnah was on secure ground; his negativism and obduracy came to the fore. Congress retreat tipped the balance in his favour. Yet he moved warily, waited for a full month—November—scanning the political horizon, studying British-Congress relations which were, of course, in the doldrums. Jinnah felt complacent. His hour was at hand. He "matched Congress negation to the British with Muslim negation to the Congress."[159] Welcoming the resignation of Congress ministries, he declared that they must never come back. On December 2, he called upon his followers to observe December 22 as has been mentioned earlier, as a "Day of Deliverance" from the "tyranny, oppression and injustice" of the Congress regime. The effrontery of this gesture left Nehru and others gasping, but it took many League members too by surprise. Some observers remarked "that Jinnah had overshot his bolt, and that his extreme tactics might even cause a split in the League."[160] He "was bitterly criticized," says Khalid Sayeed, "even by Muslim leaders for this action. But it fitted into the broad pattern of strategy that he had devised." He would use Congress lapses "to build his prestige and that of the League."[161] The Muslims all over India were to hold meetings and pass the resolution saying that the Congress ministries had left no stone unturned "to destroy Muslim culture," had tampered with the socio-religious life of the Muslims and had "trampled upon their economic and political rights," creating an impression on the Hindu public that a Hindu raj had been established. The resolution was to express deep sense of relief at the termination of the Congress regime in various provinces, and urge upon the Governor of the province in which the meeting was held to probe into the legitimate grievances of the Musalmans and make amends for them without delay.[162]

At this very time Congress seemed anxious to evolve an understanding with the League but the "Deliverance or Thanksgiving Day" "and all its implications left no room for any helpful talk."[163] The call evoked a good response from the non-Muslims as well. It was celebrated with more enthusiasm in the Congress provinces than elsewhere.[164] The Congress party was bewildered at this threatening turn. It may be recalled that in 1928, when Jinnah spoke at the All Parties Convention in Calcutta he was heckled, shouted down, almost insulted and his right to speak on behalf of Muslims was challenged.[165] After the lapse of a decade, he established his right to speak on behalf of Muslims and his call for the observance of the "deliverance day" was widely acclaimed.[166] He had steadily built himself up as the spokesman of the second Indian nation, the hundred millions as he liked to call them.

The general impression in the Congress ranks was that the Viceroy himself was responsible for the development of this communal frenzy in Jinnah. [167]

Jinnah's message on the "deliverance day" was a biting assault on the Congress party; after all the hue and cry Nehru "began to wonder if there was any common ground between them at all." He craved for "political independence and a socialist society, and the instrument of the new order was to be a constituent assembly elected by the people on the basis of adult franchise."

To Jinnah, the idea seemed "wholly utopian."[168] Apart from the "academic discussion about a constituent assembly," he said, "it shows colossal ignorance, both historic and constitutional, to expect a foreign power that is dominating this country to sign its death warrant." How could the British government have the constitution framed by an Indian assembly placed "on the Statute Book of the British Parliament?"[169] He humoured the Viceroy "that the British and not the Indian should have the final say in constitution making." However unfortunate, says Tara Chand, "this distrust of his own people and humiliating the dependence on alien masters, the fact cannot be ignored."[170]

On Socio-economic problems Jinnah seldom spoke "but he had no sympathy with Nehru's radical economics. 'All talk of hunger and poverty', he declared, 'is intended to lead the people to socialistic and communistic ideas for which India is far from prepared.' "[171] Some non-Muslims also, it has been said, joined in the thanksgiving celebrations.

Ostensibly since the launching of the Congress ministries, to Jinnah the main enemy of the Muslim League was the Congress. The League on its own could not counter the Congress. Hence, he sought to create a broad front consisting of the Muslim League and other minorities. This approach was manifest in some of the League resolutions of 1937 and 1938.[172] In its special session at Calcutta on April 18, 1938, in his presidential address, Jinnah had asserted that "the Muslim League is not only carrying on a struggle for the Muslims; it maintains that all other important minorities must have the same sense of security and a place in the sun of India, where they will enjoy their rights and privileges as free citizens, and not be ground down by caste tyranny and caste rule."[173]

Gandhi wrote to him (January 16, 1940) wondering if he intended to rally all non-Congress parties behind him. "If you succeed," Gandhi pithily observed, "you will free the country from communal incubus," and would give a lead to the Muslims and others for which he would earn the gratitude not only of the Muslims but of all the other communities and of posterity. Evidently Jinnah had no such intention for he was aware that not many could stomach his rabid communalism, or bear the salvo of his batteries against the Congress. People in general wanted to grow politically, not communally. His reply of January 21 to Gandhi was intriguing. His fellowship with other parties, he candidly admitted, was "partly a case of 'adversity bringing strange bed-fellows together' and partly because common interest may lead Muslims and minorities to combine." He went further and affirmed that India was not a nation, nor even a country. It was a subcontinent comprising various nationalities. Since religion was the basis of this appalling thesis, he did not care to elucidate "to which nationality the Christians, the Sikhs, the Parsis and many other communities belonged and how they stood in relation to the Hindus and to his own co-religionists." Jinnah was out to challenge the forces of nationalism and did not bother to find out any logic for his arguments. He found in the spineless Viceroy a tractable accessary "whose sole passion," writes Kulkarni, "was now to put down the Congress and to bleed the country white in the name of war effort."[174] According to William Phillips, President Roosevelt's special envoy in New Delhi, the Viceroy represented 'England of the old school, of the tradition of the empire, of British responsibility to govern backward peoples. To him Indians were "no better than conquered peoples."[175] Phillips came to the conclusion that the Viceroy was not in sympathy with any change in Britain's relationship to India. Indians had the impression, he felt, that the British government was determined to preserve the *status quo*.[176]

Jinnah was in close touch with such an enemy of India's dignity. Crude imperialism and impelling id joined hands to draw lines according to the predilections of the League leader. The "great national organization" asked for a national government and sat inert as the cry was unanswered.

It may be worthwhile here to note the interview of Choudhry Khaliquzzaman, a member of the working committee of the All-India Muslim League, with Lord Zetland on March 20, 1939, in London. Zaman was queried by the latter as to what was the alternative to the 1935 Act and the Federal Union. Zaman, who had discussed the matter with Choudhry Rahmat Ali, the propounder of the idea of Pakistan, promptly rejoined that the Muslim majority areas might be separated from the rest of India and the scheme of federation be implemented as far as Indian provinces were concerned "without including the Muslim areas which should be independent from the rest." Khaliquzzaman also indicated to Zetland that "this is going to be the stand of the Muslims in the next session of the Muslim League."[177] "This means," Khalid Sayeed points out, "that he must have been authorized by Jinnah to seek such an interview and put forward these ideas."[178] On meeting Jinnah, (12 May) he gave him his "impression that the British would ultimately concede partition." Jinnah was not averse to the proposal but, he felt, "it had to be examined in all its bearings."[179]

Zetland recorded the main points of his talk with Zaman in a letter which he subsequently sent to the Viceroy. Clearly, "Linlithgow knew before the Pakistan resolution was passed what next step the Muslim League was likely to take." After his talk with these two British officials, Zaman felt "that they would not oppose the demand seriously."[180] The feeling was not baseless. "Zetland's mind," says Tara Chand, "was increasingly tending towards accepting Muslim separatism."[181] Between the two diplomatic partners, the scheme was getting concocted. They would emphasize communal differences, that they should be resolved, thereby making the situation worse.

The year 1939 closed with an ominous note, without any rapprochement between the Congress and the government, or, for that matter between the Congress and the League. The war had reached a blind alley, and so it seemed had British-Indian relations.

It was the war that drove Whitehall to give a definite shape to its intentions with regard to India's future. On November, 7, Zetland asserted that Britain meant to grant India Dominion Status of the Statute of Westminster variety—"the Dominion Status of 1926" with "full status of equality within the British Commonwealth."[182] Though dominionhood had been construed as equality of status, the Cabinet still differentiated it from independence.

In January, 1940 the Cabinet asked the Viceroy to substitute the phrase "self government within the empire" for "independence within the empire" to clarify the meaning of

Dominion Status.[183] Accordingly came Linlithgow's statement on 10 January in Bombay offering India Dominion Status of the "statute of Westminster variety" at the end of the war, which impressed Gandhi as offering the hope of an "honourable settlement", and presenting a better prospect of agreement between the Congress and the government than the offers of October 18 and early November. This hope, however, proved illusory, an interview between the Viceroy and Gandhi in early February came to nothing. The Viceroy offered him the following package : a reassertion of Britain's intention to install Dominion Status at the earliest possible date; the addition of representative Hindu and Muslim politicians to the Viceroy's executive; the implementation of the federation as soon as the requisite princely adhesion was secured;[184] the revision of the federal constitution "in consultation with representatives of all parties and interests in India at the appropriate time, and shorten the transition period to the utmost extent possible." The federal scheme, it was averred, was the swiftest path to Dominion Status. The British offer was to be completed in two stages : firstly an immediate expansion of the executive council; and secondly the revival of the federal scheme to facilitate the implementation of Dominion Status after the war.[185]

In the meantime, Jinnah had met Linlithgow on 13 January and given his conditions, discussed above, for a settlement with the Congress. He had again claimed the creation of coalition ministries in the Congress provinces, and had shown his aversion to any form of democratically elected central government.[186] Gandhi would neither give in to Jinnah's provincial coalitions, nor he give up the Congress demand for a constituent assembly.

After Linlithgow's meeting with Gandhi and Jinnah in early 1940 "when Gandhi was more conciliatory and Jinnah getting more adamant", the Viceroy conveyed to the Secretary of State Jinnah's threat that "if Congress ministers did return to office under existing conditions, there would be a civil war in India."[187]

By February 1940, the situation had emerged where the negotiations with the British could proceed no further.[188] The main difference between the Congress demand and the Viceroy's offer, as Gandhi saw it, was that while the latter envisaged "the final determination of India's destiny by the British government," to Congress the Indians themselves should be the arbiter of their fate, shiva Rao says. There seemed no prospect of a congenial settlement without the elimination of this basic difference. Self determination for India, Gandhi felt, would naturally resolve all the hurdles.[189]

Linlithgow imagined that the Congress leaders had reckoned that it was an endurance test. He would not gratify the Congress, and continued playing the crescent card. Britain, he considered, had offered all that she could. At the end of February, he noted with an air of complacence that feelings towards the Congress among the minorities and the princes were "hardening rapidly." The prospects of adjustment among Indians were receding, which implied there was no likelihood of constitutional advance, and foreign rulers could be content that there seemed no scope of Britain quitting India in the "foreseeable future". Linlithgow would not estrange the Muslims; to him a Congress stoop was the necessary condition for a constitutional advance.

Zetland, more prescient, would have the Viceroy give rope to the Congress stand. However, the Cabinet was critical of his exerting pressure on Linlithgow to go further than the latter thought prudent. Linlithgow was left to himself and whilst he was in the "lie back and not move" posture, his opposite number strove to make the Cabinet realize "the need for action" to check further deterioration of the Indian situation. He was concerned that, says Moore, "some constructive plan of action" be chalked out, and discussed this matter with the Cabinet on March 11. He prepared a draft statement visualizing the formation of an all-India body to frame a constitution for India as a distinct entity of the Commonwealth. After the war, the constitution could be validated. The Cabinet procrastinated taking a decision on this count until it was conversant with Linlithgow's survey of the political scene after the forthcoming session of the Congress at Ramgarh. The Congress cry of "complete independence", followed four days later by the Lahore Resolution, was a stirring development, that led Zetland to make a reappraisal of his move. The government fell from power before he could revivify it.[190] Whether Zetland's scheme was feasible is anybody's guess.

Coming to Linlithgow, his three offers during the first six months of the war—of mid-October, early November and early February—did not purport to any change in attitude to the Indian constitutional problem. Whitehall would not go, states Moore, "beyond the policy of Dominion Status within the empire, all-India federation, and consultation (but without responsibility) through a body set up to revise the 1935 Act and in the existing central government." Democratic concessions were backlashed by the continuing protective stipulations for the minorities and the princes. Trusteeship was to endure. Linlithgow was keen that even the entry of the Indian parties to his executive must be conditional upon their antecedent agreement in the provincial field.[191]

Perhaps during the early stages of the war a generous, charismatic diplomatist might have contrived a plan to decipher the Indian tangle. Officially Britain aimed at a free and united India with effective safeguards for minorities and peripheral groups and interests. Certain ill advised schemes, discussed earlier, were initiated for this purpose but as Edwin Montague, the dedicated British Minister for India, touchingly and premonitorily remarked during the first world war, "opportunities lost in India cannot be recovered except at great cost."[192] The statements on behalf of the government were ambiguous, an attempt to avoid the main issue. Facts and figures were misrepresented. On December 14, Zetland made a statement in the House of Lords that "of the four hundred eighty-two Muslims elected to the lower chambers of the provincial legislatures at the last general elections only twenty-six stood as Congressmen." "In giving these statistics," writes Tara Chand, "the aim evidently was to deceive the ignorant Lords". He did not point out that "of 482 Muslim seats only 109 were won by the Muslim League."[193] From the statements of the government spokesmen the Muslim League was led to conclude that it had been assigned veto power on all constitutional proposals. It was natural that a vain and bitter Jinnah should make the most of it.[194]

In the early months of the war, British Policy towards India was sterile. London tried to behave as if nothing untoward was in store. The discussion initiated by the Viceroy was designedly deflected to the impasse of communal adjustment, when the issue ought to have been political. If the issue was the "settlement of the communal question," says Guha, "then the Muslim League should not have been given the status of being the sole representative of the Muslims"; there were other Muslim organizations, let alone other minorities and their political affiliations. During these discussions, the government conveniently slurred over the fact that in the 1937 elections the Muslim League had cut a sorry figure, unable to capture a majority of votes in a single Muslim majority province. Moreover, equating the Congress with the League was tantamount to Congress standing for Hindus alone, a rebuff to its national pride. This was a clever artifice to hoodwink Indian and world opinion that India was hopelessly divided, there was no room for agreement among its diverse components, and the Government, with best intentions, was helpless to smooth the discord.[195] The twists and turns in Britain's pronouncements (and actions) could not obscure the reality. The compulsions of Britain's India Policy were to assert themselves more strongly as months rolled on. The Congress demand for *purna swaraj*, if it was meaningless jargon for the Tory diehards, was becoming increasingly uncomfortable for the liberals.[196] So as far as possible, Congress- League animosity was fanned up. When a crisis of unity emerged, the self-styled champions of the integrity of the country seemed bewildered. In the absence of sincere solicitude and effective diplomacy, "the gap between British Policy and Congress demands became a gulf, the communal rift became a chasm, and party resolutions hardened into ultimate as stated by Moore.[197]

By December 1939, Jinnah's intractability was self-evident. Nehru and other Congressmen could see that he would neither settle with the Congress nor get entangled with the government. What Nehru and others did not quite foresee was Jinnah's audacious manoeuvring of the intricate situation. He might turn the growing rupture between the Congress and the government to his advantage.[198] The celebration of the "deliverance day" symbolizing freedom from "sufferings" and Jinnah's threat of a civil war if Congress came back to power, had broken a new fissure between the two political organizations. They also signified that as far as the government was concerned, he was on secure ground. He made effusive promises of Muslim aid in the war effort to a government already favourably inclined.[199] The Congress session at Ramgarh denoted the possibility of direct action and the consideration of its consequences gave the League mind a severe jolt. It feared and hated the Congress more than ever. Hence, when the League met for its Lahore session "the stage was set for the firing of the final shot."[200] The fissure was to widen menacingly. Congress and the League were now to enter the decisive phases of their careers.

Much was expected from Nehru, with his magnificent background, during this trying period. "Apart from the fact that he enjoyed," to quote Kulkarni, "immense popularity both with the masses and the intellectuals in the country, his wide-ranging mind and intimate contacts abroad helped him to appreciate better the fateful significance of the war." During his 1938 visit to Europe he had witnessed the abyssal developments bringing the world on the threshold of cataclysm. He disapproved the dictators and their fascist ideology. He wished and expected India to play her full role; using all her resources, in the stirring global happenings, to bring the war to an end, and herald the beginning of the century of the common man.[201]

Besides, Nehru was in touch with some of the renowned world figures and knew their mind on the issue of India's freedom. He must have been well aware that, thanks to the war and favourable trend in world opinion, his country's freedom was no longer in doubt.[202] Why did he cast aside, wonders C. S. Venkatachar, the fundamentals of provincial power thereby forsaking "the considerable nuisance value the Congress possessed by being in office in the abnormal situation of war time, and play directly into the hands of Jinnah?" It may be intriguing to explore this question.

In the fullness of power, as the indisputable lord of India, Nehru evinced remarkable self-control and expertise in his dealings with men and situations. However, as a nationalist leader his kaleidoscopic moodiness was often his liability.

Linlithgow was insensate but why should Nehru have fallen in the trap?. Posterity will not overlook this oversight. At this crucial moment, observes Venkatachar, "Congress should have shown patience, watched the European horizon, waited upon events, pocketed its pride," instead of taking offence and emasculating itself. The Congress in office should have kept effective armed neutrality towards government.[203] Jinnah's position was still shaky; he was still trying for recognition both from the Muslim community and from the British.[204] He could not have shoved the Congress out of power in the provinces. Nor could the British have wantonly banished the Congress governments. Had they done it, "Congress would have strengthened its position."[205]

Linlithgow had acted according to the constitution, as said before, in declaring India at war with Germany although "his manner of doing it emphasized India's dependent status."[206] After the usual tussle between right and left wings, the Congress ministries were instructed to resign on the plea that they could have nothing to do with a war high-handedly thrust upon India. "The wisdom of their departure is still a subject of dispute."[207] According to V.P. Menon a close observer with intimate inside knowledge, "this was a cardinal mistake which was instrumental in the formation of Pakistan." The Viceroy, he feels, was prone to encourage the Muslim League as a counterpoise to Congress, which gave a big push to Jinnah's still uncomfortable position. "The Congress also lost that influence which comes from being in office instead of out." Of these two factors, Menon thinks, the second was more important. "The strength of the League in the last resort was a matter of Muslim sentiment" which "was not dependent upon government patronage." By its withdrawal on the other hand, "the Congress lost an important bargaining position at a moment when bargaining was to be the order of the day." The Congress could have been at a vantage point if it had kept "the threat of resignation in reserve instead of only the threat of civil disobedience. Such a threat in wartime aroused maximum British resistance."[208]

It behoved Congress to move circumspectly, and make a realistic —sympathetic —appreciation of Britain's position. No drastic constitutional change on the Indian scene could possibly be undertaken when Britain's very existence was in peril. Britain's urge to retain her hold on India and keep the basic political structure intact during the gruesome war years is understandable; no indoor shake-up as long as out-door fighting was on. A global war was sure to make things topsy-turvy. The world was in a continual flux. If the first world war spelled the doom of four big empires, surely great and vital changes awaited the second. The post war world could not be the same. Notwithstanding Congress demands, Britain had to work according to her interests—first to labour for survival, then for the achievement of victory. She was on tenterhooks and had no patience for Congress impatience.

The main actors on the political landscape were : Lord Linlithgow for the British, Gandhi and Nehru for the Congress and Jinnah for the Muslims. In Linlithgow, the British had a man who was lacking deplorably in the art of managing men; who, said Lord Halifax, "did not really get on human terms with anybody."[209] Nehru, an ardent internationalist with touching faith in democracy, was always for action, usually against the government, but he was also anxious that India should "play her full part and throw all her resources into the struggle for a new order". The "new order" he envisaged was not an utopian conception.[210] He was keen to join in the fight against Nazism and did not believe in non-violence as an ultimate ideal, but he was under the spell of Gandhi—his mentor. "Jinnah," writes Percival Spear, "the polished Westerner who was playing on traditional Muslim mass emotions, furbished the rapier of obstructive tactics while he waited in the wings, conscious that neither side could get its way without him."[211]

In his contacts with the British Jinnah was walking on tight rope. The Congress was harbouring unconcealed antagonism to the government war effort and had renounced office. Under such situation Jinnah was likely to commit one of the two tactical errors. He could have alienated the British by trying to extract too many advantages from them, or he could have taken the other course of totally toeing the British mark including acceptance of office at the centre. "Without a Jinnah," observes Khalid Sayeed, "most of the Muslim League leaders would not have been able to resist the latter temptation." Jinnah eschewed both these options and adopted a course of action in which without much restriction on his freedom of action, he managed to obtain certain meaningful concessions from the British. He could see that the British, states Sayeed, having lost the support of the Congress, would be loath to lose the goodwill of the Muslim community as well. The Viceroy's pronouncement of August 8, 1940, stating that the British government could not transfer power to any system of government in India whose authority was disavowed "by large and powerful elements in India's national life", and asserting that they could not tolerate "the coercion of such elements into submission to such a Government"—implied an acknowledgement of the raised stature of his party. Jinnah was riding triumph, thanks to his brilliant strategy. The British had given him a valuable weapon to block any constitutional arrangement. Armed with this veto, he could bide his time, meliorate his organization, and eventually the Muslim League and the Congress representing the two communities could negotiate at the summit.[212]

Retracing a bit, the Congress was carrying on a stinging, if futile, dialogue with the government which no less pleased than when Congress was in power refused to be browbeaten. This dialogue for entering the central government, says Venkatachar, was idle as Jinnah had made things difficult having committed the League to the objective of Pakistan, and on account of the anti-Congress proclivity of the Linlithgow government. Congress tactically debilitated itself by breaking off with the government. "What is perhaps less appreciated," to quote the same author, "is that the public, realistically conscious of the rapidly changing economic situation under war time conditions, moved away from the impracticalities of the Congress leaders." War opened new vistas for employment in civil administration.[213] There was, observes K.N. Chaudhuri, "a great improvement in the volume of industrial production and the level of employment and wages" in the early phase of the war. As industrialism was triggered, businessmen prospered in war economy. "After the experience of the world depression, there was much public satisfaction at the new turn of events," Chaudhuri notes.[214] Congress, which had been clamouring for the Indianization of defence services, now started pressurizing the people not to enroll for service in a war to which it was not a party. "The public wiser than the Congress," remarks Venkatachar, "did not listen to it." In Nehru's India, one daily listened to his cherished theme: dynamism. Surprisingly he became insensate to dynamism in a war ravaged world in which the political and military situation was fast changing.[215] Gandhi had once talked of a "Himalayan blunder" over some trivial lapses of a national leader.[216] Since office acceptance, through the outbreak of war to 1942 occurrences, Congress was committing true "Himalayan blunders." There could be no escape now from Jinnah's clutches.

Slowly but surely, the Muslim leaders grew convinced that the minority safeguards conceded in the 1935 Act could no longer shield their interests and aspirations. They spoke in a desperate tone and gave a timely warning of the drift of their thought. "And yet it seems," says Z.H. Zaidi, "they were not seriously contemplating a division of India. When they talked about it, they apparently employed the threat as a counter for bargaining and settlement."[217]

Congress "large heartedly" labelled communal questions as "irrelevant issues," and did not wish "to increase their importance" by having serious, sympathetic discussion over them. Perhaps the Congress felt, if they were stoutly ignored they would perish. "As representative of the majority community," the Congress stalwarts "failed to understand the true nature of minority fears."[218] On one occasion (March 2, 1941), Jinnah replied to the argument that India's Muslims were Hindus at one time and that it was preposterous to assume that change of religion implied change of nationality.[219] Jinnah's reply, although it is a long extract, will bear perusing. He said :

> ...an Englishman, if he changes his religion in England, he, by changing his religion, still remains a member of the same society, with the same culture, the same social life, and everything remains exactly the same when an Englishman changes his faith. But can't you see that a Muslim, when he was converted, granted that he was converted more than a thousand years ago, the bulk of them, then according to your Hindu religion and philosophy, he becomes an outcaste and a *Mlechha,* and the

> Hindu ceased to have anything to do with him socially, religiously, culturally, or in any other way?... It is now more than a thousand years that the bulk of the Muslims have lived in a different world, in a different society, in a different philosophy and a different faith. Can you possibly compare this with the nonsensical talk that mere change of faith is no ground for a demand for Pakistan? Can't you see the fundamental difference?...[220]

"Issues that were by no means frivolous, and demands which in spite of a certain crudity in expression," writes Hiren Mukerjee, "touched the heart strings of Muslim India, needed therefore, "to be understood and appraised by a serious mental effort which unfortunately was not forthcoming." The result was wrangling and recriminations to the unconcealed joy of the alien lord who waxed merry on Intra-Indian clashes.[221]

Linlithgow was certainly not eager to hasten the end of the raj. If he was sluggish to make a suitable response to the Congress requirements, he did little to assuage Muslim apprehensions. Perhaps he felt that his intractability toward the Congress would instinctively calm down the Muslims. Evidently Linlithgow was more concerned to keep the League under thumb than to straighten the tangle by forging safeguards to adjust the Muslims within a united India.[222] The British "made no secret of the fact," writes Kulkarni, "that the importance of the League and its leader would be measured strictly in terms of their usefulness to the government in halting India's constitutional progress."[223]

Failing any positive British move, the Muslim mind grew nervous leaping forward "to a future, envisaged by the Congress, when the raj would be no more," says Moore. "The communal dialectic that had become the dynamic force of Indian politics between 1937 and 1939 meant that each major Congress resolution provoked a Muslim reply." The Ramgarh demand, the result of Britain's shabby deal with the Congress was duly followed by the Lahore Resolution.

War put Indian emotions in a ferment. The Congress taking advantage of the cataclysm put its claims high, and as Whitehall conceived concessions in a niggardly spirit, it felt obliged to take drastic steps. The League raised its bids too with high stakes. Nor were the British ordinary gamblers. Perhaps in the early months of the war, a great Viceroy could have managed the situation, mobilized public opinion, in a wholesome manner, bringing the parties into effective unison thereby preparing the ground for a meaningful constitutional leap.[224] But traditional British imperialism sometimes overtly "and often with a consummate sanctimonious mask of impartiality" had encouraged the conflict of interests between the two communities.[225] The Viceroy failed to mend the situation that Britain's earlier policies were bringing to "fruition", incapable or unwilling to squash the communal and separatist forces that were in the ascendant. He was too good a progeny of the imperialist past to fabricate a nation of the future. The situation duped him.[226] The two fatal Conferences presaged the break-up of India's oneness.

NOTES AND REFERENCES

1. Kulkarni, V.B. *India and Pakistan: 'A Historical Survey of Hindu-Muslim Relations,* (Bombay: Jaico Publishing House, 1973), pp. 329-30.
2. Spear, Percival, *A History of India,* (Penguin Books, 1965), Vol. II, p. 214.
3. Tara Chand, *History of the Freedom Movement in India,* (New Delhi : Publications Division, Govt. of India, 1972), Vol. IV, p. 279.
4. Mukerjee, Hirendranath, *India's Struggle for Freedom,* 3rd *rev. edn.* (Calcutta: NBA, 1962), p. 212.
5. Spear, *History of India,* p. 217.
6. Hutchins, G. Francis, *The Illusion of Permanence: British Imperialism in India,* (Princeton, New Jersey: Princeton University Press, 1967), p. 201.
7. Kulkarni, *India and Pakistan,* p. 340.
8. Linlithgow M.S.S. India Office Library, London, Vol. VII, Linlithgow to Zetland, 3.1.39, quoted in B.R. Tomlinson, *The Indian National Congress and the Raj 1929-1942—The Penultimate Phase* (London : Macmillan Press Ltd., 1976), pp. 140-41.
9. Zetland to Linlithgow, 24.1.39 Ibid, pp. 140-41
10. Zetland to Linlithgow, 3.1.39 Ibid, pp. 140-141.
11. Wallbank, T. Walter, *A Short History of India and Pakistan* (Abr.

ed.), *India in the New Era;* (rev. edn.), (New York: The new American Library, A Mentor Book, 1965), p. 191.

12. Mukerjee, *India's struggle for Freedom,* p. 211.
13. Voigt, Johannes, H. "Cooperation or Confrontation? War and Congress Politics, 1939-42," In : *Congress and the Raj; Facets of the Indian Struggle 1917-47,* Low, D.A. (ed.), (London : Arnold Heinemann, 1977), p. 350.
14. Tara Chand, *History of the Freedom Movement in India,* pp. 277-78.
15. Azad, Maulana Abul Kalam, *India Wins Freedom: An Autobiographical Narrative,* (Bombay: Orient Longman, 1959), pp. 24-25.
16. Tara Chand, *History of the Freedom Movement in India,* pp. 280.
17. Bartarya, S. C., *The Indian Nationalist Movement* (Allahabad: Indian Press Private Ltd, 1958), p. 214.
18. Voigt, "War and Congress", pp. 349-50.
19. Bartarya, *Nationalist Movement,* p. 214.
20. Wallbank, *History of India and Pakistan,* p. 191; see also, Bartarya, *Nationalist Movement,* pp. 214-15.
21. Azad, *India Wins Freedom,* p. 26.
22. Edwardes, Michael, *The Last Years of British India,* (London : Nel Mentor, 1967), pp. 78-79.
23. Ram Gopal, *Indian Muslims : A Political History 1958-1947,* (Bombay : Asia Publishing House, 1959), p. 266; Guha, A. C. *India's Struggle : Quarter of a Century (1921-46),* (New Delhi: Publications Division, Govt. of India 1982), Part I, p. 438.
24. Coupland, Reginald G. *Indian Politics 1936-42,* (New York: Oxford Univ. Press, 1943), p. 208.
25. Dutt, R.P., *India Today,* (Bombay: People's Publishing House, 1949), p. 508.
26. Philips, C.H. and Wainwright, M.D., "Introduction", In : *The Partition of India: Policies and Perspectives 1935-47,* Philips and Wainwright, (eds), (London: George Allen and Unwin Ltd, 1970), p. 17.
27. Ibid. pp. 17-18.
28. Spear, Percival. "A Third Force in India 1920-47 : A Study in Political Analysis," Ibid p. 501.
29. Mukerjee, *Recalling India's struggle for Freedom,* (Delhi : Seema Publications, 1983), p. 207.
30. Edwardes, *The Last Years,* p. 78.
31. Sahni, J.N. *The Lid Off: Fifty Years of Indian Politics 1921-1971,* (Bombay: Allied Publishers, 1971), p. 149.
32. Spear, *History of India,* p. 214.

33. Voigt, "War and Congress," p. 351.
34. Edwardes, *The Last years*, p. 79.
35. Ibid. p. 79.
36. Voigt, "War and Congress," p. 351.
37. Bisheshwar Prasad, *Changing Modes of Indian National Movement* (New Delhi : People's Publishing House, 1966), p. 132.
38. Azad, *India Wins Freedom*, p. 26.
39. Tomlinson, *Congress and Raj*, p. 143.
40. Majumdar, R.C., *History of the Freedom Movement in India*, (Calcutta: Firma K.L. Mukhopadhyay, 1963), Vol. III, pp. 597-98.
41. Tomlinson, *Congress and Raj*, p. 146.
42. Majumdar, *History of the Freedom Movement*, p. 596.
43. Guha, *India's Struggle, pp. 434-35.*
44. Majumdar, *History of the Freedom Movement*, p. 596.
45. Guha, *India's Struggle*, pp. 435-437.
46. Tara Chand, *History of the Freedom Movement in India*, p. 280.
47. Prasad, *Changing Modes*, p. 133.
48. Wallbank, *History of India and Pakistan*, p. 193.
49. Venkatachar, C.S., "1937-47 In Retrospect: A Civil Servant's View," In : *Partition of India*, Philips and Wainwright, (eds) p. 472.
50. Voigt, "War and Congress", p. 351-354.
51. Majumdar, *History of the Freedom Movement*, p. 597.
52. Ibid p. 597
53. Bose, Subhash Chandra, *The Indian Struggle-1920-1942*, (Bombay: Asia Publishing House, 1964), p. 341.
54. Sahni, *The Lid Off*, p. 151.
55. Voigt, "War and Congress," p. 352.
56. Azad, *India Wins Freedom*, pp. 26-30; Bartarya, *Nationalist Movement*, pp. 216-17; Coupland, *Report on the Constitutional Problem in India*, (London : Oxford University Press, 1944), Part II, p. 215.
57. Bartarya, *Nationalist Movement*, p. 217.
58. Voigt, "War and Congress", p. 352.
59. Ibid pp. 352-53.
60. Zetland, "Memorandum for War Cabinet," W.P. (G) (39) 53, 23 Sept. 1939, PRO, Cab 67/2, Ibid. p. 353.
61. Venkatachar, "1937-47 In Retrospect", p. 485.
62. Kulkarni, *India and Pakistan*, pp. 328-35.
63. Kabir, Humayun, *Muslim Politics 1906-47 and Other Essays*, (Calcutta: Firma K.L. Mukhopadyay, 1969), p. 46.

64. Mukerjee, *India's Struggle for Freedom*, p. 217.
65. Kabir, *Muslim Politics*, p. 47.
66. Nanda, B.R. "Nehru, The Indian National Congress and the Partition of India, 1935-47", In : *Partition of India*, Philips, (ed.), p. 186.
67. Kabir, *Muslim Politics*, p. 47.
68. Ibid. p. 47.
69. Zaidi, A.M. (chief ed.,) Shaheda Ghufran Zaidi, (ed.), and others, *Evaluation of Muslim Political Thought in India*, In : *The Demand for Pakistan*, (New Delhi : S. Chand and Company, 1978), Vol. V, pp. 182-83; Matlubul Hasan Saiyid, *Mohammad Ali Jinnah* (A Political Study), (Lahore : S. M. Ashraf, 1945), pp. 647-651; Guha, *India's Struggle*, pp. 435-436.
70. Ibid (Guha), p. 436; Zaidi, *Demand for Pakistan*, p. 182; See also Saiyid, *Jinnah*, pp. 648-49.
71. Zaidi, *Demand for Pakistan*, pp. 183-4; Guha, *India's Struggle*, p. 436; Saiyid, *Jinnah*, pp. 650-52.
72. Wallbank, *History of India and Pakistan*, p. 192.
73. Tomlinson, *Congress and Raj*, p. 142.
74. "They were oblivious to the difference in these circumstances between a Britain fighting for her life and India—a spectator at the ringside. They forgot the disastrous results of this policy in Ireland in the First World War and its nearly fatal effects in India," Spear, *History of India*, p. 217.
75. Tomlinson, *Congress and Raj*, pp. 142-143.
76. Bahadur, Lal, *The Muslim League: Its History, Activities and Achievements* (Agra : Agra Book Store, 1954), p. 254.
77. Chhabra, G.S. *Advanced Study in the History of Modern India, 1920-47*. 2nd edn. (New Delhi : Sterling Publishers Pvt. Ltd, 1977), Vol. III, p. 122.
78. Moore, R.J. "The Problem of Freedom with Unity : London's India Policy, 1917-47", In : *Congress and Raj*, Low (ed.), p. 384; Chhabra, *Advanced Study*, pp. 122-23.
79. Nanda, B.R., "Nehru, Congress and the Partition", p. 164.
80. Pandey, B.N. *The Break-up of British India* (London: Macmillan, 1969), pp. 149-150.
81. Edwardes, *The Last Years*, p. 79.
82. Tara Chand, *History of the Freedom Movement*, pp. 280-81.
83. Gandhi, Nehru, Rajendra Prasad, Bose, Jinnah, Savarkar, Ambedkar and others.
84. Sitaramayya, Pattabhi, *The History of the Indian National Congress, 1935-1947*, (Bombay: Padma Publications, 1947), Vol.

II, p. 136.
85. Voigt, "War and Congress", p. 353.
86. Tomlinson, *Congress and Raj,* p. 144.
87. Voigt, "War and Congress", p. 353.
88. Sarkar, Sumit, *Modern India 1885-1947*, (Delhi : Macmillan India Ltd., 1983), p. 376; see Coupland, *Constitutional Problem* Vol. II, p. 217; and also Chhabra, *History of Modern India,* p. 123.
89. Voigt, "War and Congress", p. 353.
90. Moore, R. J. "British Policy and the Indian Problem 1936-40", In: *Partition of India,* Philips (ed.), pp. 85-86.
91. Sitaramayya, *History of Congress,* Vol. II, p. 138.
92. Sarkar, *Modern India,* p. 375.
93. Tomlinson, *Congress and Raj,* pp. 143-44.
94. Linlithgow to Zetland, October 22, 1939, Z.C. cited by R.J. Moore, "British Policy and the Indian Problem" p. 86.
95. Sarkar, *Modern India,* p. 376.
96. *The Indian National Congress Report of the General Secretary,* March, 1939—February, 1940, p. 38; See also Saiyid, *Jinnah,* p. 677.
97. Spear, *History of India,* p. 217.
98. Philips, *Partition of India,* p. 25.
99. Spear, *History of India,* p. 217.
100. Philips, *Partition of India,* p. 25.
101. Nehru, Jawaharlal *The Unity of India,* p. 314.
102. Philips, *Partition of India,* p. 25.
103. Kulkarni, *India and Pakistan,* pp. 334-35.
104. Ibid. p. 330.
105. Nanda, "Nehru, Congress and the Partition", p. 165.
106. Wallbank, *History of India and Pakistan,* p. 194.
107. *The New Chronicle,* (London, December 11, 1939), cited by Ibid.
108. Bahadur, Lal, *Muslim League,* pp. 255-56.
109. Guha, *India's Struggle,* p. 439.
110. Zaidi, *Demand for Pakistan,* p. 184.
111. Guha, *India's Struggle,* p. 439.
112. Wallbank, *History of India and Pakistan,* pp. 194-95.
113. Saiyid, *Jinnah,* p. 679.
114. Bahadur, Lal, *Muslim League,* pp. 256-57, and citations therein; "though Jinnah later on modified his original communal cry, the Day was observed all the same" Ibid. p. 257.
115. Moore, "British Policy" p. 86.
116. Guha, *India's Struggle,* p. 439.
117. Chhabra, *Modern India,* p. 123.

118. Saiyid, *Jinnah*, p. 676.
119. Ibid. pp. 674-75; see also Chhabra, *Modern India*, p. 123.
120. Moore, "British Policy" p. 86.
121. Saiyid, *Jinnah*, p. 677.
122. Guha, *India's Struggle*, pp. 439-40.
123. Peerzada, Syed Sharifuddin, *Leaders' Correspondence with Mr. Jinnah*, p. 2.
124. Kulkarni, *India and Pakistan*, p. 338.
125. Ibid, p. 338.
126. Peerzada, *Correspondence*, p.6; Kulkarni, *India and Pakistan*, p. 338.
127. Zaidi, *Demand for Pakistan*, p. 187.
128. Peerzada, *Correspondence*, p. 14; Kulkarni, *India and Pakistan*, pp. 338-39; Menon, V.P. *The Transfer of Power in India* (Princeton New Jersey : Princeton University Press, 1957), p. 85.
129. Chhabra, *Modern India*, p. 124.
130. Sayeed, K.B. *Pakistan : The Formative Phase 1857-1948*. 2nd edn. (London : Oxford Univ. Press, 1968), p. 99.
131. Tomlinson, *Congress and Raj*, p. 145, citing from *Indian Annual Register 1939*, Vol. II, pp. 243-45; see also Guha, *India's Struggle*, p. 439.
132. Sayeed, *Pakistan*, p. 99.
133. Tomlinson, *Congress and Raj*, p. 145.
134. Sayeed, *Pakistan*, p. 99; see also Saiyid, *Jinnah*, p. 678.
135. *Indian Annual Register 1939* Vol. II. p. 418, cited by Tara Chand, *History of the Freedom Movement*, p. 282.
136. Guha, *India's Struggle*, p. 440.
137. Ibid, pp. 440-441.
138. Moore, "British Policy", p. 86.
139. Tomlinson, *Congress and Raj*, p. 144.
140. Ibid p. 144.
141. Voigt, "War and Congress", pp. 354-55.
142. Moore, "British Policy", pp. 86-87.
143. Padmasha, *Indian National Congress and the Muslims 1928-1947*, (New Delhi : Rajesh Publications, 1980), p. 239.
144. Moore, "British Policy", pp. 86-87.
145. Padmasha, *Congress and the Muslims*, p. 239, cited from *The Hindustan Times* (New Delhi : February, 1, 1973).
146. Moore, "British Policy", p. 87.
147. Ibid, pp. 87-88.
148. Guha, *India's Struggle*, p. 443.
149. Tomlinson, *Congress and Raj*, p. 144; see also Guha, *India's*

Struggle, p. 443.
150. Tomlinson, *Congress and Raj*. p. 145.
151. Guha, *India's Struggle*, p. 443.
152. Rao, Shiva, "India, 1935-47", In : *Partition of India*, Philips, (ed.), p. 423.
153. Tomlinson, *Congress and Raj*, p. 145, cited from Moore, "British Policy", p. 88.
154. Moore, "British Policy", p. 88; see also Tomlinson, *Congress and Raj*, p. 145.
155. Nanda, "Nehru and Partition", p. 165; see also Kulkarni, *India and Pakistan*, p. 335.
156. Ibid. (Kulkarni) p. 335.
157. Nanda, "Nehru and Partition", p. 165.
158. Kulkarni *India and Pakistan*, p. 335.
159. Spear, *History of India*, p. 218.
160. Nanda, "Nehru and Partition", p. 165.
161. Sayeed, K.B. "The Personality of Jinnah and his Political Strategy", In : *Partition of India*, Philips (ed.) p. 286. For Jinnah's political strategy, see Ibid. p. 283.
162. Prakasah, Sri. *Pakistan : Birth and Early Days*, pp. 5-7, cited by Chhabra, *Modern India*, p. 124.
163. Padmasha, *Congress and Muslims*, p. 181: "Though it was expected that with the resignation of Congress ministries, the communal tension would decrease and favourable atmosphere created for efforts to compose all internal differences." Ibid. p. 182.
164. Ram Gopal, *Indian Muslims: A Political History (1858-47)*, (Bombay : Asia Publishing House, 1959), p. 267.
165. "On account of a crude combination in the country's leadership of legal sophistry and political shortsightedness, a magnificent opportunity was lost", Mukerjee, *India's Struggle*, pp. 119-20.
166. Khan, Mohammed Raza, *What Price Freedom, A Historical Survey of the Political Trends and Conditions Leading to Independence and the Birth of Pakistan and After* (Madras : The Nuri Press Ltd., 1969), p. 53.
167. Chhabra, *Modern India*, p. 124.
168. Nanda, "Nehru and Partition", p. 166.
169. Saiyid, *Jinnah*, pp. 673-74.
170. Tara Chand, *History of the Freedom Movement*, p. 286.
171. Nanda, "Nehru and Partition", p. 166.
172. Sayeed, *Jinnah's Strategy*, p. 285.

173. Zaidi, *Demand for Pakistan*, p. 78; Saiyid, *Jinnah*, pp. 605-6.
174. Kulkarni, *India and Pakistan, pp. 335-37.*
175. Ibid, p. 337.
176. Rao, Shiva "India, 1935-47", p. 458.
177. Choudhry Khaliquzzaman, *Pathway to Pakistan*, (Lahore: Longman Pakistan Branch, 1961), pp. 204-206; see Tara Chand, *History of the Freedom Movement*, p. 285.
178. Sayeed, *Pakistan*, pp. 114-15.
179. Khaliquzzaman, *Pathway to Pakistan*, p. 211.
180. Ibid. pp. 207-08.
181. Tara Chand, *History of the Freedom Movement*, p. 285.
182. Moore, "London's India Policy", p 383; "Before 1926, 'Dominion Status' had still implied a measure of subordination to the British Parliament, but then Balfour had explicitly defined the Dominion as "autonomous communities within the British Empire, equal in status, in no way subordinate to another in any aspect of their domestic or external affairs, though united by a common allegiance to the Crown, and freely associated as members of the British Commonwealth of Nations, Ibid; Lord Winterton noted, Now "Dominion Status" has a very special meaning (especially since the Imperial Conference of 1926), cited by Ibid, p. 383.
183. Ibid, p. 383-84.
184. Moore, "British Policy", p. 88; Moore, "London's India Policy", p. 384.
185. Rao, Shiva "India, 1935-47", p. 423.
186. Tomlinson, *Congress and Raj*, p. 145.
187. *The Hindustan Times* (New Delhi: February, 1, 1973), cited by Padmasha, *Congress and Muslims*, p. 239.
188. Tomlinson, *Congress and Raj*, p. 146.
189. Rao, Shiva, "India, 1935-47," p. 423.
190. Moore, "British Policy," p. 88.
191. Moore, "London's India Policy," p. 384.
192. Moore, "British Policy," p. 84.
193. Tara Chand, *History of the Freedom Movement*, p. 286.
194. Ibid. p. 286.
195. Guha, *India's Struggle*, p. 443.
196. Voigt, "War and Congress", p. 349.
197. Moore, "British Policy", pp. 84-85.
198. Nanda, "Nehru and Partition", p. 166.
199. Tara Chand, *History of the Freedom Movement*, p. 286.
200. Ibid, p. 287.

201. Kulkarni, *India and Pakistan*, pp. 331-32.
202. Ibid. p. 333.
203. Venkatachar, C.S., "1937-47, in Retrospect : A Civil Servant's View", In : *Partition of India*, Philips (ed.), p. 473.
204. Tomlinson, *Congress and Raj*, p. 144.
205. Venkatachar, "1937-47 in Retrospect," p. 473.
206. Spear, Percival, *India : A Modern History*, (Ann Arbor : The University of Michigan Press, 1961), p. 401.
207. Ibid. p. 402.
208. Ibid. p. 402.
209. Viceroy as Lord Irwin, April 1926-April 1931.
210. Moore, "India's Paper Federation", p. 55.
211. Kulkarni, *India and Pakistan*, p. 332.
212. Spear, *India*, p. 403.
213. Sayeed, "Jinnah Strategy", pp. 286-87; see Sayeed, *Pakistan*, p. 100.
214. Choudhuri, K.N. "Economic Problems and Indian Independence" In : *Partition of India*, Philips (ed.) p. 309.
215. Venkatachar, "1937-47 in Retrospect," p. 473.
216. Venkatachar, "1937-47 in Retrospect," p. 473.
217. Zaidi, Z. H. "Aspects of the Development of Muslim League Policy, 1937-47," In : *Partition of India*, Philips (ed.), pp. 261-62.
218. Ibid. pp. 262-63.
219. Mukerjee, *India's Struggle*, p. 218.
220. Ibid. pp. 218-219.
221. Ibid. p. 219.
222. Moore, "British Policy" pp. 92-93.
223. Kulkarni, *India and Pakistan*, p. 340.
224. Moore, "British Policy," p. 93.
225. Mukerjee, *Recalling Freedom*, p. 102; "To say this is, by no means, to exonerate Indian responsibility. 'Divide and Rule' has always been the way of empires." Ibid.
226. Moore, "British Policy," pp. 93-94.

Chapter 6

Lahore Conference and After

The Muslim League now spoke in no uncertain voice and finally chose the most extreme proposal. The rapid growth of this idea which was scoffed at as chimerical by the Muslim leaders themselves only seven years before, "may be regarded as the most remarkable thing in contemporary Muslim politics."[1] In February 1940, Jinnah in a Press statement said that the constitutional settlement must proceed on the assumption that India was not one nation but two, and that the Muslims would not submit to the arbitration of anybody, but would themselves determine their political destiny.[2] He was preparing the Muslim mind for his theory that Muslims could not remain happy under one central government.

Blinded by its own political ideology, the Congress looked at the communal problem as a British creation, and as representatives of the majority community, failed to understand the true nature of minority fears. Merely a few safeguards provided in the constitution could not win the confidence of the Muslims, for a strongly entrenched government can always get round and nullify safeguards, however elaborately built in. The explosive situation called for skilful handling. The Muslim League was not prepared to leave their security to an uncertain future in the hands of a party which had done very little to win their trust and goodwill and which had arrogated to itself all political power and authority.

While the Congress insisted that a constituent assembly would be the answer to the communal problem, the Muslim League feared that it (the constituent assembly) would be confronted with the same issues and problems which had kept the leaders divided. Jinnah said: "Mr. Gandhi is pleased suddenly to stand for a Constituent Assembly, which, in the present condition of India, will mean a second and larger edition of the Congress." Or, "The Assembly proposed by Mr. Gandhi would at best, ... be a packed body manoeuvred and managed by the Congress caucus."[3]

When the German batteries were thundering against the Maginot Line, Jinnah called the Annual Session of the All-India Muslim League at Lahore March 22, 1940. There was expectation in the air that something momentous and important was going to be decided or demanded at the conference.[4] But none had any inkling, and everybody was left only to guess.

"There was a record gathering at the conference.... Madras was well-represented by a strong contingent of delegates. Janab Sattar Sait, the late Abdul Hameed Khan, Maulana Abdul Lateef Farooki, M. R. Wahid and the author were present at the open conference. It was impossible for Sir Sikandar to come through the main gate; he came from behind the dais and the audience shouted him down. His very presence evoked so much hostile demonstration that he had to stay away from the conference."[5] Jinnah, at the outset traced the events that led to the stand of the Muslim League vis-a-vis the war. He then spoke about his talks with the Viceroy, his demand that the whole constitution of India should be considered *de novo*, and the recognition by the Government that the League alone represented the Muslim masses. "Finally he pointed out how the Congress and its leadership were exploiting the opportunity provided by the war to secure complete power for the party and holding out the threat of a *satyagraha* before the Government."[6]

"In the course of his speech," states Mohamed Raza Khan, "Mr. Jinnah exploited to great advantage the letter written by Lala Lajpat Rai to Mr. C.R. Das which stated, it comes to this that although we can be united against the British we cannot do so to rule Hindustan on democratic lines."[7]

"The Subjects Committee of the League which met as late as

3. a.m.," to quote the same authority, "agreed upon the principle of partition. No doubt the council members from the minority provinces had their own doubts which were however cleared by the President."[8] The resolution moved by Fazlul Haq, Premier of Bengal, and seconded by Choudhry Khaliquzzaman and also to be supported by representatives from every province, was approved, Jinnah put the claim for a separate homeland for the Muslims. By the midnight of March 1940, the resolution was adopted with great enthusiasm. It was :

> Resolved that it is the considered view of this Session of the All-India Muslim League that no constitutional plan would be workable in this country or acceptable to the Muslims unless it is designed on the following basic principles, viz. that geographically contiguous units are demarcated into regions which should be so constituted, with such territorial readjustments as may be necessary, that the areas in which the Muslims are numerically in a majority as in the North-West and Eastern Zones of India, should be grouped to constitute "Independent States" in which the constituent units should be autonomous and sovereign.[9]

"This was a definite demand for the partition of India on a communal basis." Jinnah admitted that it was a "terrible solution" but averred that it was "the only one".[10]

The Lahore Resolution was subjected to searching analyses, critical discussions and debates. The expression "States" (in plural)[11] had been used in the resolution : some comments were made regarding the alleged ambiguity, thereof, specially whether the resolution contemplated one or more Muslim States. Dr. Ambedkar wrote : "It speaks of grouping the zones into 'independent states' in which the constituent units shall be autonomous and sovereign. The use of the terms 'constituent units' indicates that what is contemplated is a Federation. If that is so then the use of the word 'sovereign' as an attribute of the units is out of place. Federation of units and sovereignty of units are contradictions."[12] Prof. Coupland says: It could scarcely mean that the constituent units of the independent states were really to be sovereign, but that it did mean that the states were to be independent.[13]

No doubt the resolution was somewhat vague. Jinnah was criticized for not giving a clear picture of all the details of his Pakistan scheme. But, again, it seems that Jinnah knew what he was doing. In 1940, with the war going on, his main object was to mobilize and maximize his support among the Muslims. Inspired by this ideal of a separate Muslim state, a Muslim peasant or a city dweller in areas like the Punjab and Bengal, could hold his head high even though his material possessions were meagre and cash low as compared to the more prosperous Hindus. Jinnah had been looking for support in Punjab and Bengal. In an interview with the *Associated Press of America* in 1940, Jinnah explained and clarified the proposed Muslim State of Pakistan as follows :

> Geographically—Pakistan would embrace all of the North-West Frontier, Baluchistan, Sind and the Punjab provinces in the North-Western India. On the Eastern side of India would be the other portion of Pakistan of Bengal and Assam.
>
> Politically—Pakistan would be a democracy. Jinnah said that he personally hoped its major industrial and public utility services would be socialized. The component states or provinces of Pakistan would have autonomy.
>
> Economically—Pakistan divided into two separate zones... would be just as sound an undertaking as if it were a country with all of its States in one block; its natural resources and population would be sufficient to make it a great World Power.
>
> Most Powerful State—Pakistan would embrace a population of some one hundred million persons ... would ... become one of the most powerful States economically ... a Muslim League Committee was studying the field for developing the Pakistan State as a nation ... there was a great future for it with its still untouched iron, petroleum, sulphur, coal and other mineral deposits many of which had already been mapped, ... the Punjab was putting up one of the greatest hydro-electric stations in the world which would mean a programme for the rural electrification and industrial development.
>
> Financial Position—There would be ample revenues from "equitable taxation levied in a manner consistent with social justice" to finance good government and to allow the Muslims to have a state as good as any in the world and better than

many sovereign countries on the map of the world today.[14]

Linlithgow refused to take the claim of Pakistan seriously :

> I do not attach too much importance to Jinnah's demands for the carving out of India into an indefinite number of religious areas ... And I would judge myself that his attitude at the moment is that, as the Congress are putting forward a preposterous claim which they know is incapable of acceptance, he equally will put forward just as extreme a claim.[15]

It was, Linlithgow judged, "merely put forward... for bargaining purposes." He may have been right. But the important point is that once the Congress and the League had taken up their extreme positions of March 1940, they could not recede without loss of face. Furthermore, the longer, the more tenaciously these positions were stuck to, the greater the number of their firm adherents.

As long as Congress ministries remained in office, the League derived and extended its power by resistance to and negation of Congress rule, but when Congress ministries resigned over the war issue, negation alone left the League static. For this reason as well as any other. Jinnah and his co-adjutors had inevitably to unfold a positive procedure. The circumstances too were propitious: Congress was out of office, the government hard pressed by war, was looking for friends, the federation was shelved, and there was a clear indication of the transfer of power at the termination of war.

The news of the adoption of the resolution was flashed all over the world. Khaliquzzaman recalls : "The next morning the Hindu Press came out with big headlines 'Pakistan Resolution Passed,' although the word was not used by anyone in the speeches nor in the body of the Resolution[16]. The Hindu Press had thus supplied to the Muslim masses a slogan which immediately conveyed to them the idea of a State.... Years of labour of the Muslim leaders to propagate its full import ... were shortened by the Hindu Press in sarcastically calling the resolution as 'The Pakistan Resolution.' "[17]

The Indian press made the following comments :

> *The Hindustan Times* wrote : "History has made Muslims and Hindus in India into one people, which even the ingenuity of

the most ingenious constitution-mongers will be unable to divide. To break up the unity of India is not to satisfy the ambitions of this community or that, but ruin the peace and prosperity of the people of this country as a whole. This is a solution which the Muslim community as a whole will reject, whatever the League and its leaders do." *The Amrit Bazar Patrika* considered it to be an absurd scheme. "If the Muslims cannot live as a minority community under an All-India Government can they expect the Hindus to live under a Muslim majority? What is Mr. Jinnah going to do with the non-Muslim majority? What is Mr. Jinnah going to do with the non-Muslim minorities in the Muslim States? Unless he is prepared to make them magically disappear ... Can millions and millions of people be ... transplanted? We pause for a reply."

The Statesman, on the other hand, found Pakistan a live issue. "If India receives Dominion Status, partition seems the inevitable result in view of the attitude which the Muslim community appears ... to adopt ... If both sides will face realities and discuss them without passion, Mother India can yet be saved."[18]

Some of the comments of the British Press were :

The Times held the Congress policy responsible for the emergence of Muslims as a separate nation, but disfavoured the Pakistan proposal as "it would mean an end to Indian unity" (27 March, 1940). *The New Statesman's* opinion was that the Indians did not divide on the lines of creed but on economic lines and that communal division had been recognized and exaggerated by the white rulers for their own ends (30 March, 1940). The *Observer* appreciated that a new phase of the Indian problem had opened and read in it the implied warning that the Congress must revise its policy of "a crude democratic consultation" for all India if it wanted other Indian communities to cooperate with it (31 March, 1943). *The Economist* contented itself with saying that it was foolish to suppose, as the Congress did, that divisions of race and culture, which had created fundamental political cleavages all over the world, would India be slurred over by denying their existence (30 March, 1940). For the *Manchester Guardian* Mr. Jinnah, by getting the resolution passed, had "re-established the reign of chaos in Indian politics," the plan struck at the heart of Indian nationalism; (2 April, 1940). *Nature* gave a favourable comment. It concluded : "However impracticable the Muslim demand may be, no solution will secure the future of India in world affairs or internally which attempts to ignore or override ... fundamental differences of culture and tradition.'[19]

Various religious and political organizations of the Muslims opposed the idea of a separate Islamic state, such as two Muslim religious parties, the *Jama'at-i-islami* of Maulana Saiyad Abul'ala Maudodi and *Jamiat-ul-Ulama-i-Hind.* The latter was greatly influenced by Maulana Abul Kalam Azad.[20]

The Congress did not formally express its attitude to the demand for Pakistan until April 1942, and then, too, indirectly. Maulana Azad and some other Congressmen thought that the Lahore Resolution was not serious but just a ruse by Mr. Jinnah to get concessions from the Congress.[21] It was not taken seriously. "The only person who has made any serious attempt to criticize the Lahore Resolution", said Jinnah, "is Mr. Rajagopalacharya."[22] But the climate of Congress opinion was largely created by Gandhi and Nehru. In response to the Muslim League resolution Gandhi wrote in April 1940 :

> Unless the rest of India wishes to engage in internal fratricide, the others will have to submit to the Muslim dictation, if the Muslims will resort to it. I know no non-violent method of compelling the obedience of eight crores of Muslims to the will of the rest of India, however powerful a majority the rest may represent. The Muslims must have the right of self-determination that the rest of India has. We are at present a joint family. Any member may claim a division.[23]

Again in the same month he wrote :

> As a man of non-violence, I cannot forcibly resist the proposed partition if the Muslims of India really insist upon it. But I never can be a willing party to the vivisection.... My whole soul rebels against the idea that Hinduism and Islam represent two antagonistic cultures and doctrines... But that is my belief. I cannot thrust it down the throats of the Muslims who think that they are a different nation.[24]

During the same period Nehru's response to the "Pakistan Resolution" was to say that "if people wanted such things as suggested by the Muslim League at Lahore, then one thing was clear; they and people like him could not live together in India. He would be prepared to face all consequences of it but he would not be prepared to live with such people."[25] On another occasion Nehru was reported to have remarked : "Many knots of the Hindu-Muslim problem had been merged into one knot, which could not be unravelled by ordinary methods, but would need an operation ... he would say one thing very frankly, that he had begun to consider them (Muslim Leaguers) and people like himself, as separate nations."[26]

Commenting upon the Congress reaction to the League demand C.H. Philips aptly remarks :

> The practical effect of both taking and announcing this attitude towards the Pakistan movement was drastically to reduce Congress's power of manoeuvre vis-a-vis the Muslim League, and to place total emphasis on persuasion and negotiation, without reference to Congress's power in the land.[27]

The annoyance and distress caused in Congress circles by the "Lahore Resolution" was not unmixed with a certain amount of relief. Nehru was reported to have remarked that, instead of feeling sorry at the Muslim League's new demand, "he was pleased, not because he liked it—on the contrary he considered it to be the most insane suggestion—but because it very much simplified the problem. They were now able to get rid of the demands about proportionate representation in legislatures, services, cabinets, etc."[28]

B. R. Nanda observes :

> The 'Pakistan Resolution' ... gave a new twist to the communal problem. All the solutions hitherto thought of—separate electorates, composite cabinets, reservation of posts—suddenly became out of date.[29]

To Nehru "all the old problems ... pale into insignificance before the latest stand taken by the Muslim League leaders at Lahore. The whole problem has taken a new complexion and there is no question of settlement or negotiations now."[30]

The year 1940 may be called a turning point in the history of India's struggle for freedom. Regarding the situation in 1940, B.R. Nanda makes the following observation :

> In the spring of 1940, most serious observers of the Indian scene would have described the Pakistan plan as 'chimerical and impractical', words used by prominent Muslim witnesses before the joint parliamentary committee in August 1933. (mentioned earlier). Even after the Pakistan proposal had been embodied in a resolution of the All India Muslim League, it was no more than a political phantom. It was left to the spokesmen of the British government to give it body and soul.[31]

It is difficult to agree with the above analysis. Certainly the "Pakistan Plan" in 1940 was not *as* "chimerical and impractical" as it appeared to the Muslim delegates before the joint parliamentary committee in 1933. Much water had flown under Hoogli during the seven years. In his anxiety to exonerate Nehru and his associates, Nanda finds it convenient to throw the entire blame on the British government.

The role played by Abul Kalam Azad who became the President of the Congress from 3rd September 1939, deserves critical assessment. "In fact, Maulana Azad's presidentship of the Congress...," says Raza Khan, "was the most crucial period in the history of India and he was responsible for the failure of a settlement between the Hindus and the Muslims."[32] Azad occupied a peculiar position, a great Muslim enjoying the top Congress position. Perhaps he could have exerted vigorously and tactfully in appeasing the Muslims.[33]

NOTES AND REFERENCES

1. Majumdar, op. cit. p. 268.
2. Gopal, op. cit., p. 268.
3. Sharma, Jagadish Saran, (ed.), *India's Struggle for Freedom—Select Documents and Sources* (Delhi : S. Chand and Co., 1962), Vol. I., pp. 586-87.
4. Khan, Raza, op. cit., p. 60.
5. Ibid., p. 63. Sikandar Hayat Khan was averse to the idea of partition: hence, his unpopularity with the Muslim masses who were by this time completely under the spell of Jinnah. "Sir Sikandar placed before the Congress leaders the following proposal in the spring of 1940: 'His Majesty's Government should make a declaration making it clear that India's status would be that of a self-governing Dominion in accordance

with the Statute of Westminster. So be left to Indian themselves to formulate a scheme by mutual agreement, Shiva Rao, op. cit., p. 425. According to Humayun Kabir, the sudden death of Sikandar Hayat removed one of Jinnah's strongest opponents, Kabir, "Muslim Politics, 1942-47", Philips, *"Partition Policies and Perspectives,"* op. cit, p. 390.

6. Khan, Raza, op. cit., p. 63.
7. Ibid, p. 65.
8. "Replying to the critics of the League's resolution, Mr. Jinnah said : 'In the first place, a wrong idea and false propaganda appear to be setting in motion in order to frighten the Muslim minorities that they would have to migrate *en bloc* and wholesale. I wish to assure my Muslim brethren that there is no justification for this insidious misrepresentation. Exchange of population, however, on the physical division of India as far as practicable will have to be considered. Secondly, the Muslim minorities are wrongly made to believe that they would be worse off and be left in the lurch in any scheme of partition or division of India. I may explain that the Musalmans, wherever they are in a minority, cannot improve their position under a united India or under one central government. Whatever happens, they should remain a minority. They can rightly demand all the safeguards that are known to any civilised government to the utmost extent. But by coming in the way of the division of India they do not and cannot improve their own position. On the other hand, they can, by their attitude of obstruction, bring the Muslim homeland and 60,000,000 of the Musalmans under one government, where they would remain no more than a minority in perpetuity." "It was because of the realization of this fact that the Musalman minorities in Hindu India readily supported the Lahore Resolution. In my opinion, after the present tension created by the ambition of one community dominating over the other and establishing supremacy over all the rest is ceased, we shall find better understanding and goodwill created all round. The division of India will throw a great responsibility upon the majority in its respective zones to create a real sense of security amongst the minorities and win their complete trust and confidence. Ahmed, *Recent Speeches of Jinnah* op. cit., pp. 182-84. Jinnah did not make it clear how and why the division of India will throw a great responsibility upon the majority, *to create a real sense of security amongst the minorities and win their*

complete trust and confidence, when the same was deemed impossible in a united India? In a divided India, minorities and majorities would be still more sharply pronounced. Evidently the whole reasoning of Jinnah is illogical.

9. Ahmed, "Historic Documents", op. cit., p. 382. For details, vide Syed Sharifuddin Peerzada, *Evolution of Pakistan,* "Lahore Resolution" (Lahore : All Pakistan Legal Decisions, 1963), pp. 195-209. For the text of the Resolution, vide appendix. Peerzada, Ibid, p. 127.
10. Recently it has been alleged that the word "States" in the Lahore Resolution was a misprint. Khaliquzzaman states that at the Delhi Convention of the Muslim League held in 1946, Abul Hashim had raised the question as to the word "States" and Mr. Jinnah ruled that "States" was a misprint. Vide Khaliquzzaman, *"Pathway to Pakistan"*, op. cit. p. 344.
11. Recalling the proceedings of the Convention, Mr. Ispahani writes : "The Qaid-i-Azam said that the word 'States' was a mistake and had cropped up probably as a result of a typographical error. It was then stated that even the published records of the Central Office of the All India Muslim League carried the word in plural. The Qaid-i-Azam replied what really mattered was the intention and not the word. In fact, he directed that the records be certified." (The official records do not corroborate the versions about the alleged ruling of Mr. Jinnah), Ispahani, A.H. *Qaid-i-Azam Jinnah, As I Know Him* (Karachi : Ferozsons Ltd., 1967), p. 144.
12. Ambedkar, B.R., *Thought on Pakistan* (Bombay: Thacker Co., 1941), p. 17.
13. Coupland, R. *Indian Politics,* (London: Oxford University Press, 1944), Part II, p. 206.
14. Rajput, op cit, pp. 75-76.
15. 'Linlithgow to Zetland', March 25, 1940, Z.C. quoted in Moore, op. cit., p. 93.
16. Hasan, Syed Riyaz, In : *Pakistan Naguzir Tha,* p. 57, writes that Begum Mohammad Ali in her speech referred to the resolution as the Pakistan Resolution. This has not been substantiated by any other source.
17. Khaliquzzaman, op cit., p. 237.
18. Reproduced by M. Ashraf in *Pakistan,* (Delhi : *Adabistan,* 1940), pp. 100-106.
19. Reproduced in *"The History of the Freedom Movement"*, op. cit., Vol. IV, Part II, pp. 104-106.

20. Malik, Hafeez, *Moslem Nationalism in India and Pakistan,* (Washington DC : Public Affairs Press, 1963), p. 268.
21. Khan, Raza, op. cit., p. 80. Maulana Azad wrote : "Till perhaps Jinnah but in fighting for Pakistan, he had overreached himself." It is curious that this was what he thought three or four months before the partition and he reiterated it a decade after, in the year 1956 in his memoirs, vide Azad, *India Wins Freedom,* op cit., p. 214. In 1940 Azad declared: "I am part of the indivisible unity that is the Indian nationality, I am indispensable to this noble edifice and without me this splendid structure of India is incomplete." Azad was accused by many Muslims of hypocrisy. This was unjust. He was only guilty of expecting the Muslim nation to follow his change of heart. The pathos of the situation lies in the fact that after the 1920s he and the Muslim nation ceased to recognize each other. Malik op. cit., pp. 273-74.
22. *Document on the Foreign Relations of Pakistan—The Transfer of Power,* K, Sarwar Hasan (ed.), (Karachi: Pakistan Institute of International Affairs, 1966), "Extracts from the statement by M.A. Jinnah on the Lahore Resolution, March 31, 1940", p. 22. C. Rajagopalacharya opposed the resolution, describing it as cutting the body into two : *History of Freedom Movement,* op. cit. p. 103.
23. Tendulkar, D.C. *Mahatma : Life of Mohandas Karamchand Gandhi,* (Bombay: Karnatak Publishing House, 1952), Vol. V, pp. 333-34.
24. Ibid. pp. 336-37.
25. *Leader,* April 15, 1940 : cited by Mehrotra, op cit., pp. 210-11.
26. *Leader,* April 16, 1940: cited by Ibid, p. 210.
27. Philips, *Partition Policies and Perspectives,* op. cit., p. 26.
28. *Leader,* April 15, 1940: Cited by Mehrotra, op. cit., pp. 210.
29. Nanda, op. cit., p. 166.
30. *The Hindu,* March 27, 1940: Same authority states: "Rajagopalacharya called it "a medieval conception:" cited by Ibid, pp. 166-67."
31. Ibid, p. 167.
32. Khan, Raza, op. cit., p. 80. vide *supra,* p. 36.
33. In the words of Raza Khan : "Whatever the position and claim of the Congress as a national organisation, the issue to be solved was the Hindu-Muslim problem.... There were two Muslim leaders on either side trying to find a solution to it. Both Mr. Jinnah and Maulana Azad had no regard and respect

for each other. Azad was perhaps suffering from a complex that he, being a great scholar, well versed in Islamic Law and a typical Muslim in very sense of the term, had practically nc following while Mr. Jinnah, in a period of three years, had assumed complete control and leadership of the community. Thus there was a personal factor involved in the relations between the two leaders." Ibid, pp. 80-81.

Chapter 7

The U.P. Ministry Episode

Elections over, both the Congress and League were impelled to cast a hard look at the future. The constitutional hurdle was crossed but a grave political matter dogged the steps of the Congress. The constitution implied that while appointing the ministers, the Governors would not be oblivious of the claim of the minorities. But the matter could be controversial. Majority could import the members of the minority community belonging to the majority party in the legislature, for example the nationalist Muslims in the Congress. It would also signify the members of a minority elected by the communal electorate and belonging to a communal organisation like the Muslim League. The effects of this controversy were destined to be ominous.

The situation took a serious turn in U.P., a key province so far as Hindu-Muslim relations were concerned. The Muslims who constituted only 14 per cent of the population had played a leading role in the cultural and political development of this region for centuries. Until the recent elections the relations between the Congress and some of the important Muslim leaders were generally warm and friendly. The U.P. Muslim League was dissimilar to the other branches of the Party since it contained besides diehards, a good number of progressives.[1] The leadership of the League was in the hands of the old Khilafatists like Shaukat Ali and old Congressmen like Choudhry Khaliquzzaman. In the words of V.B. Kulkarni, "Its parliamentary board was made up of forward looking Muslims drawn from the Ahrars, the Jamiat-ul-Ulema, the Momins, the Shia Political Conference and the 'Pro-Congress

Muslim."[2] In its composition the old conservative and landlord element was no longer predominant. During the elections, the League fought the candidates of the Agriculturist Party, under the inspiration of Fazal Husain. It did not oppose the Congress candidates. The Provincial Congress leaders on their part had abstained from putting up Congress Muslim candidates against the League candidates and, in fact, had persuaded some Muslim Congressmen "to stand on the League ticket".[3] Though confident of challenging the landlord's influential position in the provincial government and legislature, the Congress was not anticipating a clear majority. Working on the assumption that a decisive majority in the U.P. legislature was out of question, the Congress Party had virtually formed a kind of alliance with the Muslim League against those who were pro-British or not dependable as nationalist, who belonged to no particular party but hoped to win the election and thereby capitalize in the political field, thus lending moral support to one another. This understanding had engendered a working arrangement between the two organisations during the elections, so as to avoid confrontation between their respective candidates in certain constituencies. Jinnah expressed sentiments of goodwill towards the Congress, and was quite willing to cooperate with it on a national programme and declared, "Ours is not a hostile movement. Ours is a movement which carries the olive branch to our sister community."[4] In one speech he went to the extent of saying: "There is no difference between the ideals of the Muslim League and of the Congress, the idea being complete freedom for India. There could not be any self-respecting Indian who favoured foreign domination or did not desire complete freedom and self-government for his country."[5] Congress virtually admitted the League's claim to represent the Muslims and contenting itself barely with nine contests in Muslim constituencies, left all the rest to the Muslim League. Losing all the nine seats, its admission was fully confirmed. But for that matter, the League also did not fully vindicate the trust the Congress had placed in it having secured only 29 of the total 66 Muslim seats. Congress won most of the Hindu seats and was in a position to form a Ministry without the assistance of any other party or the independents. The attitude of the Congress leadership to the unofficial arrangement made with the League leaders gradually changed and as the negotiations over the appointment of Muslim Ministers were going on it became crystallized "that the Congress would dictate the terms of any agreement that was arrived at."[6] There was a gap of a few months between the election results and the assumption of office by the Congress in the provinces where it had secured majorities, as the constitutional obstacle by procuring Governor's assurance had to be straightened out. During the interval, interim non-Congress Ministries were inducted into office. In the meantime, a Muslim seat happened to fall vacant and since the understanding between provincial Congress and League leaders still held good, the former influenced the latter to leave the seat alone. This manoeuvre enabled the most prominent Congress Muslim, Rafi Ahmed Kidwai, who had been defeated in the general election, an easy victory.[7] He was the lone Muslim on the Congress benches in the U.P. Legislative Assembly. Thus with the help of the League, the Congress won the only Muslim seat in the Province.

When the election results became known, it was anticipated that approaches would be made for cooperation between the two bodies. The League put forward its claim for a share in the Ministry on the ground of its pre-election understanding with the Congress. Maulana Abul Kalam Azad has detailed in his memoirs the negotiations with the Muslim League in the formation of the Ministry in U.P. Choudhry Khaliquzzaman and Nawab Ismail Khan were then the leaders of the Muslim League in that Province. They assured Maulana Azad that not only would they cooperate with the Congress but fully support its programme. They naturally expected that the Muslim League would have some share in the new set up. "The local position was such," Azad would have not believed, "that neither of them could enter the Government alone. Either of them would have to accept Jawaharlal's offer."

Azad observes ruefully : "This was a most unfortunate

development. If the U.P. League's offer of cooperation had been accepted, the Muslim League Party would for all practical purposes have merged in the Congress. Jawaharlal's action gave the Muslim League in U.P. a new lease of life. All students of Indian Politics know that it was from the U.P. that the League was re-organised. Jinnah took full advantage of the situation and started an offensive which ultimately led to Pakistan."[8]

Apparently becoming wise with the Vantage Coign of Lindsight, Azad shifts the blame on Jawaharlal Nehru for this break.[9] But it was his idea to see that the Muslim League was dissolved and in return one or two Muslims got place in the Cabinet. If he had really felt that it was not a correct step, he could have suggested to the Congress to accept a sort of a coalition with the League. But that was not to be and the terms he himself offered to the League "do not vindicate", as Ram Gopal points out, "but implicate him". The terms were :

> "The Muslim League group in the United Provinces Legislature shall cease to function as a separate group. The existing members of the Muslim League Party in the U.P. Assembly shall become part of the Congress Party. They will be subject to the control and discipline of the Congress Party."
>
> The policy laid down by the Congress Working Committee for their members in the legislatures along with the instructions issued by the competent Congress bodies pertaining to their work in such legislatures shall be faithfully carried out by all members of the Congress Party including these members.
>
> The Muslim League Parliamentary Board in the United Provinces will be dissolved and no candidates will thereafter be set up by the said Board at any by-election. All members of the Party shall actively support any candidate that may be nominated by the Congress to fill up a vacancy occurring hereafter.[10]

This document was nothing but an ultimatum to surrender. No surprise the League leaders characterized this as the death warrant of "the League, which curiously enough, they of all people, were asked to sign". Was it, it was asked, for this that the League had assiduously built itself up as an all India organisation, issued an election manifesto, sought the support of the Muslim voters and contested the election? And having miserably failed to capture Muslim vote, was it morally appropriate for the Congress "to suggest that the Leaguers should virtually enter the Congress through the backdoor?" Why the Congress would not accommodate the League? No square answer to these questions was ever given, though observes Ram Gopal, "the anxiety of the Congress to make its actual form reflect its creed was an answer; but it was an answer which was naturally more repulsive to the League."[11]

The Congress in U.P. was undoubtedly, tactless in not taking two Leaguers into the Ministry, but in the opinion of C.S. Venkatachar, the distinguished Indian civil servant, the action of the Congress is not altogether unjustifiable. Let us follow Nehru's line of thinking in 1937: "He had had no understanding with Jinnah on an all India basis for a coalition with the League." In principle there was no case for such a coalition after the poor performance of the League and the magnificent success of the Congress at the polls. To Nehru, Ministry making was of secondary importance. Being the creation of the Congress they could be set aside any time. His attention was riveted on the impending contest with the British to wrest power at the centre. In this contest, the League Muslims' bonafides were questionable, as they did not share Congress ideology.

This was the reasoning on part of Nehru; these were theoretical considerations. They sound plausible. In action, Nehru was led, says Venkatachar, "by his friend Rafi Ahmed Kidwai, a curious influence in U.P. politics." Kidwai could not get elected straight away but was made to slip in and Nehru would not prevent his nationalist Muslim friend from the U.P. Ministry. "Nehru's attachment to his friend from U.P. led by winding and devious steps," states Venkatachar, "to the creation of Pakistan."[12]. In the opinion of Shiva Rao, if the Congress Party had stuck to its pre-election intention of forming a coalition Ministry, "the Hindu-Muslim problem might not have assumed formidable dimensions. But it preferred to exercise the right of forming a party government, since that was held to be the verdict of the electorate."[13]

A party government! That was another snag, a fresh one.

While the negotiations between the Congress and the U.P. Muslim League were in process, the idea of evolving the party system of government suggested itself to some of the Congress leaders. Eventually this view prevailed, and the final offer made to the League was on this basis, namely that Khaliquzzaman would be taken in the Cabinet provided he signed the Congress Party pledge. He refused arguing that the League as such should be represented in the Cabinet but agreeing that if that was done, he would not only acquiesce in the Congress programme, but persuade all the Leaguers in the Legislature to have common benches with the Congress Party. "That was the end of the negotiations", observes Ram Gopal, "and the beginning of extreme provocation."[14]

Nehru and the Congress had their reasons too for the stand they took. Nehru truly felt that communalism—the ogre let loose by the British—had been beaten at the polls. Unison with the League would revive it. Besides what was the sense in forming coalition when the Congress had secured an absolute majority? Why not take Congress Muslims? Congress feared that the induction of League members into the Cabinet would mar their cohesion. Nehru was eager that the Congress should introduce land reforms in the United Provinces and the League, which represented some big landowners, would be disinclined to the abolition of landlordism. The Congress was determined to give a fair deal to the common man. In pursuance of its socialist goal, the Congress was prepared to go to any length vending the Constitution if it proved non-resilient. Obviously the League would not have gone thus far. Further the Muslim League soon after the election seemed to be disintegrating. For instance in U.P., the Jamiat-ul-Ulema which had joined the League on the eve of the election deserted it and joined the Congress in May 1937.

The Congress procedure could be justified constitutionally and by normal parliamentary standards. The League contention however was that as the Muslim Ministers were being appointed not on account of their personal claims but as representatives of Muslims, they should be persons who commanded the confidence of the majority of the Muslim members of the Legislature.[15] The Congress' inability to accommodate the League was one of the most "distressing failures in the political history of India; it gave strength to the belief, held by some adventurous Muslim leaders, that the Muslims should have a separate homeland."[16]

The original conditions offered by Maulana Azad for including the League members in the Ministry were Khaliquzzaman maintained, tantamount to the suicide of the League. These were later modified and he was willing "to accept them provided the League Ministers were permitted to vote according to their conscience on communal matters." On this, the talks floundered.[17]

It seems that during the elections the Congress flirted with the League because it was not sure of its success in the elections. But with their spectacular victory the Congress, then had no more need to seek the assistance of the League for running governments. The fact that the League had fared badly in the Muslim majority provinces showed that it did not enjoy much hold on the Muslim community and desertions were already taking place in its ranks. Its support was thus of little consequence.

Moreover, Nehru asserted that Hindu-Muslim problem did not exist in the minds of the masses. It was cooked up by a few Muslim intellectual landlords and capitalists. He derided the idea of Muslims having any separate entity within Legislatures. Nehru claimed to have come into closer touch with the Muslim masses than most members of the Muslim League. He felt he knew "more about their hunger and poverty and misery than those who talk in terms of percentages and seats in the Councils and places in the State Service."[18] He wrote to Jinnah haughtily that there were only two forces in India at that time—British imperialism and the Congress representing Indian nationalism.[19] From this lofty pedestal, the Congress dictated its terms to the League.

Nehru or the Congress could have ameliorated the situation. The Muslims of the U.P. had great personal softness for Nehru, whom they considered their friend, an idealist in politics who due to naivete had been caught in the trap of communalist Hindus. "Even today", Venkatachar is prone to believe, "Nehru is entitled to the benefit of doubt on the

Ministry Question". Where he erred was in his failure to gauge the extent to which the faith and the confidence of the Muslims in the majority party had been shaken. They argued that if this was the behaviour of the Congress in the limited sphere of provincial autonomy, what could they expect when it would be at the citadel of the central Government.[20]

To quote V.P. Menon :

> When the Congress decided to accept office there was a proposal that it should form coalition ministries with the Muslim League.......the Congress decided to have homogeneous ministries of its own and chose Muslim Ministers from amongst those who were members of the Congress Party. This was the beginning of a serious rift between the Congress and the League and was a factor which induced neutral Muslim opinion to turn to the support of Jinnah."[21]

In the opinion of Prof. M. Mujeeb the Congress victory was overwhelming and a Ministry could be formed without the aid of any other party or the independents; so "the attitude of the Congress leadership to the informal arrangement made with the Muslim League leaders gradually changed" and as the negotiations proceeded, "it became more and more obvious that the Congress would dictate the terms of any agreement that was arrived at." As for the draft of the agreement proposed by Maulana Azad to be sent to Khaliquzzaman, Mujeeb reflects; "The immediate reaction on reading it was that the Muslim League was being asked to abolish itself. This was an attack not on the persons who wanted to become Ministers but on the whole class that had painfully organised itself and was still feeling very shaky." Jawaharlal Nehru made matters still worse, Mujeeb adds, by writing to the League president, that there were only two forces in India at that time—British Imperialism and Indian Nationalism. "It was very poor statesmanship that transformed a difference of opinion over a Ministerial post or two into a national struggle" in which a class felt that its very existence was at stake. "It would not have shattered Nehru's prestige if, because of him," Mujeeb affirms, "the Muslims had got one Ministerial post more than they were entitled to."[22] To cast a close look at the matter: Were the differences between the Congress and the League really substantial? The main points of differences were :

Although both the Congress and the League were ready to fight the election of 1937 to achieve full responsible self-government or *Swaraj*, there was a difference in their attitudes. The Congress would accept office in order to wreck the Constitution of 1935. The League would enter into office to work the Constitution for what it was worth. To Jinnah the Congress' attitude was hypocritical and unrealistic. He reminded that in the early 20's the Swaraj Party had put forward the same aim but rot in the party could not be stopped. Motilal Nehru's tremendous personality and prestige notwithstanding, some of his followers succumbed to official blandishments. Thus in practice, the conduct of the Swaraj Party negatived its profession. The subsequent functioning of the Congress Ministries in the provinces proved the truth of Jinnah's views. Concerning the Communal Award, the attitude of the Congress was ambiguous. The League wanted the award to be accepted provisionally and meanwhile efforts should be made to replace the award by a mutually acceptable settlement through negotiation. The greatest hit was the Congress' refusal to recognise the distinct entity of the Muslim League and with it the concomitant entity of the Muslim community as a political group or nationality.[23]

Obviously there were misunderstandings, hurdles and snags. These were not reduced by the Congress' attitude towards the setting up of a Ministry in the United Provinces.

Nor was the Congress' approach to the principle of the homogeneity of the cabinet unassailable. For it brought to the fore, the question whether the Congress was a political party or a national movement "In which groups with varying shades of opinion had collected together to achieve the object, viz. independence." In the words of Tara Chand : "There were to be found within its fold rightists like Malaviya, centrists like Patel and Rajendra Prasad, leftists like Jawaharlal Nehru, socialists like Jayaprakash Narayan and Narendra Dev and communists." It was very doubtful whether they all appreciated Jawaharlal's economic or land reform programme.[24]

Moreover, the idea of the Congress party in assuming office

in the year 1937, for the first time was not to work the parliamentary form of Government to perfection, but only to consolidate the warring elements within the country and try to satisfy the minorities, particularly the Muslims in order that they might join with it to exert pressure on the British to concede their demand of independence.[25]

It may be mentioned that even in England, the mother of Parliamentary system of government, "not absolute sanctity attaches to the principle of collective responsibility." Not to trace back on the basis of separate electorates and reservation of seats for Muslims, how could a party on the threshold of assumption of office demands the surrender of another party? It was a sordid deal to say the least.[26] The progressive conversion of the Congress into a Hindu organization contrary to the wishes of the best elements in that body "was attributed by some to communal electorates and by others to the lack of contact of Congressmen with the Muslims." But the broad fact that emerged on the conclusion of elections was that, observes Ram Gopal, on the one side stood the Congress with its Hindu seats and on the other the Muslim League trying to increase its members and asserting that no other Muslim or secular organisation had come to the fore to lay claim to Muslim representation.[27]

The Congress attitude towards the League was illustrated in a letter by the Congress President, Jawaharlal Nehru, to the League President M.A. Jinnah—referred to earlier—in January 1937: "In the final analysis there are only two forces in India today—British Imperialism and the Congress representing Indian nationalism... The Muslim League represents a group of Muslims no doubt highly estimable persons, but functioning in the higher regions of the upper middle classes and having no common contact with the Muslim masses and few with the Muslim lower middle class."[28] The League retorted that the Congress did not represent even the upper classes of Muslims, let alone the lower classes and affirmed that it alone could rightfully speak for the Muslims.[29]

On this ground, the League was aspiring for a share in the Ministries in Hindu majority provinces more so in U.P. when it had captured a sizable number of seats and where there had been a tacit understanding with Congress leaders. The League however was making its demand not so much on the strength of any alliance "as on a statutory provision", which according to its rights authorized Governors to choose Muslim Ministers from among Muslim representatives in the Assemblies."

According to Clause VIII of the Instruments of Instruction to the Provincial Governors, the Governor would select his Ministers "in consultation with the person who in his judgement is likely to command a stable majority in the legislature to appoint those persons (including so far as practicable members of important minority communities), who will best be in a position collectively to command the confidence of the legislature." But in so doing, he would do his best to promote a sense of joint responsibility among his Ministers.[30]

This instruction visualized a party system of Government, and accordingly Congress leaders in the Hindu majority provinces were asked by the Governors to form ministries. The risk for the Congress party was great. It was only after this that the League took up a more militant attitude. Frustrated League leaders carried on propaganda against the Congress telling their co-religionists that the Congress version of the party system was odd, ruling party benches would all be occupied by the Hindus and on the opposing benches would sit all the Muslims, the oddity consisted in the fact that the opposition could never hope to replace the ruling party. The propaganda brought good dividends.[31]

"In U.P. affairs", observes A.C. Guha, "Jawaharlal Nehru had to take the major share of responsibility".[32] In the words of C.H. Philips : "The sad fact was that temperamentally and perhaps, through his upbringing and early eduction in the cosmopolitan setting of Oudh and England, Nehru seemed incapable of evaluating the difference between Hindus and Muslims or of appreciating the full force of the Muslim case."[33]

Had the Congress "behaved more wisely and met the Muslim League half way and formed a coalition Government in the United Provinces, the way could have been opened for Hindu-Muslim collaboration throughout India. Power corrupts and absolute power corrupts absolutely." (Sinha)[34]

The Congress High Command wanted no truck with Jinnah. Kanji Dwarkadas reveals a similar attitude to the High Command in Bombay where it demanded that the Muslim Leaguers must resign from the Muslim League and join the Congress and then only would they be taken as Ministers. This was a humiliating condition. Jinnah therefore, summarily rejected the Congress suggestion. He wanted to cooperate with the Congress Ministry but not at the price of liquidating and sabotaging his own party.[35]

R.C. Majumdar is critical of the Congress intransigence: "To sacrifice collaboration with the Muslim League in the name of ideals which did not at all correspond with existing facts was an extreme unwise—almost fatal—step for which India had to pay very dearly.... The Muslims now fully realized that as a separate community they had no political prospects in future. The Congress ultimatum was the signal for the parting of ways which by inevitable stages, led to the foundation of Pakistan."[36]

Beni Prasad expresses the same feelings :

> "Orthodox Parliamentarianism led the Congress leaders to forget that the one-party theory, even if true of political agitation, was not in the absence of an accomplished revolution, applicable to Ministerial office. The change from extra-constitutional action to governmental responsibility to which the Congress assented in 1937 was a change of scale and methods of the profoundest significance and called for a fresh evaluation and rearrangement of political forces. The country was passing through a crisis, and crises have usually been surmounted even in England through coalitions, for instance in 1915, 1931 and 1940.... The majority principle is at bottom not an ethical maxim but a rule of expanding and has always to be so interpreted as to command minority affirmation. Orthodox parliamentarianism, however, carried the day and excluded the Muslim League from a share in power."[37]

The failure of the talks between Khaliquzzaman and the Congress leaders in summer 1937, though regretted by some, caused little surprise and elicited few comments at that time. Khaliquzzaman commentary of the whole episode was typical of his slippery personality: "I am afraid I was trying to accomplish the impossible."[38]

NOTES AND REFERENCES

1. Kulkarni, V.B., *India and Pakistan: A Historical Survey of Hindu-Muslim Relation*, (Bombay: Jaico Publishing House, 1973), p. 318.
2. Ibid. p. 318.
3. Tara Chand, *History of the Freedom Movement in India*, (Publications Division, Ministry of Information and Broadcasting, Govt. of India, Nov., 1972), Vol. IV, p. 229.
4. Sayeed, K.B., *Pakistan : The Formative Phase* (London : Oxford University Press, 1968), p. 83.
5. Ibid, p. 84.
6. Mujeeb, M. "The Partition of India in Retrospect", In : *The Partition of India, Policies and Perspectives 1935-1947*, Philips C.H. and Wainwright M.D. (eds), (London : George Allen and Unwin Ltd., 1970), p. 411.
7. Ram Gopal, *Indian Muslims : A political History, 1858–1947*, (Bombay : Asia Publishing House, 1959), p. 247.
8. Azad, Maulana Abul Kalam, *India Wins Freedom–An Autobiographical Narrative*, (Bombay : Orient Longman, 1959), pp. 160-61.
9. Nehru tried to wriggle out by stating at a later date that "there were accounts of certain events which were not correct as Maulana had recalled them from memory": Jawaharlal Nehru, 'Speech in Lok Sabha', March 27, 1959; cited in Tara Chand, op. cit., p. 231.
10. Gopal, op. cit. p. 248.
11. Ibid, p. 249.
12. Venkatachar, C.S. "1937-47 in Retrospect : A Civil Servant's View", In : *Partition of India, Policies and Perspectives,* Philips and Wainwright (eds) op. cit., p. 470.
13. Rao, B. Shiva, "India, 1935-47", in Ibid. p. 419.
14. Gopal, op. cit., p. 249.
15. They returned to the precedent of the Punjab, where the Muslim Premier, Sir Sikandar Hayat Khan, in spite of having an overwhelming majority in the house, invited "the leader of the Hindu Mahasabha to nominate a Minister".
16. Ibid. p. 248.
17. Tara Chand, op. cit., p. 232.

18. Sayeed op. cit., p. 85.
19. Ram Gopal, op. cit., p. 251.
20. Venkatachar, op. cit. p. 470.
21. Menon, V. P., *The Transfer of power in India,* (Princeton New Jersey : Princeton Univ. Press, 1957), p. 56.
22. Mujeeb, op. cit., pp. 411-12.
23. Tara Chand, op. cit., pp. 233-34.
24. Ibid, p. 239.
25. Ibid, p. 239.
26. Many of whom were in due course won over to the League.
27. Ram Gopal, op. cit., p. 250.
28. Ibid., p. 251.
29. Ibid. p. 251.
30. Ibid. p. 251-52.
31. Ibid. p. 252.
32. Guha, A.C., *India's Struggle Quarter of a Century 1921-1946,* (Publications Division, Ministry of Information and Broadcasting, Government of India, June, 1982), Part I, p. 341.
33. Philips, C.H., *The Partition of India 1947,* (Leeds; Leeds Univ. Press, 1967), p. 14.
34. Sinha, Sasadhar, *Indian Independence in Perspective,* (Bombay : Asia Publishing House, 1964), p. 96.
35. Dwarkadas, Kanji, *India's Fight for Freedom 1913-1937, An Eyewitness Story* (Bombay : Popular Prakashan, 1966), pp. 466-67.
36. Majumdar, R.C., *History of the Freedom Movement in India* (Calcutta : Firma *K.L. Mukhopadhyay, 1962),* pp. 563-65.
37. Ispahani, M.A.H., "Factors Leading to the Partition of British India", In : *Partition of India, Policies and Perspectives,* op. cit. p. 343.
38. *Leader,* August 4, 1937 : cited by Mehrotra, S.R., "The Congress and the Partition of India," in Ibid, p.199. See also Khaliquzzaman, *Pathway to Pakistan,* (Lahore: Longman Pakistan Branch, 1961), pp. 160-63.

Conclusive Corollary

During this great metamorphosis of Muslim politics in India, neither the Congress nor the Hindu public men outside it seem to have devoted to it the serious attention it deserved. The Congress had been harping on the one idea of a "Constituent Assembly" as the only remedy for all political dissonance and discontent. From this high pedestal, the Hindu leaders never came down to discuss in detail, in a friendly spirit, even the most moderate suggestions of a lose federation. The tragic aspect of the situation was that the Congress party failed to grasp a valuable opportunity in refusing to examine the basic idea behind the resolution. Gandhi condemned it in a long article in the *Harijan*,[1] and the Hindu Press attacked it in varying degrees of bitterness. "But there was no constructive suggestion or attempt of a compromise, conciliation or even mutual understanding, till it was too late."[2] At the outset, many Muslims not only in the minority but also in majority provinces, had their own misgivings about the new plan.[3] But the Congress attitude only helped them to support it strongly. By now the feeling had developed among the Muslim masses and even among the intelligentsia "that regarding any issue involving the Muslims of India, if the Congress opposed it, it was really good for Muslims, and if they supported it, it was very bad for them."[4]

In their evaluation of the Muslim League, Nehru and the Congress committed the same type of mistake as the Britishers did in respect of the Congress when they belittled its importance by describing it as the organization of the English-educated classes constituting a microscopic minority. Nehru's idealism atleast in respect of the Muslim community had absolutely no relation to actual facts.[5]

The year 1937 had offered the most valuable opportunity to the Congress Party, which in the full glow of a resplendent victory had to decide how to use it. Jinnah was keen "to work as equal partners for the welfare of India."[6] But Nehru and the Congress remained scornful and Jinnah's offer "to work as equal partners" was ignored. Sir Percival Griffiths, a former leader of the European Group in the Indian Central Legislature, has written of this "grave tactical blunder". He says : "Spiritual arrogance grew a pace and conditioned the approach of the predominantly Hindu Congress to the Muslims at the one time above all when conciliation was required."[7]

Griffiths further states :

> It is undoubtedly true that the real creators of the demand for Pakistan were the Congress High Command. If they had been prepared to abate their claims to be the sole spokesmen for India and had tried to allay Muslim fears even slightly, Pakistan might never have come to brith.[8]

The British historian Reginald Coupland considers it not only feasible but very desirable for the Congress to have secured the League's cooperation. "In fact, the Congress made the Muslim League a great power."[9]

"In the past eight hundred years of their relationship," says the socialist leader R. M. Lohia, "the Hindus and Muslims have continually suffered from a see-saw of estrangement and approximation.... Among the unforgivable crimes of the Congress government is precisely its failure to bring together the estranged souls; in fact, its unwillingness to attempt the task."[10]

Congress, under the influence of Mahatma Gandhi, who confessed himself bewildered by the emergence of the two-nation theory, denounced and denied the validity of Jinnah's thesis. India, they affirmed, was one nation and the Congress stood for its unity; but at the same time Gandhi made it clear that in no circumstances would Congress forcibly resist Pakistan—perhaps assuming, along with most Congressmen, that British policy and presumably force of arms would, in the last analysis, always be thrown on the side of maintaining the unity of India.[11]

It was indeed unfortunate that the Congress party and its leadership chose to adopt an attitude which was, to say the least, very unrealistic and unhelpful. It was one thing to have an ideal and work for its realization, but consideration of practical politics should not be lost sight of. Even as in any industry or a battle field and in politics the law of causation is inexorable. One wrong step leads to a series of others resulting in difficulties and problems. Looking back into the pages of the history of the Indian Freedom Movement, one comes across several painful instances wherein one has reason to feel that the Congress party as the leading party and the oldest, due to wrong moves and careless action, had to face ominous consequences.

Faced with a human problem involving large numbers of people with a different way of life and outlook, nay, different set of values, the major communities should in their own interest and in the larger interest of the country as a whole, have adopted a conciliatory and sympathetic attitude which would make for a friendly response. The lessons of history seem to have been lost on the Congress leadership, and, as months and years rolled on, whether one liked it or not, partition became inevitable and a *fait accompli*.

"The Lahore Resolution was the beginning of the end of the administrative unity of the entire subcontinent, which had been created by the Muslim Emperors and continued by the British."[12] In the coming years, Pakistan became the "goal" of the Muslim League. Its policy and programme were formulated to achieve that objective. At the annual session of the League held in April 1941 at Madras, the Lahore Resolution, in a slightly amended form, was adopted as one of the aims and objects of the All India Muslim League.[13] Thus Pakistan came to be regarded the symbol of Muslim nationalism and their ultimate destiny. Prodigious indeed had been the increase in the power and the prestige of the League since the debacle of 1937.

Pakistani patriots and the Pakistan government however, are prone to exaggerate too much the importance of the resolution.

According to the official history: "The importance of the Lahore Resolution as a constitutional document cannot be overemphasized."[14] Such statements have to be accepted with reserve.

Was Jinnah working consistently and single-mindedly for partition from 1940 onwards? Was his strategy thought out and consistently followed, with the one aim of achieving Pakistan? Perhaps he merely reacted to events, taking advantage of his opportunities as they occurred.

It is doubtful if the resolution determined finally Jinnah's political objective.

NOTES AND REFERENCES

1. *Harijan.*
2. Majumdar, op. cit. p. 616.
3. Khan, Raza, op. cit. p. 70.
4. Ibid. p. 70.
5. Majumdar, op. cit., p. 592.
6. Bolitho, Hector, *Jinnah—Creator of Pakistan,* 1st edn. (London: J. Murray, 1954), p. 114.
7. Griffiths, Percival, *The British Impact on India,* (London : Macdonald, 1952), p. 340.
8. Ibid, p. 342.
9. Coupland, op. cit. pp. 13-14 : As he further says : "Stupidity of the Congress was the cause of the growth of the Muslim League and its growing power."
10. Lohia, Ram Manohar, *Guilty Men of India's Partition,* (Hyderabad: Samata Vidyalaya Nyas, Publication Dept., 1970), pp. 4-5.
11. Philips, *Partition of India* 1947, op. cit. p. 22.
12. Qureshi, *History of Freedom Movement,* op. cit., p. 73.
13. Sayeed, *Pakistan : The Formative Phase,* 1857-1948, 2nd. edn., (London : Oxford Univ. Press, 1968), p. 124.
14. Qureshi, *History of Freedom Movement,* op. cit. p. 115.

Appendix

Resolution Adopted by the All India Muslim League at Lahore, 23 March, 1940[1]

While approving and endorsing the action taken by the Council and the working committee of the All India Muslim League, as Indicated in their resolutions dated 27th August, 17th and 18th September, and 22nd October, 1939, and 3rd February, 1940, on the constitutional issue, this session emphatically reiterates that the scheme of federation embodied in the Government of India Act, 1935, is totally unsuited to, and unworkable in the peculiar conditions of this country and is altogether unacceptable to Muslim India. It further records its emphatic view that while the declaration dated 18th October, 1939, made by the Viceroy on behalf of His Majesty's Government is reassuring in so far as it declares that the policy and plan on which the Act, 1935, is based will be reconsidered in consultation with the various parties, interests and communities in India. Muslim India will not be satisfied unless the whole constitutional plan is reconsidered *de novo* and that no revised plan would be acceptable to the Muslims unless it is framed with their approval and consent.

Resolved that it is the considered view of this session of the All India Muslim League that no constitutional plan would be workable in this country or acceptable to the Muslims unless it is designed on the following basic principles, viz., that geographically contiguous units are demarcated into regions which should be so constituted, with such territorial readjustments as may be necessary, that the areas in which the Muslims are numerically in a majority as in the North-

West and Eastern zones of India should be grouped to constitute "Independent States" in which the constituent units shall be autonomous and sovereign: that adequate, effective and mandatory safeguards should be specifically provided in the constitution for minorities in these units and in the regions for the protection of their religious, cultural, economic, political, administrative and other rights and interests in consultation with them and shall also be applicable in other parts of India where the Muslims are in a minority.

This session further authorizes the Working Committee to frame a scheme of constitution in accordance with these basic principles, providing for the assumption finally by the respective regions of all powers, such as defence, external affairs, communications, customs and such other matters as may be necessary.

NOTES

1. Hasan, K.S., 'The Transfer of Power—Documents, (Karachi : Pakistan Institute of International Affairs), pp. 19-20.

Bibliography

Contemporary Source Material

Ahmad, Jamiluddin. 1946. *Some Recent Speeches and Writings of Mr. Jinnah*, Vol. I., Lahore: S.M. Ashraf.

Ahmad, Jamiluddin, 1970, (Comp.), *Historic Documents of the Muslim Freedom*, Lahore: United Publishers.

Alexander, H.G., 1938, *Congress Rule in India : A Study in Social Reform*, London : Fabian Research Bureau Publication.

Ali, Chaudhri Muhammad. 1967. *The Emergence of Pakistan*, New York: Columbia University Press.

Ali, Chaudhry Rahmat. 1940. *The Millat of Islam and the Menace of 'Indianism'*, Cambridge.

Ambedkar, Bhimrao Ramji. 1945. *Pakistan or Partition of India*, 2nd ed., Bombay: Thacker and Co. Ltd.

Ambedkar, B.R. 1941. *Thoughts on Pakistan* (Report submitted to the Executive Council of the Independent Labour Party), Bombay: Thacker and Co. Ltd.

Ashraf, K.M. 1940. *Pakistan : Foreward (sic)*, Delhi: Adabistan.

Azad, Maulana Abul Kalam, 1960, *India Wins Freedom* (An Autobiographical Narrative), Ist American ed., New York: Longman Green and Company.

Bose, Subhas Chandra. 1964. *The Indian Struggle 1920-1942* (Comp. by the Netaji Research Bureau, Calcutta), Bombay: Asia Publishing House.

Coupland, Reginald. 1944. *Indian Politics, 1936-1942*, London: Oxford University Press.

Coupland, Reginald. 1945. *Report on the Constitutional Problem in India*, 3 parts, New York: Oxford University Press.

Dwarkadas, Kanji. 1966. *India's Fight For Freedman 1913-1937*, Bombay: Popular Prakashan.

Griffiths, Percival. 1952. *The British Impact on India,* London: Macdonald.

Gwyer, Maurice L. and Appadorai. A. 1957. (eds, *Speeches and Documents on the Indian Constitution 1921-1947,* 2 Vols, London: Oxford University Press.

Halifax, The Earl of. 1957. *Fullness of Days,* 2nd Imp, London: Collins.

Hamza, E.l. 1946. *Pakistan : A Nation,* 4th Imp, Lahore: S.M. Ashraf.

Haq, S. Moinul. 1963. *A History of the Freedom Movement :* 1906-1936, Vol. III, No. 19, Karachi: Pakistan Historical Society.

Haq, S. Moinul. 1970. *A History of the Freedom Movement :* 1936-1947, Vol. IV, No. 56, Parts I and II, Karachi : Pakistan Historical Society.

Hasan, K. Sarwar and Hasan, Zubeida. 1966. *The Transfer of Power—Documents on the Foreign Relations of Pakistan,* Karachi: Pakistan Institute of International Affairs.

Ispahani, M.A.H. 1967. *Qaid-i-Azam As I knew Him,* Karachi: Ferozsons.

Jack, Homer A. (ed.). 1956. *The Gandhi Reader—A Source Book of His Life and Writings,* Bloomington: Indiana University Press.

Kabir, Humayun, 1969, *Muslim Politics 1906-1947,* Calcutta: Firma K.L. Mukhopadhyay.

Kahliquzzaman, Choudhury. 1961. *Pathway to Pakistan,* Lahore: Longman Pakistan Branch.

Khan, Mohamed Raza. 1969. *What Price Freedom,* Madras: The Nuri Press.

Kulkarni, V. B. 1944. *Is Pakistan Necessary?* Bombay: Jaico Publishing House.

Lateef, S. Abdul. 1947. *The Great Leader.* Lahore: Lion Press.

Linlithgow, The Marquess of. 1945. *Speeches and Statements 1936-43,* New Delhi: Bureau of Public Information, Govt. of India.

Lohia, Ram Manohar. 1970. *Guilty Men of India's Partition,* Hyderabad: R. Lohia Sameta Vidyalaya Nyas, Publication.

Menon, V.P. 1957. *The Transfer of Power in India,* New Jersey: Princeton University Press.

Mitra, Nripendra Nath, (ed.), *The Indian Annual Register,* Vol. I (Jan to June 1936) and Vol. II (Jan to June 1937) Calcutta: The Annual Register Office.

Nehru, Jawaharlal. 1936. *India and the World,* London: George Allen and Unwin, Ltd.

Nehru, Jawaharlal. 1948. *Nehru on Gandhi—Selection from Writings and Speeches,* New York: John Day Company.

Nehru, Jawaharlal. 1958. *Toward Freedom,* (The Autobiography of Jawaharlal Nehru), Boston: Beacon Press.

Nehru, Jawaharlal. 1962. *An Autobiography*, Bombay: Allied Publishers.

Noman, M. 1942. *Muslim India : Rise and Growth of the All-India Muslim League*, Allahabad: Kitabistan.

Philips, C.H. 1962. *The Evolution of India and Pakistan, 1858 to 1947—Select Documents*, London: Oxford University Press.

Prasad, Rajendra. 1947. *India Divided*, 3rd ed., Bombay: Hind Kitabs Ltd.

Rajput, A.B. 1948. *Muslim League-Yesterday and Today*, Lahore: S.M. Ashraf.

Rauoof, A.A. 1947. *Meet Mr. Jinnah*, 2nd ed., Lahore: S.M. Ashraf.

Saiyid, Matlubul Hasan. 1953. *Jinnah, Muhammad Ali*, 2nd ed., Lahore: S.M. Ashraf.

Sharma, Jagdish Saran. 1962. *India's Struggle For Freedom–Selected Documents and Sources*, Vol. I, Delhi: S. Chand and Company.

Sitaramayya, Pattabhi. 1947. *The History of the Indian National Congress—1935-1947*, Vol. II, Bombay: Padma Publications.

Vairanapillai, M.S. 1946. *Are We Two Nations Nationalities in Indian Politics*, Lahore: Herbert Milton Williams.

Young, Desmond. 1965. *Try Anything Twice*, London: Cassell.

Zetland, Lawrence John Lumley Dundas, 2nd Marquess of. 1956. *Essays and Memoirs*, London: J. Murray.

Secondary Works

Aggarwala, R.N., 1962, *National Movement and Constitutional Development of India*. 4th ed., Delhi: Metropolitan Book Company.

Ahmad, Jamiluddin. 1964. *Final Phase of struggle for Pakistan*, Karachi: International Press.

Aziz, Abdul. 1964. *Discovery of Pakistan*, 2nd rev. ed., Lahore: Sh. Ghulam Ali.

Bahadur, Lal. 1954. *The Muslim League–Its History, Activities and Achievements*, Agra: Agra Book Store.

Bhagat, K.P. 1959. *A Decade of Indo-British Relations 1937-1947*, Bombay: Popular Book Depot.

Bolitho, Hector. 1954. *Jinnah—Creator of Pakistan*, London: J. Murray.

Bose, Nemai Sadhan. 1965. *The Indian National Movement–An Outline*, Calcutta: Firma K.L. Mukhopadhyay.

Brecher, Michael. 1959. *Nehru–A Political Biography*, London: Oxford University Press.

Fischer, Louis. 1950. *The Life of Mahatma Gandhi*, New York: Harper.

Gopal, Ram. 1959. *Indian Muslims–A Political History (1858-1947)*, Bombay: Asia Publishing House.

Ikram, S.M. 1965. *Modern Muslim India and the Birth of Pakistan 1858-1951*, rev. and enl. ed., Lahore: S.M. Ashraf.

Kulkarni, V.B. 1969. *The Indian Triumvirate—A Political Biography of Mahatma Gandhi, Sardar Patel and Pandit Nehru*, Bombay: Bharatiya Vidya Bhavan.

Lumby, Esmond Walter Rawson. 1954. *The Transfer of Power in India, 1945-47*, London: G. Allen and Unwin Ltd.

Mahajan, Vidya Dhar. 1970. *Fifty Year of Modern India 1919-1969*. Delhi : S. Chand and Company.

Majumdar, R.C. 1962. *History of the Freedom Movement in India*, Vol. III., Calcutta: Firma K.L. Mukhopadhyay.

Majumdar, R.C. 1969. *Struggle For Freedom*, Vol. XI, of *History and Culture of the Indian People*, Bombay: Bharatiya Vidya Bhavan.

Majumdar, S.K. 1966. *Jinnah and Gandhi—Their Role in India's Quest for Freedom*, Calcutta: Firma K.L. Mukhopadhyay.

Malik, Hafiz. 1963. *Moslem Nationalism in India and Pakistan*, Washington DC: Public Affairs Press.

Menon, Vapal Pangunni. 1965. *An Outline of Indian Constitutional History*, Bombay: Bharatiya Vidya Bhavan.

Mukerjee, Hirendranath. 1962. *India's Struggle for Freedom*, 3rd rev. ed., Calcutta: NBA.

Philips, C.H. 1949. *India*, New York: Hutchinson's Univ. Library.

Philips, C.H. 1967. *The Partition of India 1947*, Leeds: Leeds Univ. Press.

Philips, C.H. 1970. *The Partition of India—Policies and Perspectives, 1935-1947*, Massachusetts: The M.I.T. Press.

Pirzada, Sharifuddin Syed. 1963. *Evolution of Pakistan*, Lahore : All-Pakistan Legal Decisions.

Qureshi, I.H. 1969. *The Struggle for Pakistan*, 2nd ed., Karachi : University of Karachi.

Qureshi, I.H. 1962. *The Muslim Community of the Indo-Pakistan Sub-continent 1910-1947*, S' Gravenhage, Mouton : Columbia University Publication.

Sayeed, Khalid Bin. 1968. *Pakistan: The Formative Phase, 1857-1948*, 2nd ed., New York: Oxford University Press.

Sinha, Sasadhar. 1964. *Indian Independence in Perspective*, Bombay: Asia Publishing House.

Spear, Percival. 1961. *India—A Modern History*, Ann Arbor: Michigan : The University of Michigan Press.

Srinivas, M.N. 1971. *Social Change in Modern India*, Berkeley: University of California Press.

Swarajya, 1968. Annual Number (India).

Symonds, Richards. 1950. *The Making of Pakistan*, London: Faber and Faber.

Tendulkar, D.G. 1952. *Mahatma: Life of Mohandas Karamchand Gandhi*, Vol. V., Bombay: Karnatak Publishing House.

Zakaria, Rafiq. (ed.), 1959-60. *A Study of Nehru*, 2nd ed., Bombay: *Times of India* Publications.

Index

A

Abdul Aziz, Syed, 10
Abdul Hashim, 184
Aden, 120
Africa, 120
Agriculturist Party, 188
Ali, Mohammad, 40, 81
Aligarh Muslim University, 56
  Upsurge, 41
Aligarh School, Political
  Ideology of, 32
All India Congress Committee,
  8, 92 Hindu Mahasabha, 124
  Muslim Conference, 9 Politics,
  53 Muslim League, 1, 9, 103,
  131, 175-6, 182, 203, 205
All Parties Conference, 31, 54
  Convention, 150
Amba Prasad, 144
Ambedkar, 173, 176
Anandmath, 80-1
Anti-Partition Movement, 80
Assam, 20, 67, 177
Attlee, Clement, 133
Aurengzeb, 61
Australia, 120
Azad, Abul Kalam, 3, 20-1, 24,
  97, 118, 121, 123-4, 177, 179-
  80, 182, 185-7, 189-90, 193-94
Azad Party, 10, 82

B

Baluchistan, 177
Bande Matram, 80-3
Bankim Chandra, 80
Basic Education, 82 Wardha
  Scheme of, 73, 83
Bengal, 10, 16-9, 67, 80, 124, 139,
  176-7
Beni Prasad, 195, 198
Bhartarya, S C, 120
Bihar, 10, 16, 20, 77
Bipin Chandra, 71
Blasphemy, 71
Bombay, 1, 20, 25, 52, 111, 154,
  198 Assembly, 82 Press
  Conference in, 105
Bose, Subhash Chandra, 123-4,
  126, 129 Election of, 60
Britain, 85, 99, 118, 120, 122-4,
  126, 129, 134, 137-8, 142, 147,
  155, 160
British Bureaucracy, 139
  Civilization, 32 Common-
  wealth, 154 Empire, 116
  Freedom Policy, 126
  Impact, Reaction of, 41
  Imperialism, 9, 24, 39, 128,

164, 191, 193-4, 196 Appendage of, 119 India, 92, 99, 121 Labour Party, 136 Parliament, 120, 130, 151 Policy, 4, 132, 148, 154, 199, 202 Power, Establishment of, 76 Press, 79 Rule, 42, 71, 77, 110, 128, 146
Burma, 120

C

Cabinet Mission Plan, 105
Calcutta, 52, 150-1 University, Crest of, 108
Carlyle, 35
Cause of Hindu-Muslim Unity, 30
Chakrabarthy, Atulananda, 37-40, 46, 69-70
Chamberlain, Neville, 133, 144, Appeasement, 118
Chatterji, Bankim Chandra, 80-1
Chauduri, K N, 159, 162
Churchill, Winston, 134, 146
Civil Disobediance, 148 Threat of, 157, War, 155, 158
Coker, F W, 40
Communal Politics, Growth of, 53 Problem, 98 Aggravation of, 34 Question, 142 Settlement of, 157
Communalism, 47, 49, 68, 192 Growth of, 53 High Priest of, 64
Complete Independence, 96, 153, 156
Confield, Conrad, 100
Congress Agrarian Programme, 27 Government, Establishment of, 71 High Command, 24-5, 45, 88-90, 126, 198-9, 202 Ideology, 22 Monopoly of, 39 Movement, 45, 70, 88 Opinion, 4 Party, 20, 23, 26, 63, 69, 76, 89, 93, 99, 188, 190-1, 198-9 Success of, 17-8 Policy, 123, 126, Power, Foundation of, 3 Propaganda, 49 Raj, 89 Rule, 102, 140 Crest of, 3, 78 Resolution Secularism, 25 Victory, 16, 23, 68, 194
Congress-League Accord, 1 Agreement, 54 Coalition Government, 148 Relation, 27
Congress Working Committee, 89, 108, 123-4, 126, 130, 147, 190
Conservative Party, 100
Constituent Assembly, 8, 105, 127, 146-8, 151, 155, 175, 201
Constitution, 195,
Contitutional Plan, 176
Contemporary Muslim Politics, 174
Corfield, Conrad, 99
Coupland, Reginald, 89, 121, 176, 199, 202
Cripps, Stafford, 146
Czechoslovakia, 78, 118

D

Das, C R, 31, 172, 175
Death Warrant, 190
Delhi, 5, 13, 101, 117, Convention of Muslim League, 184
Deliverance Day, 101, 141, 143, 150-1, 155, 158
Democracy, Betrayal of, 118, 126
Dissension, Source of, 75
Divide and Rule, 85, 133, 148
Dividing India, 70
Dominion Status, 117, 140, 152, 154, 156, 172, 176, 179

Dutt, R P, 43, 45, 52-3, 59, 121
Dwarkadas, Kanji, 24, 34, 38, 195, 198
Dyarchy, Opening of, 53

E

Education, 48
Edwardes, Michael, 121, 123
Egypt, 120
Election Manifesto, 8, 37
England, 1, 10, 24, 38, 53, 125-6, 160, 193, 163, 196, 198
English Education, 75
Erikson, Erick, 36
Ethiopia, 118
Europe, 7, 123, 127, 131, 139, European Rule, 41

F

Faizpur Session, 9
Farooki, Abdul Lateef, 175
Fazal Husain, 185, 188
Fazlul Haq, 10, 17, 67, 77, 90, 176
Federal Plans, 131
First World War, 46, 157, 168
Fisher, Louis, 39
Forward Bloc, 124
France, 125-6, 131
Free India, 130-2
Freedom Movement, History of, 26
Freedom, Struggle for, 66, 77, 181
Future India, 143

G

Gandhi, 4-5, 14, 19, 31, 34-5, 38, 44, 60, 67-70, 73-4, 78, 81, 86-9, 96-9, 111-2, 123, 125-6, 128, 134, 141-2, 148-9, 152, 154-5, 161-2, 172, 175, 177, 180, 201-2
Gankousky, 73
General Election, 27
Germany, 43, 79, 96, 119, 121, 123, 126, 134, 157, 159
Global War, 158
Gokhale, 31
Government of India Bill, 7
Great Britain, 127, 131 War, 127
Griffiths, Percival, 78, 99, 199, 202
Guha, A C, 67, 78, 94, 97, 102, 124-5, 140-1, 151, 194, 197
Guiana, 120

H

Hailey, 132
Halifax, 12, 161
Harijan, 125, 201
Haripura, 126
Hasan, Mumtaz, 2
Hegel, 35
Hidayatullah, Ghulam Husain, 17
Himalayan Blunder, 162-3
Hindu Communalism, 18, 92 Commission Report, 61 Congress, 202 Domination, 94 India, 95, 183 Mahasabha, 54, 64, 93-6, 110, 200 Movement, 44 Nationalism, 44 organization, 196 Press, 178, 201 Raj, 3, 32, 46, 71, 78-9, 90, 94, 96, 102-3, 150 Idea of, 43 Rashtra, 93
Hindu-Muslim Bitterness, 76 Communalism, 53, Conflict, 52, Cooperation, 11, Coordination, 1 Culture, 87 Discord, 75 Problem, 23, 97, 185, 191, 93 Relations, 42, 91, 187 Riots, 90 Settlement, 96 Unity, 38
Hinduisation, 94

Hitler, Aims of, 116
Hoare, Samuel, 77
Hoogli, 182
House of Commons, 7 Lords, 157
Hugh, Tinker, 105
Hutchins, Francis, 116

I

Ill-Starred August Resolution, 60
Imperialism, 51, 119, 124, 139
Independence Day, 148 Declaration of, 123 Independent India, 32, 102
India, 1, 4-5, 7-8, 18-9, 24-5, 27, 32-3, 38-44, 50, 68-9, 74, 77, 85, 93-5, 116-9, 121, 126-8, 133-4, 140, 143, 146-7, 152, 159, 174, 202-3 Constitutional History of, 12, Division of, 183, Ordinance, Defence of, 121 Liberal Federation, 124 Policy, 132, 134 Self-determination for, 153, 155 Sun of, 152
Indian Constitutional Problem, 156 Freedom, Declaration of, 142, Dominion Status, 134-5
Indian Freedom Movement, 5 History of, 203, Muslim, 30, 34, 129-30 Nation, 95
Indian National Congress, 1, 7, 33, 47, 72, 79, 139, 140 Movement, 115, 118
Indian Nationalism, 24, 39, 43-4, 50, 128, 193-4, 196 Attitude of, 127
Indian Politics, 36 Press, 178
Ireland, 46,
Islamic League of Nations, 32
Ispahani, M A H., 2, 90, 181, 184

J

Jama'at-i-Islami, 180
Jamiat-ul-Ulema-i-Hind, 9, 64-5, 67, 102, 180, 187, 189
Jamshed, 58
Jayaprakash Narayan, 192, 196
Jinnah, M A, 1-4, 10-1, 19, 21-2, 24, 26, 30-40, 44-7, 53, 56, 58, 64-5, 67, 69-70, 74, 78-82, 90-3, 96-9, 101-2 105, 129-30, 138-41, 143-5, 147, 148-53, 161-3, 174-7, 180-1, 183-4, 188, 191, 195-6, 198, 202
Joint Parliamentary Committee, 180

K

Kabir, Humayun, 65, 72, 106, 128-30, 180, 183
Karachi Resolution, 9
Khadi, 102
Khaliquzzaman, 20-1, 24-5, 153, 173, 178, 184, 187, 189, 192-4, 199
Khan, Abdul Ghaffar, 63, 107
Khan, Abdul Hameed, 172, 175
Khan, Abdul Qayyum, 107-8
Khan, Aga, 34
Khan, Mohamed Raza, 21, 27, 172, 175, 182, 185
Khan, Nawab Ismail, 20-1, 189
Khan, Shafaat Ahmed, 77
Khan, Sikandar Hayat, 17, 67, 179,182, 196, 200
Khan, Syed Ahmed, 41, 74
Khan, Yaqub, 72
Kher, Bála Saheb, 111
Khilafat Movement, 81
Kidwai, M H, 34
Kidwai, Rafi Ahmad, 22, 186, 188-9, 191

Krishak Praja Samity, 10 Party, 17
Kulkarni, V B, 35, 66, 152, 158, 161, 164, 184, 187

L

Lahore, 172, 175, 177 Resolution, 38, 141, 153, 156, 161, 164, 173, 176, 180-1, 183-4, 200-1, 203-4
Lal Bahadur, 70, 72, 140-1
Land Reforms Programme, 196
Lasswell, Harold D, 35-6
League Subject Committee Manifesto, 12 Resolution, 130, 151, 183
Liaqat Ali, 107
Liberal Democracy, Concept of, 47
Linlithgow, 3, 20, 99-100, 103, 117, 120-2, 133, 135-7, 139, 141-2, 145-6, 153-6, 159, 161, 164, 178
Local Hindu Mahasabha, 108
Lohia, R M, 199, 202
London, 13, 132, 134, 154, 157
Lucknow, 24, 80-1, Pact, 12 Session, 708, 64, 67
Lamby, E W R, 96

M

Macaulay's Dreams, 31
Madras, 16, 20, 52, 67, 175, 200, 203
Maharashtra, 94
Mahudabad, Raja of, 26, 73, 76
Majid Sindhi, Abdul, 10
Majumdar, R C, 48-9, 66-7, 72, 79-80, 93-4, 98, 103, 109, 195, 198
Manifesto, 11
Mass Contact, 69-70 Movement, 71 Scheme, 27
Maudodi, Abul'ala, 177
Menon, V P, 23, 26, 160, 194
Moin Shakir, 31-2, 37, 37, 44, 49
Montford Constitution, 51
Moon, Penderal, 66, 70-1
Moore, R J, 161, 169
Morley, 41
Morley-Minto Reforms, 62
Mughal Empire, 51
Mujeeb, M, 23-4, 191, 194-5
Mukerji, Hirendranath, 63, 87, 97-8, 161, 164
Muslim Communalism, 18, 93, 138 Growth of, 133 Leader, Growing Alienation of, 45 Politics, 198
Muslim League, 1-2, 4-5, 9-11, 17, 19-21, 23-7, 39, 50, 53, 56, 63-4, 66-7, 79, 92-4, 97, 102-3, 124, 129-30, 140, 142, 151, 157, 171-2, 174, 188, 195-6, 198, 201-2 Demand of, 133 Growth of, 45 Parliamentary Board, 10, 22, 187, 190 Party, 187, 190 Performance of, 16 Programme, 11
Muslim Mass Contact Programme, 25-6, 71, 83, 89 Nationalism, 1-2, 43-4, 97, 200, 203 Emergence of, 40 Nationalist Movement, 2, 55 Politics, 106, Provincialism, 54 Separatism, 41, 49-50, 55, 86, 91, 97, 144, 153 State, Creation of, 30
Mutiny, 41
Myrdal, Gunnar, 44

N

Nanda, B R, 78, 80-1, 130, 133, 178, 181-2

Naoroji, Dadabhai, 31, 48
Narendra Dev, 192, 196
Narrow Communalism, 94
National Government, 90 Movement, 195
Nationalism, 40 Birth of, 109 Forces, 152 Growth of, 41 Hindu View of, 32 Political Idea of, 2 Political Level of, 91
Nationalist Movement, 41-2, 63, 82, 91
Nazi Agression, 127 Germany, 43 Propaganda, 96
Nehru, Jawaharlal, 3-5, 7, 9, 14, 17-9, 21-7, 32-3, 35-9, 44, 66, 68-70, 77, 82-4, 87-8, 92-3, 97-9, 101, 103, 105, 107, 112, 123-6, 128, 138, 141, 149-51, 158-9, 161, 180-2, 190-4, 196-99, 201-2 Influence of, 45 Report, 34 Totalitarianism, 39
Nehru, Motilal, 195
New Constitution, 7
Nizam, 103
Non-Cooperation Movement, 87
Non-Violence, 125, 145, 161

O

Open conference, 175
Orissa, 16, 20
Oudh, 24, 198

P

Page, David, 50-5
Pakistan, 2, 5, 26, 50, 101-2, 107, 110, 177-8, 190, 202-4 creation of, 23, 86, 191 Demand for, 39 Foundation 06, 25, 198 Idea of, 153 Making of, 110 Movement, 4-5, 91 Muslim State of, 177, Plan, 179, 182 Resolution, 153, 175, 177-8, 180-1, 184
Palestine, 42
Pandey, B N, 68, 71, 78
Panikkar, K M, 41
Pant, Gobnind Ballabh, 99
Parliamentary System, 85
Partition, Demand for, 99, 107, 202 Formation of, 160, Idea of, 182 Principle of, 176
Partition of Pakistan, Demand for, 176
Patel, Vallabhbhai, 111, 196
Permanent Settlement Act, Abolition of, 17
Philips, C H, 1, 24, 33, 56, 97, 122, 137-8, 178, 181, 197
Phillips, William, 152
Pirpur, 107 Committee, 74, 85 Report, 77, 85, 92, 94, 110
Poland, 127, 131
Political Independence, 151, Party, 63, 195
Power, Desire for, 40, Transfer of, 134, 178
Programme of Muslim Mass Contact, 20
Provincial Autonomy, 89 Impact of, 52 Congress Committee, 108
Public Settlement, 20
Punjab, 16-9, 67, 124, 139,. 177, 200
Purna Swaraj, Demand for, 158

Q

Qaid-i-Azam, 181, 184
Quit India, 3
Qureshi, I H, 1, 12, 101

R

Rahmat Ali, 150
Rai, Lajpat, 172, 175

Raja Gopalachari, C, 99, 180, 182
Rajendra Prasad, 110, 137, 141-2, 192, 196
Ram Gopal, 12, 21, 25, 79, 83, 95, 188, 190-3, 196
Ram Raj, 44, 87
Ramgarh, 153, 156, 158, 161
 Demand, 164
Rana Pratap, 61
Rao, Shiva, 23, 93, 153, 183, 188, 191
Religious Fanaticism, 31
Republican Party, National Committee of, 89
Round Table Conference, 10, 32, 34, 38
Royal Commission, 110
Russia, 42, 119
Ruttie, 34-5

S

Saadullah, Mohammad, 67
Sait, Sattar, 172, 175
Saiydain, KG, 73
Sakkur, 108
Sanatanist Hindu, 44
Sarkar, Sumit, 51, 134, 136
Satyagarh, Threat of, 175
Savarkar, Threat of, 175
Savarkar, Vinayak Damodar, 94-5
Sayeed, Khalid B, 31, 36, 40, 42, 46, 51, 64, 83, 86-7, 107, 110, 150, 153, 158-9
Second World War, 96, 116, 120-1, 126, 128
Sharif Report, 77, 85
Shaukat Ali, 184
Shia Political Conference, 184, 187
Shivaji, 61
Sikandar, 175
Sind, 10, 16-8, 67, 124, 139, 177
Singapore, 121
Singhvi, L M, 49-50
Sinha, 198
Slavery, Charter of, 7
Social Welfare Scheme, 86
Socialism, 98
Socio-Economic Problems, 151
Spear, Percival, 100-1, 116, 161
Surendranath, 31
Swaraj Parly, 192, 195
Symond, Richard, 85, 110

T

Tarachand, 100, 134, 151, 153, 157, 195
Templewood, 13
Thompson, Edward, 123, 125
Tomlinson, B R, 63, 143
Tripura, 126
Two Nation Theory, 38, 47, 202

U

Unionist Party, 17, 67
United India, 77, 99, 143, 134, 161, 184 Party, 10, Provinces, 1-2, 17, 22-5, 27, 55-6, 77, 187, 190-2, 195, 198 States, 89, 129
Unity of India, 203
University of Sabarmati, 14

V

Venkatachar, C S, 22-3, 91, 127, 129, 156-7, 156-60, 188, 190-1, 194
Veto Power, 146
Vidya Mandir, 83-4 Scheme 82
Voigt, Johannes H, 120, 123, 126, 128, 134

W

Wahid, M R, 175

Wain Wright, M D F, 56, 98, 122, 137-8
Wall bank, Walter, 89, 138
War Advisory Board, Creation of, 133 Declaration of, 137 Proclamation of, 127
Wazir Hasan, 72
Wedgewood, Veromica, 35
Whitehall, 116-7, 156, 161, 164
White paper, 135
Willingdon, 13
World Power, 177

Y

Young, Desmond, 125

Z

Zaidi, Z H, 11, 66, 71, 107, 160, 163
Zakir Hussain, 73
Zetland, 100, 103, 117, 134-7, 141, 146-7, 153-7
Zionism, 42